Coerced

Coerced

WORK UNDER THREAT OF PUNISHMENT

Erin Hatton

UNIVERSITY OF CALIFORNIA PRESS

University of California Press
Oakland, California

Library of Congress Cataloging-in-Publication Data

ISBN 978-0-520-30539-7 (cloth : alk. paper)
ISBN 978-0-520-30541-0 (pbk. : alk. paper)
ISBN 978-0-520-97340-4 (ebook)

Manufactured in the United States of America

27   26   25   24   23   22   21   20
10   9   8   7   6   5   4   3   2   1

For Felix

You must always remember that the sociology, the history, the economics, the graphs, the charts, the regressions all land, with great violence, upon the body.

—Ta-Nehisi Coates, *Between the World and Me*

Contents

Tables

Acknowledgments

I have many people to thank for supporting me as I researched and wrote this book. Most of all, I am indebted to the workers who shared their experiences with me. They gave me their time, they gave me their stories. Thank you.

I also owe many thanks to the experts in the field who helped me understand their respective institutions and the people who labor within them; particularly Jerome Wright, Grace Andriette, Jennifer Hadlock, Amy Dvorak, Barbara Young, Ivan Soto, and Kyle Rowley.

I received much-needed financial support from various institutional gems at the University at Buffalo: Errol Meidinger and the Baldy Center for Law and Social Policy; Erik Seeman and the Humanities Institute; Kari Winter and the Gender Institute; and Laura Mangan and UB Civic Engagement and Public Policy. Thank you; this research would not have been possible without your support.

Over the years, a number of students (student workers!) worked on this project. My thanks to Paul Durlak, Kiera Duckworth, Matt McLeskey, and Colin Walsh. Thanks also to Nicolas Penchaszadeh for document translation work.

While I was developing this project, I had many mentors—both formal and informal—to whom I could turn for advice and support. Jamie Peck, Erik Olin Wright, Steven Vallas, Steve Lopez, and Anna-Maria Marshall, I'm looking at you. Thank you. And Erik, rest in peace. You will be missed, but in so many ways you are still with us.

The Baldy Center at UB hosted a manuscript workshop so that scholars from around the country and university community could read and comment on my book in progress. This workshop was invaluable. Thank you, Errol Meidinger and the Baldy Center, and a million thanks to the three experts who traveled from afar to attend it: Adia Harvey Wingfield, Allison Pugh, and Noah Zatz. You were my scholarly dream team. Thanks, too, to my scholar-friends at UB who attended the workshop: Marion Werner, Susan Cahn, Victoria Wolcott, Abigail Cooke, Hanna Grol-Prokopczyk, Chris Mele, Jessica Su, Amanda Hughett, Errol Meidinger, Martha McCluskey, Carl Nightingale, Camilo Trumper, Dalia Muller, Katja Praznik, Mary Nell Trautner, Sarah Robert, David Herzberg, Maggie Rex, Jared Strohl, Matt McLeskey, Kiera Duckworth, Ayşegül Balta, and Vinay Kumar. To all of you, your insight was incredible. This book is better because of you.

Extra-special-beyond-the-call-of-duty thanks to David Herzberg, Nicole Fox, Allison Pugh, Adia Harvey Wingfield, and Hanna Grol-Prokopczyk for reading multiple drafts of some or all of this book's chapters. I am so thankful.

To my inner circle, David and Nicky, you are an amazing combination of academic and personal love and support. Felix, you are my daily dose of joy.

And to my beloved family, David, Rex, Leo, and Felix. You are my heart, you are my home.

Foreword

After three-plus decades of consecutive incarceration and now more than a decade on post-release community supervision, one might think there would be little that anyone, much less an academic, could enlighten me about concerning the prison industrial complex. However, after reading this wonderfully and comprehensively researched book, I confess that the lived prison experience alone cannot adequately educate one about some of its more subtle facets. Erin Hatton delves into how the "work" aspect of prison permeates so much of the history of economics in this country as well as the distinct and purposeful perpetuation of a second-class, third-world "employment" paradigm that is also inherent in academia, athletics, and social welfare programs.

My prolonged and seemingly endless incarceration forced open my eyes to the insidious nature of prison labor and its attendant malfeasance. This book expounds upon and fully exposes the involuntary servitude and slave-like character of this industry as well as several others not in the least associated with the prison experience. To be able to so cogently juxtapose such divergent industries as criminal justice (prison), higher education, athletics, and welfare speaks volumes about the artistry of this work and why reading it is essential. If we are to honestly and seriously address one of the most pressing social and economic injustices plaguing our already discriminatory systems of "employment," crime and punishment, and economic subjugation, then there is no better place to start than with this reading. Yet the subtle nature of these intertwined economic injustices makes clear that even more research on this subject matter is sorely needed.

My decades-plus time on community supervision has allowed me to be heavily involved in criminal justice advocacy and reform, which is why I was able to meet and work with Erin Hatton, a person who I knew from our very first encounter was, in spite of her academic achievement, a committed and compassionate student of life. This allowed me (and others) to take her on a journey through a system that most know very little about and care even less to understand.

The prison system returns to society men, women, and children who are ill-prepared to be employable citizens and fails to reduce recidivism or promote economic sustainability. It is an economic drain on state coffers and does not even remotely provide a meaningful return on the investment. My personal story aside, I continually witness how this failure plays itself out in the decimation of predominantly black, brown, and Latinx communities without the faintest hint of concern from society at large. It is my sincerest hope that reading this book will foster a greater interest in these systems of economic exploitation. Unlike those who believe these systems are broken, I believe we must break them because, in fact, currently they are working just the way they are intended to. And that's definitely not to the benefit of working people in or outside of this convoluted occupational conundrum.

Though thoroughly researched, this book is not just an exercise in academic posturing or liberal gobbledygook. It is an entertaining read that replaces scholarly supposition with truths that would be comical if they weren't painfully and graphically authentic. To know Erin Hatton is not only to love her work but also to see through her eyes the stories of those with whom she has engaged in exploring this country's uncomfortable history of economic subjugation. Slave-like indentured servitude in one system (academia) seems perfectly acceptable, while in another (prison) seems unnervingly exploitative but gratuitously necessary. After reading this book, it is clear that both cases are equally injurious and unethical.

I am pleased to have been just a small part of the effort for this book so that others in academia and society can gain the insights of this intimate and astute work. May it not only enlighten you but also motivate you to be an agent of change.

Jerome R. Wright, Community Organizer
Campaign for Alternatives to Isolated Confinement (CAIC)
Buffalo, New York

Introduction

Apache is compact and muscular.[1] He talks fast and low in an eloquent rumble. At 34 years old, the Black American man recently finished his second stint in a New York State prison where he was incarcerated, he explained philosophically, for "a certain lifestyle"—an ontological way of being in the world—rather than for any single crime. "In order to change that lifestyle," he said, "it's a process. . . . You have to get stripped down to look at yourself." For Apache this process was accelerated by the birth of his third child while he was in prison. "For me to miss his birth and have him visit me in a prison and then not get to touch him, just see him through a glass. That took, like, mad layers off." He was emotionally "stripped down."

Like all able-bodied prisoners in New York State, Apache was required to work in prison. He worked six hours a day in the mess hall—preparing and serving food, washing dishes, scouring the kitchen—for which he was paid 15¢–17¢ an hour, nearly $13 every two weeks.[2] Earning these wages in prison, Apache said,

> You convince yourself that you in a good position as far as, you know, getting by. Because you locked down, you ain't got to pay no light bill and this, that, and the other. But it's still slave labor at the end of the day . . . because you don't get to call off, you don't get sick days, you don't get a union. You don't

get none of the benefits of a normal worker. You can't really even advance. You can't aspire to be the boss one day. And, I mean, you're getting paid fifteen cents an hour.

Yet even as Apache described prisoners' work as "slave labor," he argued that it should not be otherwise. Prisoners should not earn the higher wages and other "benefits of a normal worker," he said, because the purpose of prison labor is punishment. "It's not supposed to be a camp," he explained. "It's not supposed to be a happy place. . . . We're in prison. We're not supposed to come in and kick our feet up."

> I mean, I think the best thing is to stay out of prison. I couldn't really conjure somebody getting a lot of money working in prison. It wouldn't really make sense to me. . . . I mean, you're in prison, people are paying taxes and you're not doing nothing. I mean, like, even my wife and my moms, they're out there working and they were sending me money, and that didn't make me feel good . . . and, if you really look at the grand scheme of things, *you* were out there working for me, to take care of me. I mean, the tax they took out of your check, they put it somewhere, and somewhere down the line it came in [the prison]. So, my best advice—even though I *am* an advocate [for prisoners] and I don't want to sound like a hater, but—*just don't go*. If you don't want to be put in that position, *then don't go*.[3]

Whether or not one agrees with Apache's view of prisoners, his description of their labor captures their contradictory position as *workers* in American citizenry: they are "slave labor" yet they are also "doing nothing" while others are "paying taxes" and "working for" them. For like all Americans, prisoners are culturally expected to fulfill a moral obligation to work, the shirking of which—perceived or real—has long been used to justify exclusion from the rights of productive citizenship.[4] Yet prisoners work not only to avoid a stigmatized state of dependence. They also have to work *because* they are dependent. They are the sole exception to the U.S. Constitution's prohibition of slavery. As the 13th Amendment states, "Neither slavery nor involuntary servitude, *except as a punishment for crime* . . . shall exist within the United States."[5] In short, prisoners can be forced to work. Their incarceration not only justifies the compulsion of their labor; it also serves as the legal rationale for their exclusion from employment rights and protections, including the federal minimum wage, overtime pay, and collective bargaining.[6] Because they are prisoners, they can be required to work but, because they are prisoners, they are not protected as workers under labor and employment law. Like enslaved people in years past,[7] American prisoners can be compelled to work while being denied the rights and protections of productive workers, while also condemned for not being such workers. As Apache said, they are at once "slave labor" and "doing nothing." It is this cultural and legal intersection of *working* but not being recognized as *workers* that allows prisoners' labor—and that of others, as we will see—to be characterized by the coercion that I examine in this book.

Prisoners are, in many ways, exceptional. They have been convicted of crimes; they are institutionally confined and therefore physically and economically dependent on the state; and as noted above, they can be legally forced to work. Even still, prisoners' contradictory position at the crossroads of compulsory labor ("slave labor") and culturally constructed idleness ("doing nothing") is not unique. Take, for example, workfare workers: welfare recipients who are required to work 25–35 hours a week in order to receive public assistance. They are assigned to jobs—often janitorial or bookkeeping in nature—in public parks, nonprofit organizations, government agencies, and (in New York City at least) subway stations, but their labor is construed as "work experience" rather than work.[8] As a result, instead of wages their work garners a relatively meager combination of cash benefits, rental and utility assistance, and food stamps (now SNAP), along with childcare during work hours.[9]

There are many dynamics unique to this labor relation, of course, as there are for prisoners. Yet there are also important economic, legal, and cultural parallels between workfare and incarcerated labor. On a structural level, in fact, the U.S. welfare system can be conceptualized as the feminized counterpart to the masculinized criminal justice system, as both are highly racialized, gendered, and classed institutions of social control and subjugation in the United States.[10] Within this system, moreover, workfare workers—much like prisoners—are compelled to work, as their labor is a prerequisite for their continued access to key elements of the social safety net. Meanwhile, the labor of both of these groups yields financial returns for their respective institutions. Workfare workers provide cost savings to the nonprofit organizations and government agencies that use their labor at no cost. Likewise, because incarcerated workers do much of prisons' everyday operations and upkeep work (e.g., food service, cleaning, utilities maintenance), their low- or no-wage labor generates substantial cost savings for prisons and state agencies, while also generating revenue through the sale of prisoner-made goods and services.

Despite their labor, workfare workers—like prisoners—are seen as dependent on the state and are culturally disparaged as being a "drain on the economy" and a "burden" on taxpayers.[11] Indeed, workfare workers themselves often take part in this disparagement, echoing Apache's reprobation of prisoners. As workfare worker April Smith said of other welfare recipients, "A lot of people lay around, they don't do anything." To the contrary, studies suggest that most welfare recipients, like most Americans, believe deeply in the importance of work.[12] Even still, welfare recipients are seen as uniquely economically dependent on the state (in contrast to other demographic groups who, for example, receive Social Security benefits or federally subsidized student loans), and as with prisoners, this socially constructed dependence is used to justify their exclusion from many legal protections as "employees." In both cases, these workers' economic dependence is reified, and even intensified, by the extra constraints of their labor relations. For instance, both workfare and incarcerated workers cannot freely choose whether and for whom they work, nor can they freely change or quit their jobs. Yet in the (white) American imagination, such restrictions are justified by welfare recipients' and prisoners' (interrelated) criminalization and marginalization. As convicts, prisoners are overtly criminalized, while welfare recipients' criminalization is the product of the more insidious "criminalization of poverty," a political, legal, and cultural superstructure built on the presumption of their fraudulence and enacted through their punitive surveillance and bodily regulation.[13] For both of these groups of workers, this criminalization is at once cause and consequence of their social marginalization, as they each confront high levels of stigmatization, pathologization, and subjugation at their particular intersections of race, class, and gender disadvantage.[14]

Thus, in America's convoluted raced, classed, and gendered cultural logic, both welfare recipients and prisoners can, *and should*, be compelled to work because they are convicted or suspected criminals and because they are deemed to be unduly dependent on the state. Because of such dependence, workfare and incarcerated workers are not seen as "real" workers—regardless of their labor—and are therefore not protected by labor and employment laws. In fact, their economic independence is overtly curtailed by the institutions for which they labor. Yet all the while they are culturally condemned for being idle.

These parallels are perhaps not surprising. Scholars have persuasively argued that the carceral and welfare states in America comprise a "single policy regime,"[15] which has taken a "resolutely punitive turn" in recent decades with carceral expansion and social welfare contraction.[16] This two-pronged policy regime has been built at the state level through political discourse, legislation, and budgetary spending (and cuts).[17] On the ground level, as I have argued elsewhere, it has been rolled out through the dual expansion of workfare and incarcerated labor—"punitive labor regimes"[18]—in which welfare recipients and prisoners experience firsthand the penalizing and paternalistic power of what Loïc Wacquant has called the neoliberal "centaur state."[19]

As this book will show, however, understanding the U.S. carceral and welfare states as a single policy regime—and workers' marginalized labor within it—does not fully explain these workers' contradictory position as "slave labor" and "doing nothing." In fact, focusing solely on the points of intersection between prison labor and workfare, as important and compelling as they are, may obscure their parallels to other *very different* categories of work that can be found beyond the "carceral archipelago."[20]

Take university student workers, such as college football and basketball players and graduate student researchers in the sciences. To be sure, these students are *far removed* from prisoners and welfare recipients in many (almost innumerable) ways. While the latter groups are scapegoated as cultural exemplars of personal and moral failure, college athletes and PhD students are the opposite: they are cultural role models, and as a result, their day-to-day lives, as well as their future trajectories, are vastly different. The stigmatization, criminalization, and punishment which characterize daily life for many prisoners and welfare recipients differ dramatically from the near hero worship of some college athletes, whose ardent fans don replicas of their jerseys, hang their action shots on dorm-room walls, and cheer for them wildly from the sidelines. And though graduate students are not nearly such campus and cultural icons, they too occupy a position of social privilege, walking the halls of the "ivory tower" in pursuit of new knowledge and advanced educational degrees.

Despite these important differences, there are also parallels between these groups in their interstitial status as workers. For instance, though there is controversy about whether these student workers should be legally categorized as "employees"—just as there is about incarcerated and work-fare workers[21]—they arguably perform labor: for hours a day, athletes sweat in sports arenas, and graduate students run experiments and analyze data in science labs. Like incarcerated and workfare workers, both student groups have professional counterparts who *are* considered rights-bearing workers: professional athletes in the NFL and NBA, science researchers in industry and academia. Furthermore, like incarcerated and workfare workers, these students' labor yields substantial financial returns, not for themselves but for their institutions and other stakeholders. In fact, the athletic labor of Division I football and basketball players can generate multimillion-dollar salaries for their coaches and even more for their universities, athletic conferences, and the NCAA itself.[22] Private companies as well have profited handsomely from athletes' labor by commodifying their names, photographs, likenesses, jersey numbers, and equipment, although court rulings have begun to proscribe some of these practices.[23]

In the academic sciences, PhD students and postdocs conduct much, and sometimes all, of faculty research. While faculty members design and oversee research projects in the lab, graduate students typically do the labor necessary to carry out such projects. Yet the products of their labor—publications, inventions, patents, and more—are owned by the faculty member in charge of the lab. As a result, faculty in the sciences are often bosses as well as teachers, and these students' graduate education is often a labor relation as well as a learning one. This stands in contrast to my own discipline of sociology, for example, in which graduate students generally devise and pursue their own research agendas (not their advisors'), and so their PhD research is not a labor relation in the same way. Yet it is also true that many graduate students across academic disciplines, including sociology, work under their advisors as teaching and research assistants, so that their labor would indeed be characterized by the type of coercion I examine in this book. In the sciences, such dynamics are often more acute, not least because graduate student labor is the foundation of the scientific enterprise in the academy. As Slaughter and colleagues write in their study of science and engineering faculty, "one cannot be a professor unless he or she does research, and a professor cannot do research without graduate students."[24] Such research, fueled by graduate student labor, is the primary driver of the research-publication-grant cycle, which generates substantial financial returns for universities and faculty alike. For their part, graduate students are paid less than market value for their labor—indeed, they are widely referred to as "cheap"[25]—and their labor is largely paid for by the external grants it helps obtain. Yet such grants pay for much more than graduate student stipends; they supplement faculty salaries and subsidize universities' "indirect costs" (e.g., administrative support and facility maintenance). Beyond these immediate financial returns, graduate student labor helps universities cultivate their reputation as generators of scientific innovation, enabling them to recruit faculty and students, and thereby sustain the cycle.

Despite their labor, graduate students and college athletes have been legally deemed "primarily students" rather than workers.[26] Although workers, activists, and even judges have challenged this sociolegal construction, both groups are still broadly considered trainees instead of employees: apprentices in the lab, amateurs on the field. As a result, they are paid in education and training rather than wages, though they often also receive basic stipends.[27] As students, moreover, their earnings outside of the lab and off the court can be capped. For graduate students in the sciences, for example, the general expectation is that they will not hold any other job, and this expectation can be formalized and enforced by granting agencies, universities, departments, and faculty advisors alike.[28] Regardless, the science graduate students I interviewed said that long hours in the lab rendered other employment out of the question. This was also the case for the college athletes I interviewed, who said that their intensive training and traveling schedules precluded them from taking other jobs. In any case, the NCAA explicitly restricts what kind of employment Division I athletes can accept and how much they can earn.[29] Indeed, with the very recent exception of California, athletes (along with their families) are not allowed to profit from their athletic labor in any way: aside from any university stipend they might receive, they cannot accept money, gifts, or meals for their athleticism or any activities that stem from it, such as selling autographs or endorsing products.[30] Such nonpayment is the underpinning of college athletes' "amateurism," NCAA officials assert, which "is crucial to preserving an academic environment in which acquiring a quality education is the first priority."[31] Thus, in a true tautology (recalling that of prisoners), college athletes cannot profit from their athletic labor because they are students, and because they are students they cannot profit from their athletic labor. Moreover, football and basketball players in particular are effectively required to play at the collegiate level before playing professionally.[32] In these revenue-generating sports, athletes are compelled to perform unpaid athletic labor before they can be paid for it.

Like incarcerated and workfare workers, then, college athletes and graduate students work but are not seen as workers.[33] They cannot earn (or earn much) from their labor, and their economic independence—their ability to sell their labor and expertise—is restricted. They too are culturally and legally constructed as economic dependents: amateurs and trainees gaining education and experience. Yet *unlike* incarcerated and workfare workers, for whom the cultural condemnation of their racialized and gendered criminality and poverty justifies such dependence, college athletes' and graduate students' relatively privileged status as university students justifies theirs. For while incarcerated and workfare workers are socially constructed as *immoral* dependents who require punitive state intervention to attend to their criminality and poverty, college athletes and graduate students are constructed as *moral* dependents who benefit from paternalist state intervention. They are seen as being gifted—even uplifted through—education. Yet for football and basketball players, the majority of whom are racial minorities,[34] the racialized overtones of such "uplift" cannot be ignored. In fact, as I show in chapter 1, they echo the paternalism of 19th-century slave owners in the American South,[35] thus pointing to even more parallels between college athletics and the racialized regimes of workfare and incarcerated labor in America today.

.   .   .   .   .

Broadly speaking, then, there are surprising parallels across these diverse cases: graduate students, college athletes, workfare participants, and prisoners are all sociolegally constructed as something other than "workers" doing something other than "work." Rather than rights-bearing employees, they are dependents whose economic independence is constrained, as they cannot freely seek additional or alternative employment. They do not earn free-market wages for their labor and in fact are often paid in something other than money altogether.

This book does not argue, simplistically and narrowly, that all of these groups should be legally categorized as "employees." Their legal exclusion is the starting point of this analysis, not its endpoint. My task is at once larger and messier. Through a comparative analysis of these strikingly different labor relations, I identify key similarities between them: not just their status as nonworkers, but how this status shapes the power dynamics that define their workplaces.

I find that in all of these cases, as different from each other as they are, workers' status as something other than rights-bearing employees allows for their supervisors to have unusually *expansive punitive power* over them. For instance, if prisoners do not comply with officer demands, the consequence is not just being fired from the job, though that may also happen. They can be fined a week's pay, lose their eligibility for parole, and be put in solitary confinement, that is, within an enclosed and segregated cell for 23 hours a day without human interaction. Indeed, any form of noncompliance, large or small, can land prisoners in the "box" (as those in New York State often refer to solitary confinement),[36] making it a relatively common occurrence. Although precise data are not available, it is estimated that 80,000–100,000 people in the United States (and 4,500 in New York) are held in some type of isolation at any given time, and often for significant periods of time: an average of 5 months in New York and 18 months in Colorado, though in fact solitary sentences can be indefinite.[37] The mental and physiological consequences of such prolonged isolation are well documented and severe: PTSD, anxiety, depression, suicide, paranoia, insomnia, hallucinations, psychosis, dizziness, headaches, lethargy, heart palpitations, and more.[38] At least one bioethicist has called solitary confinement "the worst kind of psychological torture."[39] Yet such "torture" is a routine consequence that officers—as labor supervisors as well as guards—can mete out to prisoners.

For the other workers I studied, the punishments that their bosses can impose are usually less severe, but the reach of their bosses' power is similarly expansive. For instance, if workfare workers do not comply with their caseworkers' or workfare supervisors' demands, they can be "sanctioned," which means that they lose access to public assistance programs, such as cash benefits, rent and utility subsidies, Medicaid, childcare and transportation assistance, and SNAP benefits—elements of the social safety net which are crucial to families in poverty.[40] Although such sanctions are usually temporary, their effects are permanent. In addition to any long-term consequences for themselves and their families, including those of homelessness and extreme poverty,[41] welfare sanctions reduce their lifetime allotment of public assistance under TANF (Temporary Assistance for Needy Families).[42]

For the university student workers in this study—college athletes and graduate students—the punitive power their bosses can wield is less severe still, though nonetheless far-reaching. For instance, if Division I athletes do not comply with their coaches' directives, they may lose their playing time, that is, the much sought-after chance to compete at an elite collegiate level and the professional recruitment opportunities it provides. They may also lose their scholarships and thus their education and undergraduate degrees. Likewise, the education, degree conferral, and future employment of science graduate students are in the hands of the faculty advisors for whom they labor. Such advisors can dismiss them from the PhD program as well as delay their graduation because they have become productive workers in the lab. Advisors also have total authority over students' academic record in the sciences, particularly their publications, which in combination with letters of recommendation give them immense power over students' futures.

Of course, not all faculty advisors, coaches, case workers, and corrections officers deploy these punitive powers. But those who do are not "bad apples." They are not exceptions to the rule. They are the rule. Their access to such expansive punitive power is simply a matter of course in these labor relations and, as a result, often remains unquestioned by workers and supervisors alike. This is simply "how things are done" in these workplaces. If a prisoner does not comply with an officer's orders, he will likely be put in the "box." If a workfare worker does not adhere to her supervisor's directives, she may very well be sanctioned. If an athlete does not comply with her coach's dictates, she will likely lose playing time. If a graduate student does not follow his advisor's directives, he may well lose his advisor's support for future employment. Thus, graduate students, college athletes, workfare workers, and prisoners not only labor in the absence of most employment protections and remedies; they labor *under the threat of punishment.* Whether or not they experience such punishment, they are acutely aware of the punitive power that their supervisors can wield and this awareness pervades the workplace, fundamentally shaping their actions and experiences.

To be sure, bosses in all workplaces wield substantial, and expansive, power over their subordinates. Most often, they do so through their capacity to hire, promote, schedule, and fire workers, that is, the economic coercion that Karl Marx identified as endemic to capitalist labor relations.[43] Because the "economic whip of the market" is ever present for workers in this system, the fear of losing one's job may compel—indeed, coerce—their compliance.[44] This form of coercion is particularly acute in this era of resurgent labor precarity. For although the market's lash can be softened by strong worker protections and a sturdy social safety net, such is not the case for American workers at the start of the 21st century, who face rising employment insecurity and welfare retrenchment along with intense social stigmatization of unemployment and welfare. Even the nontraditional workers in this book face economic coercion, at least to some degree, as their "wages"—prison earnings, public assistance, and student stipends—are often essential to their material well-being.

But the workers in this book face a different form of coercion as well. For their bosses can do more than harness the lash of the market by firing them or assigning them worse work schedules. Their bosses can also disrupt their familial relationships (e.g., through solitary confinement or, much less severely, through long work hours in the lab); they can harm their health and well-being as well as that of their families (e.g., through solitary confinement, welfare sanctions, or pressure to play through injuries); and they can thwart their education, aspirations, and future employment (e.g., by withdrawing or withholding scholarship/funding, playing time, graduation, or positive letters of recommendation). Thus, in these labor relations bosses' punitive power extends beyond the immediate job and its wages to affect workers' lives in even more expansive ways. For incarcerated, workfare, athlete, and graduate student workers, then, the primary threat is not that they will lose their jobs, though that may also be of concern. Rather, it is what might happen to their bodies, families, and futures if they refuse to comply with their bosses' demands.

In existing scholarship there is no term that adequately captures this type of punitive power. In my search to find such a term, I looked to Marxian frameworks where the most productive tools for such analysis have been developed. Initially, the Marxian term "extra-economic coercion" seemed to capture this type of expansive employer power, as it is *beyond economic* in nature. Yet in the literature, this term is not usually used in this narrow, literal way. Instead, "extra-economic" has been used to distinguish (purportedly) precapitalist types of labor coercion from capitalism's economic coercion.[45] As a result, it has become an umbrella term for an array of coercive employer powers, including physical coercion (violence and threats thereof, as in chattel slavery), economic and legal limits on worker mobility (as in debt peonage and vagrancy laws), and political and economic limits on land use (as in feudalism).[46] As the latter examples suggest, such coercion was at least somewhat economic in nature, despite being labeled "extra-economic."[47] Similarly, as scholars have argued, "economic coercion" itself is not strictly economic in nature, as it also has social, legal, and political dimensions.[48] Thus, as used in the literature at least, "economic" and "extra-economic" coercions pertain more to their context—capitalist versus precapitalist—than to the nature of the coercion itself. This is in spite of the fact that, as scholars have shown, extra-economic coercion was not necessarily precapitalist at all.[49] As demonstrated by studies of U.S. slavery, for example, this violent and brutal system of forced labor was essential, not antithetical, to America's emergence as a modern, industrial, capitalist economy.[50] Then, after slavery was abolished and free labor was ostensibly universalized, forced and coerced labor remained entrenched, as evidenced by the persistence of sharecropping, debt peonage, indentured servitude, and prison labor as American capitalism developed.[51] Meanwhile, even purportedly "free" labor was underpinned by coercion through the 19th century. Because of employers' widespread use of criminal sanctions and wage forfeiture to enforce employment contracts, "free" workers were not actually free to quit their jobs.[52] Therefore, although the term "extra-economic" might seem definitionally appropriate to the type of coercion I analyze here, the term itself is used otherwise, while also implicated in outdated binarisms between economic and noneconomic, capitalist and precapitalist, and free and unfree labor, all of which have been disrupted in the scholarly literature.

Beyond intervening in such debates, I believe it is more analytically productive to identify what this type of coercion *is* rather than what it is not (e.g., economic), for doing so highlights the mechanism by which it operates. In this vein, "economic coercion" is aptly named because it operates primarily through pecuniary compulsion. The same is true of "physical coercion," which operates through corporal compulsion. While the workers in this book experience some degree of economic coercion and, in the case of prisoners, physical coercion, the type of coercion that permeates their labor does not operate through either pecuniary or corporal mechanisms. Rather, it operates through *status*. Their supervisors have the power to discharge them from a particular status—as prisoner, welfare recipient, college athlete, or graduate student "in good standing"—and thereby deprive them of the rights, privileges, and future opportunities that such status confers. Thus, I argue that these labor relations are characterized by *status coercion*.

Status is a foundational sociological concept. Developed by anthropologist Ralph Linton in the 1930s, the term refers to individuals' positions in society, both ascribed and achieved, such as female, parent, professor, and prisoner.[53] Such statuses come with important (though sometimes conflicting) rights, obligations, limitations, and expectations ("roles"), which are often normative in nature but which can also be codified in law. The workers in this book, for example, do not occupy the status of "worker," and therefore do not have access to the cultural standing and legal rights and protections that this status usually yields. Instead, they occupy a variety of other statuses, each of which comes with its own obligations, constraints, rights, and privileges (however attenuated). To be sure, such statuses are not always desirable. It is likely that no one desires to occupy the status of prisoner. But once in it, retaining one's status as *prisoner in good standing* is of utmost importance, because it gives prisoners access to the many human entitlements that become "privileges" behind bars—privileges which can be revoked. For example, being in good standing allows prisoners to sustain relationships with family and friends (through phone use, visitation, and interaction with fellow prisoners), while also giving them access to activity, recreation, and freedom of movement (albeit constrained), money, food, and consumer goods (through work assignments and commissary purchases), and sometimes early release from prison (through parole or commutation). Thus, although "prisoner" is not a desirable status, as it imposes many more constraints than privileges, when one is living behind bars, maintaining one's status as a "good" prisoner is desirable indeed.

The other statuses that I examine in this book are similar, for even when they impose constraints on their worker-occupants, they also offer important rights and privileges. For workfare workers, for example, being a welfare recipient in good standing is a prerequisite for their continued access to key safety net programs and even homeless shelters. For Division I college athletes, occupying that status in good standing gives them access to subsidized university education and the credentials it confers, as well as the chance to play the sport they love and, for some, professional recruitment opportunities (perhaps even fame and future fortune). Likewise, being a graduate student in good standing offers access to subsidized graduate education as well as high-status credentials, experience, training, and professional opportunities. Even though these statuses do not confer the right to a minimum wage or collective bargaining, as would the status of "worker," they offer rights and privileges that are highly valued within their respective institutions. Yet in each of these cases, supervisors have the capacity to revoke such rights and privileges, the consequences of which extend beyond the job to affect these workers' lives, families, and futures in far-reaching ways. This control over status—status coercion—is the basis for supervisors' expansive punitive power in these labor relations.

But, of course, these workers do not experience this type of coercion to the same degree. Much like the differing degrees of economic coercion across jobs and workers in the conventional labor market, the status coercion that these workers experience is similar in kind but not intensity. Indeed, the severity of the punitive power that their bosses wield differs dramatically across these groups: solitary confinement is *far removed* from losing playing time on the field; welfare sanctions are *far removed* from being dismissed from PhD programs. As in conventional jobs, moreover, workers' demographic characteristics—their particular identity at the intersection of race, class, gender, sexuality, and more—may make them more or less likely to be targets of their bosses' punitive power, and their vulnerability to such power can be mitigated (or intensified) by their personal circumstances.[54] There is significant variation, then, both within and across these labor relations in the severity of workers' experience of status coercion. The goal of this book, however, is not to document such variation, but to delineate the contours of this form of labor coercion.

To be sure, the labor relations I examine in this book are not the only ones characterized by status coercion. Take, for example, foreign guest workers and undocumented immigrant workers, both noncitizen workers for whom U.S. employers have de facto power of deportation. Because guest workers are legally bound to a single employer, the Southern Poverty Law Center reports, "At any moment, the employer can fire the worker, call the government and declare the worker to be 'illegal.'"[55] A similar dynamic is in effect for undocumented workers, because under U.S. immigration law employers are empowered—and in fact obligated—to verify workers' citizenship status.[56] This means that at any point they can "discover" workers' undocumented status and contact immigration authorities. In both cases, then, employers can convert workers into criminals ("illegal aliens")—directly for guest workers and indirectly for undocumented immigrants by exposing their illegality—leaving them subject to detention and deportation. In short, employers have power over noncitizen workers' status as *worker* or *criminal* and the privileges or punishments that each yields. Thus, like the labor relations I examine in this book, noncitizen labor is characterized by status coercion. And as studies of noncitizen workers have shown, employers' access to this legal form of punitive power seems to facilitate their use of illegal exploitation and coercion, such as paying subminimum wages, providing unsafe working and living conditions, seizing passports, and blacklisting.[57] In fact, this also seems to be true of the labor relations in this book: bosses' licit power of status coercion seems to open the door, at least for some, to illicit abuse.

Status coercion is not relegated to such extreme or unusual labor relations. Many conventional workers also experience status coercion, at least to some degree. At the most basic level, being fired from one's job means being ejected from one's status as *worker* and the considerable rights and privileges it confers. Such loss of status can have significant psychological and physiological consequences in addition to economic consequences, especially for those who are culturally or financially expected to be "breadwinners."[58] For many workers, however, this loss of status is temporary, as they are free (within constraints) to find and accept other employment. For such workers, the threat of losing income (economic coercion) often overshadows the threat of losing one's employment status (status coercion). But this is not the case for everyone. For workers who are bound by noncompete clauses, for example, employers have power over their status as that particular type of worker.[59] According to reporting by the *New York Times*, an increasingly broad array of workers is bound by such clauses—including, for example, tree service workers. As one such worker told reporters, "It's one thing to have a bump in the road and be in between jobs for a little while; it's another thing to be prevented from doing the only thing you know how to do."[60] For this worker, his employer controlled not only his wages and working conditions, but also his ability to leverage his labor market experience and obtain future employment. This is status coercion.

Such coercion can be found anywhere an employer has power over a worker's social position—not their immediate income but their status in society. It may be particularly prevalent among those who labor in "total institutions," such as military and religious organizations, in which one's status, as Marine officer or Catholic nun, for example, is equally as important as (or even more important than) one's income.[61] Status coercion may also be prevalent in occupations characterized by high degrees of social closure or tight labor markets. For instance, as I was writing this book, actors' pushback against sexual harassment and assault in Hollywood revealed (once again) the expansive power that gatekeepers in exclusive occupations wield over subordinates' access to an elite status—in this case, Hollywood actor—and its many privileges.[62]

For those workers whose freedom from incarceration is predicated on their employment, such coercion may be even more acute. As Noah Zatz and collaborators have shown, people who are under criminal justice supervision but not incarcerated—parolees, probationers, and those with court-ordered debts—can be required to maintain employment on threat of incarceration.[63] In such "carceral labor," as Zatz calls it,[64] employers have power over workers' status as *worker* or *criminal* (as for noncitizens) and all of the privileges and punishments associated with each. As a judge in a court supervision program told a defendant's employer, "Okay, I'll make a deal with you; you take him back and I'll add another weapon to your arsenal. If he doesn't come to work when he is supposed to, doesn't come to work on time . . . I'll put him in jail, on your say-so." Then, to the defendant, the judge said, "Your employer is now on the team of people who are reporting to me. When he calls up and tells me that you are late, or that you're not there, I'm going to send the cops out to arrest you."[65] Thus, for such workers the threat of incarceration is an explicit employer "weapon," rendering their labor deeply coercive. As for noncitizen workers, moreover, studies suggest that this licit form of status coercion facilitates illicit coercion and exploitation as well, all of which suppresses workers' resistance and enforces their productivity.[66]

As all of these examples suggest, status coercion is not only common practice; it is legal and legitimate. Employers are legally empowered to govern workers' behavior on threat of incarceration; they are legally responsible for verifying workers' citizenship status; and in most states, they can legally impose and enforce noncompete clauses for any type of worker. Likewise, for the workers in this book, employers are legally empowered to put them in solitary confinement, push them off public assistance, and obstruct their education and future employment. In short, employers' powers of status coercion are *sanctioned* by the state.

This state sanctioning of status coercion stands in contrast to state efforts to curb—at least to some degree—employers' powers of economic coercion. Through various hard-won labor protections and social welfare programs, the state protects workers (however minimally) from economic coercion. If workers lose their jobs, for example, they may have access to unemployment benefits, cash assistance, and other social welfare programs; if they fall ill or adopt a child, they may have access to Family and Medical Leave Act benefits. Such protections offset the economic coercion at the heart of those labor relations. But this is not the case for the type of coercion I examine in this book, which is endorsed, not mitigated, by state and institutional policies.

Thus, in this book I argue that work in America is not only characterized by precarity and the "dull compulsion" of economic coercion.[67] It is also characterized by coercion of another sort: employer power over workers' status in society—whether as "worker" or as something else—and therefore power over their access to meaningful rights and privileges. Studies of work and employment need to look beyond precarity and flexibilization to understand all of the "weapons" that employers can wield against workers. Doing so will not only provide a more complete accounting of employers' "arsenal." It will also provide a better understanding of how such weapons can be combined, compounding one another to amplify employers' power over workers.

The labor relations I examine in this book reveal this type of coercion in high relief. Yet some might object to the comparison of these groups, because they are simply so different. Indeed, on the surface, it seems absurd to link PhD work to prison labor. Thus, it is important to state again, as clearly as possible, that I do not argue that these groups are the same. They differ on so many levels, including their levels of social stigmatization and economic marginalization, as well as the severity of their coercion. Yet even with such important differences between them, I believe that highlighting their similarities yields analytical advantages. By showing how this type of coercion operates for the criminalized as well as the privileged, for the powerless as well as the potentially powerful, and for those who are racialized Black as well as those racialized white, this book shows that this type of employer power is not unique to any one of these groups. Status coercion is not the idiosyncratic byproduct of, say, mass incarceration or the NCAA. It is an entrenched and pervasive form of labor governance, one that intersects with other regimes of social and labor control—including both race and precarity—to disadvantage workers, albeit in different ways and to different degrees.

Examining the common power dynamics across such divergent cases offers political and methodological advantages as well. By highlighting the connections between these typically siloed domains—criminal justice, welfare, sports, higher education, and work—this book lays the foundation for future alliances between scholars, workers, and activists who have, until now, understood their circumstances as unique. Methodologically, by comparing these divergent cases, this book fulfills the two primary functions of comparative research identified by French sociologist Michel Wieviorka.[68] First, it deconstructs "what common sense takes to be unique or unified"[69] by interrogating the presumed distinctiveness of each of these categories of work, as well as the presumed unity of "work" as it is traditionally defined. Second, by identifying status coercion as the unifying thread across these (and other) seemingly dissimilar labor relations, it constructs "unity of what seems to be broken up into practical categories."[70] In so doing, this study continues the long sociological tradition of making what George Steinmetz describes as "odious comparisons."[71] Scholars in this tradition, who include Everett Hughes, Erving Goffman, and Howard Becker, have compared radically different cases, identifying the often-surprising points of intersection between them in order to elucidate broader social phenomena. This is the goal of this book. By comparing the dramatically disparate cases of incarcerated, workfare, college athlete, and graduate student labor, this book uncovers the dynamics of a previously unidentified type of labor coercion: what status coercion is, how it works, and the ways that workers experience—and resist—it.

.   .   .   .   .

Coerced both complements and extends previous studies of work, power, and social control. Foremost, it adds to Marxian analyses of labor coercion by identifying control over status as an additional form of coercive employer power that overlaps with, but is distinct from, economic and physical coercion. In so doing, it contributes to the now sizable scholarly literature documenting the persistence of not-strictly economic coercion in advanced capitalism.[72] In fact, by documenting such coercion in modern-day America, this book explicitly extends this literature, which has generally focused on either historical forms of unfree labor (particularly chattel slavery[73]) or present-day trafficked, forced, and enslaved labor from the global South,[74] while also documenting the continued prevalence of economic coercion, especially among low-wage workers.[75] Yet such research, though important, might mistakenly lead readers to conclude that labor coercion is, variously, a historical relic premised on regimes of extreme racial violence and subjugation, a byproduct of contemporary globalization and transnational labor migration, or a customary component of capitalist labor relations. This book draws from each of these literatures while also diverging from them to show that labor coercion is not only a thing of the past, an import from the global South, or a common characteristic of "bad" jobs. In the form of status coercion, it is also a distinct and well-established mode of labor governance in America today.

This book thus transforms our understanding of work in contemporary America. For simply put, labor coercion has not been a part of this understanding. Instead, the problem of precarity has dominated accounts of work and labor in America—with good reason, to be sure, as precarious employment has produced instability, insecurity, and vulnerability for a significant and growing population of workers.[76] But this book shows that precarity is not the only force shaping work in America today. Labor coercion is alive and well, and not simply in the widely accepted (even expected) form of economic coercion. Employers' power over workers' status is a pervasive and often potent type of labor control, one that seems to be growing with the criminal justice system's deepening reach into the low-wage labor market; the upsurge in citizenship audits, deportation arrests, and immigrant detention; the rise of noncompete clauses, and more.

Yet status coercion is not just operating alongside, and separate from, precarity. The two systems of labor control intersect, shaping and reinforcing one another. For as we will see in this book, status coercion helps *create* the vulnerable and compliant workers on whom neoliberal precarity relies. Whether priming workers for undervalued and insecure positions as adjuncts and postdocs (as does graduate school) or as day laborers and fast-food workers (as do prison labor and workfare), the coercive labor regimes I examine in this book actively produce the "precariat."[77]

This book thus identifies a new mechanism by which the state has expanded its punitive power in the context of neoliberalism. For as scholars have noted, neoliberalism in the United States has entailed not only state contraction but also state expansion—a strategic shrinking of government combined with a surge of authoritarianism.[78] The recent spread of labor precarity is associated with the former: state withdrawal from (some categories of) work through de- and reregulation, declining labor standards, and deunionization.[79] The labor coercion I analyze in this book is associated with the latter: the insertion of punitive state power into (these and other categories of) work. In such coercive labor regimes, the punitive arm of the "ambidextrous" neoliberal state has flexed its muscle.[80]

In this way, status coercion not only intersects with other systems of labor control, such as precarity; it also intersects with other systems of social control, such as race. Its overlap with the racialized criminal justice system is a case in point. As scholars have shown, racial logics have been woven into the very fabric of this system, designating some (explicitly or implicitly) racialized people, drugs, crimes, and neighborhoods as "worse" and more "dangerous" than others and therefore deserving of increased surveillance, policing, and sentencing.[81] This has produced the profoundly racialized regime of mass incarceration, in which a vastly disproportionate share of the skyrocketing carceral population is African American, which has reentrenched America's racial caste system.[82] The same is true of the welfare system, a profoundly racialized institution that has also produced and sustained deep racial disparities.[83] Racial logics have been woven into the fabric of this system as well, as racism has long been a guiding principle for administering—and denying—public assistance.[84] Status coercion directly intersects with both of these racialized regimes of social control through prison labor and workfare, as well as through the "carceral labor" that Zatz has identified.[85] In all of them, status coercion exploits and amplifies their punitive racial logics.

Indeed, I would argue that racial logics have been woven into the coercive labor regimes I examine in this book—logics which seek to explain who should be subject to such coercion and why. As I show in chapter 1, for prisoners, welfare recipients, and athletes alike, cultural constructions (and assumptions) of their Blackness intersect with presumptions of their criminality, or their (not quite deserved) privilege, to justify their bosses' expansive punitive power over them. Whether they are construed as wayward crooks (as are prisoners and welfare recipients) or as potentially wayward kids (as are college football and basketball players), such workers are framed as needing extensive surveillance, control, and discipline. Meanwhile, for graduate students, cultural constructions (and assumptions) of their whiteness intersect with presumptions of their (mostly deserved) privilege, to justify but also mitigate their bosses' punitive power over them. Rather than wayward kids, they are seen as smart novices who require direction and surveillance, perhaps, but not punitive discipline. Therefore, just as racialized logics form the substructure of the American criminal justice and welfare systems, they also profoundly shape the institutions at the center of this book, and therefore workers' experiences within them.

This book thus builds on analyses of social institutions, particularly work organizations, as fundamentally raced, gendered, and classed. As scholars have shown, these intersecting axes of inequality are embedded in organizations' culture, policies, and practices in ways that are distinct from (though not unrelated to) the particular bodies that inhabit them at any given time.[86] This is certainly true of the institutions at the center of this book. For despite the demographic diversity of prisoners in the United States, prisons are culturally constructed as Black, lower-class, masculinized institutions.[87] Similarly, despite the demographic diversity of people receiving public assistance, the American welfare system is coded as a Black, lower-class, feminized institution.[88] College football and basketball teams have a somewhat more complex race-class designation: regardless of athletes' diversity, both sports are construed as relatively poor Black spaces situated (sometimes uneasily) within white upper-middle-class universities, though both are masculinized.[89] By contrast, the cultural construal of university graduate programs—in the sciences and otherwise—broadly aligns with universities' race-class-gender designations, despite the diversity of those who learn and labor within them.[90]

Even though such designations are cultural constructs rather than demographic facts, their effects are powerful, shaping many aspects of these institutions, including their policies and practices of worker governance. Thus, for example, prisons' everyday practices of coercion and subjugation, which all prisoners experience, at least to some degree, are shaped by their designation as Black, lower-class, masculinized institutions and the social construction of this identity as criminal and dangerous. This is not to deny that racial minorities experience unequal and discriminatory treatment in U.S. prisons. They do.[91] But at the same time, I contend that all prisoners experience prisons' particular race-gender-class designation through the institution's policies and practices. The same is true of the other labor regimes I examine in this book. Even though race and gender minorities experience disparate treatment within these work organizations,[92] these organizations' institutionalized practices of worker governance are shaped by their socially constructed race-class-gender designations. Therefore, just as Cynthia Cockburn argued in her early study of occupational gender segregation that "jobs ... have a gender character that rubs off on the people that do them,"[93] I argue that each of these labor regimes has a race-class-gender character that "rubs off" on the people who labor within them. Indeed, in this book I uncover at least some of the mechanisms by which such "rubbing off" occurs: for these institutions' race-class-gender character is actively "rubbed onto" workers' bodies through the raced, classed, and gendered technologies of coercion and subjugation that I examine.

Ultimately, *Coerced* revises our understanding of labor governance and social control in contemporary America. By identifying a previously unrecognized type of power that (at least some) employers can wield over workers, it shows how those employers are able to affect workers' lives, families, and futures in far-reaching ways. Moreover, though this book's analytical lens is centered on how workers' experience this power in four particular types of work—from prisons to PhD programs—it also looks beyond these workplaces to consider how this coercive power intersects with other systems of social control. But this book is only the beginning: a first step toward a broader and deeper understanding of work and power in America today.

.   .   .   .   .

For this book I interviewed more than 120 workers over the course of five years.[94] Of those workers, 42 were workfare participants and 41 were ex-prisoners, both from cities across New York State: New York City, Albany, Rochester, and Buffalo. Interviewing these two types of workers from just one state—New York—was necessary to control for the substantial state-level variation in poverty and prison policies. For both, moreover, New York is an ideal site of analysis. New York has been a national leader in the implementation of workfare, particularly in the years after welfare reform, and therefore offers greater insight into workers' experiences of this labor regime. At the same time, New York's prisons and prison practices are neither particularly extreme nor particularly controversial. New York does not have (the often infamous) private prisons, as do Texas, Indiana, Colorado, and Oklahoma; its prison conditions have not been deemed in violation of prisoners' constitutional rights, as have California's;[95] and its prisoners are paid wages for their labor, however minimal, unlike Georgia, Texas, and South Carolina, where they are not paid at all.[96] In short, New York represents a middle-of-the-road case of prisons and prison labor in the United States.

I also interviewed 18 former NCAA Division I football and basketball players and 20 former PhD students in the sciences. Unlike workfare and incarcerated workers, these former student workers were recruited from sites across the country. (In fact, in order to ensure their anonymity, I did not interview any student connected—past or present—with my own university.) Not only had these former student workers attended many different universities; they had also labored in different work environments within those universities. I interviewed women as well as men basketball players, for example, and I interviewed graduate students from a variety of labs and science departments, including chemistry, biology, pharmacology, and neuroscience. Yet like incarcerated and workfare workers, all of these student workers had labored under a single policy regime, because their governing bodies are at the national (rather than state) level. Athletes' labor is primarily governed by the NCAA, while graduate students' labor is governed by an amalgamation of court rulings and federal granting institutions, particularly the National Institutes of Health, which is the primary funder of bioscience research in the academy.[97] Within each of these groups of workers, then, any differences between them stem not from structural variation but from the particularities of their bosses and work environments, that is, the dispositions of their faculty advisors, coaches, workfare supervisors, and corrections officers, and the organizational cultures that such bosses have cultivated. (As I discuss in chapter 2, supervisors in these labor regimes often have exceptional latitude to shape workers' lives.)

Aside from those in workfare, most of the workers in this study had moved on from these particular employment relations, either recently released from prison or recently graduated from their universities.[98] For many, such distance enabled them to speak more freely about their work. Despite such distance, however, a few expressed fear of reprisal in doing so, particularly athletes and graduate students, who often continue to rely on their coaches and lab bosses for postgraduate employment. Although the ex-prisoners I interviewed did not generally share this concern, their distance from prison was also essential to their ability to talk openly, given the totality of their surveillance and control behind bars. Workfare workers were the exception: even though most of them were still laboring for workfare at the time of our interview, they did not express any concerns of reprisal. Nonetheless, for all of my informants I have taken numerous measures to protect their privacy and confidentiality, including changing key but inconsequential details and using pseudonyms, which the workers themselves chose so that they can identify themselves in my writing.

In our interviews, a worker and I typically talked for an hour or more— me with a digital recorder in hand—most often in person but sometimes over the phone. My interview questions were broad and wide-ranging. I asked about their labor in college sports arenas, university science labs, public parks and thrift stores, prison mess halls and dormitories. I asked about their everyday tasks, work schedules, and remuneration. I asked about the best and worst aspects of their jobs, what they gained from their labor, and what (if anything) they would change if they could. I asked if they ever had any problems with coworkers or supervisors and, if so, how they handled them. Throughout, I was careful to utilize the workers' own language in discussing their labor, so as not to introduce my own perspectives or politicized rhetoric into the conversation. If they described their supervisors as "like family," "bosses," or "slave drivers," for example, I would inquire about their word choice and then, in some (less inflammatory) cases, use it myself; but I never introduced such language. I wanted to learn how *they* conceptualized their work, how *they* experienced their labor.

Thus, in this book I draw heavily on these workers' words: their own interpretations of their experiences, their own views of their labor. And as much as possible, I have tried to use their voices to tell their own stories.[99] For they are not simply data. They are people, and their stories are their own.[100] Despite the personal and idiosyncratic nature of their stories, however, in this book I only present findings with high levels of saturation. For though these workers' stories are unique, the ones in this book are not anomalous. In fact, I have deliberately not detailed the worst aspects of their jobs and lives; this book is not intended to be a journalistic exposé. I have tried to avoid casting them as passive victims, while not overlooking the ways in which they are sometimes victimized. Indeed, like most workers, those in this book sought to find meaning and pleasure in their labor, even as they also faced difficulties.

Finally, because I did not set out to study labor coercion, as detailed in appendix A, in many of my interviews with these workers I did not delve directly into the coercive power that would eventually become the centerpiece of this book. Thus, on the one hand, my findings bolster the centrality of status coercion to these workers' lives as it emerged organically from talking to them about their labor. On the other hand, my findings should be understood as only a first step in understanding this form of labor governance and its consequences for workers and their families.

. . . . .

Status coercion is recursively produced and reproduced at three levels: cultural, institutional, and individual. Its foundation is laid in the realm of culture, the realm in which narratives are circulated (and contested) about why some groups—despite their labor—are not "real" workers and therefore require extra regulation, surveillance, and discipline. Such ideas are operationalized at the institutional level. Prisons and college athletic programs, for example, act as chutes that channel these cultural narratives into policies and practices, thereby institutionalizing employers' powers of status coercion.[101] Within such institutions, employers enact these powers on workers' bodies through individual-level actions. At all of these levels, workers themselves challenge such narratives, policies, and practices.

In reality, of course, such levels are not so neatly divided, nor do social phenomena unfold linearly from one level to the next. Rather, culture, institutions, and individual actions are ever-changing, mutually constitutive components of dynamic social systems, continually pushed and pulled, shaped and reshaped by the actors within them. Yet differentiating these levels is useful for analyzing how such messy real-world dynamics operate.

In this book, my primary focus is the third level, the individual: how workers experience, and resist, status coercion in these labor regimes. But before delving into their individual experiences, I briefly explore the other levels at which coercion is produced and sustained: culture and institutions. In chapter 1, "'Wicked' and 'Blessed': Cultural Narratives of Coerced Labor," I analyze the role that ideologies of *immorality* and *privilege* play in constructing, justifying, and sustaining status coercion and the labor regimes predicated on it. I begin with a brief history of such narratives, examining how they were deployed during America's Industrial Revolution to characterize enslaved people, Native Americans, and white housewives. By highlighting this narrow slice of their cultural history, I seek to expose the artificiality of these narratives of immorality and privilege. I then jump to the contemporary era, exploring how recent changes in America's criminal justice, welfare, and higher education systems have made it more likely for such narratives to be culturally affixed to their respective populations. In short, I show how narratives of immorality and privilege have been embedded in the structure of these institutions. Then, through analysis of hundreds of cultural documents, I analyze how these narratives have been applied to incarcerated, workfare, college athlete, and graduate student workers. In doing so, I find that despite important differences in how they exploit logics of race, class, and gender, narratives of immorality and privilege use similar methods to produce similar results. By portraying their targets as subordinate, dependent, childlike figures who require extensive direction, control, and (often) punishment, these narratives cast them as something other than "workers" doing something other than rights-bearing "work." As a result, such narratives not only justify workers' exclusion from the rights and privileges of employment; they also justify their bosses' legal, culturally accepted, and institutionally expected power over their position in those institutions—that is, their status coercion. Thus, I argue that narratives of "wickedness" and "blessedness" are two sides of a single ideological apparatus used to delegitimize and discipline workers.

With this cultural and institutional framework in place, I explore workers' experiences of status coercion in chapter 2, "'Either You Do It or You're Going to the Box': Coercion and Compliance." Such experiences are diverse and vary significantly in their intensity. They include, for example, PhD students' graduation dates being delayed because they had become productive workers in the lab, and prisoners being put in solitary confinement because they refused to clean up feces. Yet for all of these workers, such coercive penalties are not rarities, nor are they reserved for extreme cases of wrongdoing. To the contrary, the possibility of punishment is omnipresent, and even when their bosses do not wield such punitive powers, these workers are well aware of their capacity to do so. This is how coercion works: everyone knows what is possible and such knowledge is usually enough to compel compliance. Thus, I argue that the coercion at the center of these labor relations creates and sustains "a relation of docility-utility," as Michel Foucault said of another context,[102] which not only pervades these particular labor regimes but also reaches beyond them into the mainstream economy.

In chapter 3, "'They Talk to You in Any Kind of Way': Subjugation, Vulnerability, and the Body," I continue this analysis by exploring how status coercion interacts with other forms of worker subjugation, particularly surveillance, degradation, and dehumanization. These types of subjugation are not unique to these labor relations, of course. In fact, they are common modes of labor control across work organizations. But when bosses have access to the expansive and punitive powers of status coercion, I find, such forms of subjugation take on new shape and intensity. For example, routine labor surveillance—the regulation and monitoring of workers' actions and bodies—both creates and catches worker missteps to be punished, and in these labor relations such punishments are the same punitive technologies of status coercion. In these workplaces, then, even routine modes of labor governance increase workers' vulnerability to employers' coercive power.

Despite their vulnerability to such power, these workers regularly resist it. In chapter 4, "'Stay Out They Way': Agency and Resistance," I examine their strategies of resistance. To do so, I identify four interrelated axes by which resistance can be analyzed: its level of action (individual vs. collective), the openness of its defiance (covert vs. overt), the narrative frames workers use to explain it (e.g., sovereignty), and its goal (e.g., "respect" vs. justice). From these I construct and analyze three categories of resistance, which I call "getting by" strategies, "standing up" strategies, and mobilization strategies. Yet while there are analytical differences between these resistance strategies, they are not so distinct in workers' everyday lives. Indeed, the same worker is likely to deploy different strategies in different situations. This analysis thus underscores the ways in which context fundamentally affects the form that resistance takes.

In chapter 5, I continue this study of resistance by examining workers' ideological dissent. In "'I'm Getting Ethiopia Pay for My Work': Hegemony and Counter-Hegemony," I explore how the workers in this book justify and challenge hegemonic constructions of "work" and their exclusion from it. While some of them outright accept or dispute these ideological tenets, others take a more nuanced stance through partial accessions and dissensions. Yet in doing so, nearly all of them draw on the same two ideological frames: work and citizenship. This is not surprising, perhaps, as these interrelated ideologies are the conceptual foundation of work in America, jointly built on raced, classed, and gendered notions of morality and immorality, independence and dependence, productivity and idleness, rights and rightslessness.[103] Whereas in chapter 1 I analyze how cultural narratives stemming from these ideologies have been used to construct these categories of labor as something other than "work," in this chapter I examine how workers themselves deploy these ideologies. Through this analysis, I show how long-standing hegemonic ideals—such as the veneration of productive labor and the abhorrence of idleness—can be rearranged toward counter-hegemonic ends.

In the conclusion, I discuss how this study transforms our understanding of work in America, expanding our notions of employer power while deepening our grasp of already-familiar power systems. In appendix A, I tell "The Story of This Book," charting its analytical development and detours, including my interviews with domestic workers, which do not appear in these pages. In appendix B, "People qua Data," I provide more detail about the workers at the heart of this study: their demographic characteristics and their jobs, as well as how they compare to their broader populations. Yet even as these workers have become "data" in this book, I urge readers to keep in mind Ta-Nehisi Coates's words while reading these chapters, as I sought to do while writing them. "You must always remember that the sociology, the history, the economics, the graphs, the charts, the regressions all land, with great violence, upon the body."[104]

1 "Wicked" and "Blessed"

CULTURAL NARRATIVES OF COERCED LABOR

We're trying to make them into taxpayers instead of tax burdens. . . . No rest for the wicked.[1]

—Steve Smith, then director of Colorado Correctional Industries, describing its prison labor program

Exploited? Try blessed. Here's hoping they spend this weekend counting their blessings while ignoring the members of the chattering class who are trying to convince them to walk away.[2]

—Seth Davis, senior writer for *Sports Illustrated,* discussing the possibility of University of Oklahoma men's basketball players boycotting the 2016 NCAA Final Four

"No rest for the wicked," then director of Colorado's prison industry program said of prisoners. Apache agreed, as you will recall. "It's not supposed to be a camp," he argued. "We're in prison. We're not supposed to come in and kick our feet up." "If you do bad," Apache said, "you get bad." Meanwhile, *Sports Illustrated* writer Seth Davis described college athletes as "blessed," not "exploited." Haley, one of the athletes I interviewed, agreed. Having played for one of the best women's college basketball teams in the country, she described herself as "100% blessed." "I still don't know how it all happened," she told me, "but I'm forever grateful for that opportunity."

These tropes of immorality and privilege—being "wicked" and "blessed"—dominate American cultural narratives of incarcerated and college athlete labor, respectively. Prisoners, by virtue of their incarceration, are deemed to be fundamentally immoral, and their labor is construed as punishment, reparation, or rehabilitation for their "wickedness."[3] Athletes, by contrast, are not seen as performing labor at all. Instead, they are viewed as privileged—"blessed"—to play their sport and are therefore expected to be "grateful" for their good fortune.

On some level, these portrayals make sense and not only because we— as writer and reader—are of the culture in which such tropes prevail. In point of fact, prisoners have been convicted of crimes, sometimes heinous ones, and Division I athletes are an elite set, sometimes achieving fame and access to future fortune at a young age. Therefore, although neither group is perceived to be entirely "wicked" or "blessed," these characterizations likely ring true for many Americans.

Yet these tropes of immorality and privilege are not unique to these groups, for they are also used to characterize the other workers in this study. Like prisoners, workfare workers are culturally construed as immoral, while PhD students, like athletes, are seen as privileged. In fact, these tropes extend well beyond these four groups, dating from (at least) the 18th and 19th centuries when they were applied to enslaved and indigenous people, as well as white housewives in the United States. Thus, the repeated use of these narratives over time and across groups suggests that rather than apt descriptors of such groups, they are cultural artifacts themselves worthy of study.

In this chapter, I unpack these cultural artifacts. I begin with a brief examination of how narratives of immorality and privilege were deployed during the American Industrial Revolution. In highlighting this narrow slice of what is in fact a much broader cultural history, I seek to expose the artificiality of these narratives. Indeed, from today's perspective the claim that—for example—the violently brutal system of slavery would benefit the enslaved by remedying their inherent laziness is not only a racist and farcical anachronism. It is also an unambiguous strategy to exploit their labor by justifying their exclusion from rights-bearing "work" and legitimizing their bosses' power over them. In short, claims of enslaved people's immorality— their laziness as well as their ignorance and criminality—served as the cultural scaffolding for their violent exploitation, subjugation, and coercion.

Having highlighted the social engineering behind such narratives, I then jump from the distant past to the contemporary era to analyze how narratives of immorality and privilege are used to govern the workers at the center of this book. I do so in two analytical steps. First, through a rereading of secondary literature, I show how recent institutional changes in the U.S. criminal justice, welfare, and higher education systems have made it more likely for such narratives to be culturally affixed to their respective populations. Second, through analysis of hundreds of cultural documents—newspaper and magazine articles, government and institutional publications, court rulings, and online discussion boards—I explore how these narratives of immorality and privilege are applied to incarcerated, workfare, college athlete, and graduate student workers.

Despite important differences in how these narratives exploit logics of race, class, and gender, I find that they use similar methods to produce similar results. By portraying their targets as subordinate, dependent, childlike figures who require extensive direction, control, and (often) punishment, narratives of immorality and privilege cast them as something other than "workers" doing something other than rights-bearing "work." As a result, these narratives not only justify workers' exclusion from the rights and privileges of "employment." They also justify workers' status coercion: their bosses' legal, culturally accepted, and institutionally expected power over their positions in those institutions and in society. Thus, I argue that narratives of "wickedness" and "blessedness" are two sides of a single ideological apparatus used to delegitimize and discipline workers in America.

IMMORALITY AND PRIVILEGE IN THE INDUSTRIAL REVOLUTION

The Industrial Revolution of the 18th and 19th centuries not only produced modern forms of work; it also produced modern ideas about work. For it was through industrialization that work in America came to be narrowly defined as "wage labor," a newly constructed category that was deeply entwined with emerging notions of economic independence, morality, and citizenship.[4] The fulcrum of this new definition of work was white masculinity, and so, in a looping cycle of exclusion and stigmatization, women and nonwhite workers were excluded from wage labor and associated with economic dependence, immorality, and noncitizenship, or at least a lesser citizenship. As a result, by the end of industrialization a broad range of workers, from enslaved people to housewives, were—despite their labor—neither culturally nor legally deemed to be productive, rights-bearing "workers."

It is thus illustrative to examine the cultural tropes of nonwork during that time, when such tropes were relatively new and raw, rather than naturalized and normalized as are today's versions. To do so, I draw on Nancy Fraser and Linda Gordon's analysis of what they call the three "icons of dependency" in 19th-century America: the "pauper," the "slave and colonial native," and the white middle-class "housewife."[5] My reinterpretation of their findings, as well as my own analysis of primary documents and secondary literature, reveals that tropes of "immorality" and "privilege" were central to discursively framing all of these groups as economically dependent noncitizen nonworkers.

In the case of paupers, for example, narratives of immorality were the sine qua non of their 19th-century cultural construction. As Fraser and Gordon write, "Paupers were not simply poor but degraded, their character corrupted and their will sapped through reliance on charity."[6] More than just vaguely immoral, paupers were associated with several particular brands of immorality: indolence, "feeblemindedness," criminality, and (for women) sexual promiscuity.[7] As the latter suggests, such allegations were not only classed but also gendered and raced, and they were disproportionately levied at those deemed deficient in fulfilling gender roles as well as racialized others, including those with "tainted whiteness" (such as immigrants of Irish, Italian, and Jewish descent).[8]

To redress their purported immorality, 19th-century paupers (along with people with physical and mental disabilities) were often confined in workhouses, also known as "poorhouses" or "almshouses," the conditions of which were deliberately abhorrent in an effort to deter claims for relief.[9] In such institutions, all remotely able-bodied occupants were compelled to work, for it was broadly believed that labor was the antidote to paupers' immorality and that because of their inherent laziness, compulsion was required. If they did not adequately perform such labor, or if they broke any of the workhouses' many moral codes, they would be punished. In one New York poorhouse, for example, such punishment entailed solitary confinement with only bread and water as sustenance.[10] As its 1831 "Rules & Regulations" stated,

> If any persons shall neglect to repair to their proper place to work, or being there shall refuse to work, or shall loiter, be idle or shall not well perform the task of work wet them, or shall waste or spoil any of the materials or tools, or shall deface the walls, or break the windows, or shall disturb the house by clamorous quarrelling, fighting or abusive language, or shall bring any strong liquors into the house without leave, or shall behave disrespectfully to any, or shall be guilty of lying, or in any other respect act immorally, they shall be punished by withholding their regular means, not exceeding one days [*sic*] allowance, or by being confined in a cell, or some solitary place and supported on bread and water, at the discretion of the keeper, not exceeding seventy two hours: unless the board of superintendents order a longer confinement, or proceed against them before a justice of the peace, there to be dealt with according to law.[11]

As this passage suggests, labor was not only the cornerstone of American poorhouses; it was the cornerstone of American morality. Work was explicitly equated with morality—and idleness with immorality—despite unequal access to culturally defined "work." For paupers, then, compulsory labor was both punishment and remedy for their perceived moral failings.

Immorality was also the central tenet of 19th-century cultural constructions of enslaved and indigenous people. In fact, the only significant difference was the role of race: while paupers were an implicitly racialized emblem of immorality, slaves and Native Americans were explicitly racialized as such. Simply by virtue of their race, they were presumed to be immoral. Yet they were charged with the very same brands of immorality as were paupers: indolence, moral depravity, promiscuity, and feeblemindedness.[12] Just as these allegations were used to justify paupers' confinement and compulsory labor, they were used to justify Black enslavement in the American South. "Since blacks were inferior," historian Eugene Genovese writes, "they had to be enslaved and taught to work, but, being inferior, they could hardly be expected to work up to Anglo-Saxon expectations."[13] In fact, proponents of slavery argued that this sadistic system of forced labor would morally "elevate" this "degraded race." For instance, as South Carolina politician William Harper proclaimed in his 1853 *Pro-Slavery Argument,*

Slavery . . . has done more to elevate a degraded race in the scale of humanity; to tame the savage; to civilize the barbarous; to soften the ferocious; to
enlighten the ignorant, and to spread the blessings of Christianity among
the heathen, than all the missionaries that philanthropy and religion have
ever sent forth.[14]

Harper then went on to elaborate the many ways that he believed slavery
had redressed the particular strands of enslaved people's purported immorality. He argued that slavery "enlightened" slaves by teaching them *how* to
work. "They are undergoing the very best education which it is possible to
give," he explained. "They are in the course of being taught habits of regular
and patient industry."[15] In fact, in Harper's view, slavery was a system of
care, not cruelty. By virtue of their enslavement, he argued, slaves were
"saved . . . from the responsibility of self-government"[16] and cared for during the "wants and sufferings of infancy, sickness, and old age."[17] For these
reasons, Harper avowed, slavery was less exploitative than wage labor in the
American North. Thus, in his construal, slavery was a means of moral uplift
as well as one of paternalist benevolence, both of which enslaved people—
portrayed as lazy, ignorant, immoral, and childlike—desperately needed.

These narratives of Black immorality, particularly indolence, persisted
long after slavery ended.[18] After emancipation, historians Eric Foner and
Olivia Mahoney write,

Among white Southerners, the question "Will the free Negro work?" became
an all-absorbing obsession. . . . It was widely believed that African-
Americans, naturally lazy, would work only when coerced. Charges of "indolence" were often directed not only against blacks unwilling to work at all,
but at those who preferred to labor for themselves rather than signing contracts with whites. In the strange logic of plantation society, African-
Americans who sought to become self-sufficient farmers seemed not examples of industriousness, but demoralized freedmen unwilling to work—work,
that is, under white supervision on a plantation.[19]

From today's perspective, of course, it is clear that the desire to preserve
this stratum of cheap (or free) labor was at the heart of the South's "strange
logic." To do so, white southerners deployed numerous strategies. Culturally,
as Foner and Mahoney suggest, they portrayed the formerly enslaved as
indolent and immoral and therefore in need of the moral discipline of

(white-controlled) labor. Then, on the basis of such cultural narratives, white southerners built a variety of economic and legal structures that secured former slaves' coerced or unpaid labor, such as debt peonage and convict labor.[20] For instance, as historian Douglas Blackmon writes, after emancipation the crime of vagrancy—not being able to prove at any particular moment that one is employed—became a "new and flimsy concoction dredged up from legal obscurity" and enforced "almost exclusively" against Black men (and boys).[21] Once incarcerated, they could be forced to labor without remuneration under threat of violence. "For whites no longer able to mete out arbitrary punishment to their former black chattel," historian Alex Lichtenstein writes, "the criminal justice system served as a prime means of racial control and labor exploitation in the New South."[22] Indeed, it was arguably *because* of this use of the criminal justice system to subjugate and exploit Black labor that cultural claims of Black criminality increasingly accompanied—and ultimately overshadowed—claims of Black indolence over the course of the 20th century.

The third emblem of 19th-century nonwork was the white middle-class housewife. Through industrialization, women's domestic labor was increasingly excluded from new conceptions of work, while white women's opportunities for wage labor were increasingly curtailed. As a result, white middle-class women went from being white middle-class men's economic equals in household subsistence to their economic dependents: from "partners to parasites," as policy scholar Hilary Land notes.[23] (Of course, poor white women and women of color were also deemed "parasites," but more because of their cultural association with poor and enslaved people than their culturally constructed economic dependence on men.) Thus emerged the white middle-class "housewife" in American culture.

To justify the social construction of white middle-class women as nonworking dependents, these women of relative privilege were cast as weak and vulnerable.[24] As historian Alice Kessler-Harris explains, it was argued that (white) women should be kept out of wage work because their "fundamentally weaker" constitution was unfit for physical hardship, and due to their "laxity of moral fiber," their presumed innocence would be jeopardized by exposure to unseemly influences in the workplace.[25] In both cases, then, these women's purported vulnerability was linked to their race-class privilege as well as their gender disadvantage. By contrast, poor and nonwhite women were seen as neither physically weak nor morally innocent, and therefore not in need of protection from physical hardship or moral lapse.[26] In this way, the symbiotic tropes of vulnerability and protection, which stemmed from both privilege and disadvantage, were used to construct white middle-class women as dependent nonworkers.

Thus, multiple and contradictory narratives were deployed to justify the exclusion of these groups from the new category of productive rights-bearing "work" in 19th-century America: immorality as well as privilege, laziness as well as weakness, criminality as well as innocence, the need for domination as well as the need for protection. Though in isolation such narratives might seem to be anachronistic portrayals of idiosyncratic groups, taken together they shed new light on the cultural construction of "work" in America when its modern architecture was being built. For at the broadest level, this analysis shows how narratives of immorality and privilege were used to delegitimize and discipline all three groups—paupers, slaves, and housewives—by constructing their labor as something other than rights-bearing work. Yet there were also important differences in how these cultural narratives were used, particularly in how they capitalized on social constructions of race, class, and gender. While immorality narratives were deployed against those with race-class disadvantage, privilege narratives were deployed against (and sometimes for) those with race-class privilege.[27] In both cases, however, they exploited and reified race-gender-class stereotypes, reentrenching already-stalwart systems of social inequality. In short, narratives of immorality and privilege were powerful cultural tools of labor governance and social control during the Industrial Revolution.

IMMORALITY AND PRIVILEGE IN CONTEMPORARY AMERICA

Though these "icons of dependency" are no longer cultural archetypes of nonwork, the narratives used to construct them continue to shape the politics of work and employment in America today. Such narratives are likely deployed against a variety of populations, of course, but here I examine how they are used to govern incarcerated, workfare, college athlete, and graduate student workers. Because of broader changes in the institutions for which they labor—the criminal justice, welfare, and higher education systems in the United States—narratives of immorality and privilege have become increasingly effective tools of governance for these groups of workers.

For both the criminal justice and the welfare systems in America, such changes revolved around their transformation from being culturally associated with whiteness in the mid-20th century to being associated with Blackness by century's end. For its part, the criminal justice system at mid-century was framed by the "rehabilitative ideal," the belief that prisoners—largely presumed to be white and male—could and should be reformed into law-abiding citizens.[28] At times, prisoners were even idolized in American culture, as evidenced by the acclaimed 1967 film *Cool Hand Luke*, starring Paul Newman as a (white) prisoner who refuses to submit to an unjust authoritarian system. Due to sociopolitical sea changes already underway, however, the criminal justice system's cultural whiteness would soon change. The "race riots" of the late 1960s, combined with civil rights activism, particularly the Black Power movement, increased the visibility, and *fear*, of Blackness in the white American imagination.[29] This fear was often fixated on Black violence and crime and was therefore fueled by rising crime rates in the 1960s and 1970s,[30] and then ignited by the racially targeted "War on Drugs" in the 1970s and 1980s.[31] Such dynamics helped produce mass incarceration—the skyrocketing of the prison population, particularly the Black male prison population[32]—as well as the cultural association of the criminal justice system with Black (male) immorality. Thus, by the turn of the 21st century, prisons were no longer seen as sites of rehabilitation for white people presumed to be fundamentally moral; they were seen (and sometimes used) as semipermanent warehouses for Black and Brown people presumed to be fundamentally immoral.[33] And so, as we will see in the sections below, the same narratives of immorality that were once used to characterize 19th-century poor and enslaved people came to dominate modern-day portrayals of prisoners.

The American welfare system followed a similar cultural trajectory, but with one key difference. Whereas for a time after emancipation prisons had been associated with Black (male) immorality, the welfare system—since its modern inception in the 1930s at least—had always been associated with (female) whiteness, the perceived immorality of which varied depending on the program and the era.[34] This presumption of whiteness was because traditionally defined "welfare" was reserved almost exclusively for white mothers, while Black women and their families, despite pervasive poverty, were largely excluded from public assistance programs.[35] Indeed, African American women did not have access to other less stigmatized forms of public assistance either, because of their near-total exclusion from the Social Security Act and therefore from old-age insurance and widow benefits. For although white mothers (and widows in particular) were seen as "deserving" of government assistance, Black mothers—widows or otherwise—were not. They were deemed "employable."[36]

In the 1960s and 1970s, however, Black women's exclusion from social welfare programs, and thus the welfare system's cultural whiteness, began to change. During that time, the problem of poverty, particularly Black urban poverty, gained new visibility in the United States. In 1964, President Johnson famously declared an "unconditional war" on poverty and for a relatively short time welfare programs expanded.[37] By the end of the 1960s, class action lawsuits began to curb racial bias in these programs so that African Americans gained unprecedented access to the new and growing forms of public assistance.[38] Such access, combined with Black women's activism in the welfare rights movement, increased Black visibility—and stigmatization—in the welfare system.[39] But it was Ronald Reagan's persistent promotion of the "welfare queen" trope in the 1970s and 1980s, equating welfare receipt with Black (female) fraudulence and indolence, that decisively attached this racialized immorality narrative to welfare in America.[40] As a result, by the start of the 21st century traditionally defined welfare had been gutted and rebuilt as a highly restrictive and punitive system centered on reducing welfare receipt rather than poverty itself.[41] Such changes were justified because in the American cultural imagination the welfare system, much like the criminal justice system, had become defined by Black immorality.[42]

In comparison to narratives of immorality, those of privilege have been less straightforwardly used as tools of governance in American culture. In part this is because rather than unambiguously pivoting on race, these narratives are used to target groups with varying combinations of advantage and disadvantage. Moreover, as a disciplinary tool, "privilege" is less potent than "immorality" in American culture, and therefore privilege narratives have been less strongly attached to social institutions and their inhabitants. Nonetheless, such narratives have indeed been deployed to delegitimize college athletes' and graduate students' claims for worker rights, just as they were used to delegitimize white middle-class women's standing as workers.

To understand how this came to pass, it is first necessary to understand that in the second half of the 20th century, universities became places where some students saw themselves as "workers." This was likely a byproduct of the neoliberalization of higher education in the United States; that is, universities' uneven yet broad-based push toward marketization, driven (at least in part) by state cuts in educational funding.[43] Thus, university officials sought to transform their institutions' education and research functions into revenue generators by, for example, partnering with private industry, replacing faculty with low-wage adjuncts and other insecure workers, and positioning students as consumers.[44] In the realm of athletics, university officials sought to capture a share of the significant (and growing) returns from their "revenue-generating" sports, football and basketball.[45] Their efforts to do so were facilitated by (though sometimes also in tension with) those of NCAA officials, who sought to capture their own share of this revenue as well.[46] For it was the NCAA's creation, promotion, and staunch protection of the principle of "amateurism" that meant that college athletes were the only entities who could not profit from their athleticism.[47] The considerable and growing disparity between athletes' scholarships and others' profits, particularly in football and basketball, generated dissatisfaction among at least some athletes, giving rise to a new sense of worker consciousness and new claims to worker rights.[48] Such dissatisfaction was further compounded by the issue of race. For as critics have argued, when the concentration of African American athletes in these revenue-generating sports is situated in the long history of Black unfree labor and Black bodies being made spectacle for white entertainment and profit, these sports can be reconceptualized as modern-day iterations of southern plantations.[49]

Though these dynamics make athletes' position unique in many ways, the neoliberalization of higher education has had similar effects on many graduate students; namely, reconstructing the university as a workplace and therefore producing a new sense of worker identity. In the academic sciences, such neoliberalization has been enacted through a series of inter-related measures. Partially because of state funding cuts, science faculty and their labs have increasingly had to rely on "soft money" from government agencies and corporations to fund their research,[50] as well as on the "cheap" labor of graduate students and postdocs to do the research and writing necessary to sustain such funding.[51] As a consequence, the number of science graduate students has grown dramatically; but at the same time, university officials have disinvested in tenure-track faculty positions, so that a declining fraction of PhD graduates have been getting faculty jobs.[52] All of this has increased at least some students' dissatisfaction with their graduate education and labor, leading to a rise in worker conscious-ness and rights claims.[53]

Yet this neoliberal milieu not only produced new arenas of worker iden-tity and activism among PhD students and college athletes. It also increased the financial pressure on universities to push back against their activism, for these students' labor—their scientific research and their athleticism—is a critical component of the new "academic capitalism."[54] In this pushback, as we will see, university officials (along with others) have revitalized time-honored narratives of privilege to argue that graduate students and ath-letes are not performing labor and are therefore not rights-bearing "work-ers," similar in effect to the use of immorality narratives against incarcerated and workfare workers.

In the sections that follow, I examine the cultural discourse surround-ing each of these groups in turn, revealing how narratives of immorality and privilege have been used in similar ways to govern them all.

Incarcerated Workers

Narratives of immorality are the centerpiece of cultural justifications for prison labor. Over and again, politicians and prison officials (along with laypeople) claim that labor will rehabilitate prisoners' immorality in at least three ways: (1) by preventing their idleness and correcting their indolence, (2) by redressing their economic dependence, and (3) by remedying their criminality. These are discrete charges of immorality—laziness, depend-ence, and criminality—but in such rhetoric these tropes are often intertwined. In this analysis, I disentangle these discursive threads to examine how each of these charges of immorality serves to legitimize compulsory prison labor and delegitimize prisoners' rights claims, all the while echoing 19th-century portrayals of poor, enslaved, and indigenous peoples.

In the first case, mandatory labor is said to prevent prisoners' idleness and indolence, underscoring the centrality of work and disdain for laziness in American culture. The primary purpose of prison labor, institutional officials repeatedly proclaim, is to "reduce idleness."[55] "We don't want inmates sitting around idle doing nothing," asserts the director of Arizona's Department of Corrections.[56] "We believe offenders should not just sit idle while they serve their time in state prison,"[57] argue proponents of expanding Washington State's prison labor program. At the heart of this argument is the contention that prisoners should be required to work simply to make them do something; not working is equated with laziness, and laziness is not acceptable.

Yet in such rhetoric forced labor will not only forestall idleness and indolence; it will cure these moral vices by teaching prisoners "good work habits" and "positive work ethics."[58] "Inmates are gaining a work ethic and a sense of value and self worth," avow officials of South Dakota's Department of Corrections.[59] "What we want to do," the director of Indiana's prison industries says of incarcerated workers, is

> When they're released, for them to feel unnatural not to be working. . . . For you and I, if we go a long period of not working, something's wrong. But they have not lived their life that way. We're trying to change that habit to where they need to work, mentally, just as much as you and I do.[60]

In this formulation, prisoners are fundamentally different from most people: "you and I." They are constructed as "the Other."[61] As such, they purportedly do not have a "habit" of working ("they have not lived their life that way"), and therefore they need to be taught how to work, by being required to work, in order to gain a "sense of value and self worth." In other words, compulsory labor will (supposedly) give prisoners the moral compass they lack.

Dependence is the second brand of immorality that prison labor is said to remedy. Although prisoners are dependent on the state by virtue of their incarceration, it is argued that their compulsory labor will compensate for their dependence in at least two ways: directly, by offsetting the costs of their incarceration, and indirectly, by decreasing state expenses overall. In these ways, prison labor proponents repeatedly argue, compulsory labor will reduce prisoners' financial "burdens" on "taxpayers" and "society."[62] As economist Robert Atkinson writes,

> The majority of Americans support prison labor because they believe that prisoners should help offset some of the costs of incarceration. It costs approximately $40 billion annually to incarcerate prisoners in local, state, and federal prisons. That works out to approximately $20,000 a year per prisoner. Surely prisoners can work and contribute something to help pay for this so taxpayers don't have to spend as much.[63]

In his limited economic formulation, Atkinson does not question the sheer number of prisoners and its effect on the costs of incarceration. Instead, he asserts that prisoners, as criminal dependents, should be required to work (implicitly at low or no pay) to "offset" such costs.

In a similar vein, the sheriff's office in Pasco County, Florida, proclaims that its prison labor programs are "designed to save taxpayer's dollars, raise the work ethic of selected inmates and give them a productive way to spend their court-ordered sentences."[64] While this statement deploys several immorality tropes—idleness and indolence as well as dependence— official descriptions of the county's prison labor programs repeatedly emphasize the latter by enumerating the monetary returns and work output of each. For example, the agricultural prison labor program reportedly yielded "15,465 heads of cabbage valued at $16,238.25."[65] Prison officials in Jackson County, Georgia, use a similar tactic, detailing the economic returns of their prison labor programs:

> The Road Department uses on average 70 inmates per day on its details. Based on 2,000 work hours per year per person this amounts to 140,000 man hours per year! If you could hire civilian workers to perform the work done by inmates at a cost of $10 per hour (and you couldn't), this department alone would have to spend $1,400,000 per year.[66]

In this calculation, Georgia prisoners—who are not paid for their labor— work full-time on the road crew (often in the blistering southern heat), 40 hours a week, 50 weeks a year. As compared to even relatively low-wage workers performing this labor, Jackson County officials proudly proclaim that this single unit of prison labor (and there are twelve others) saves the local government well over one million dollars.

Indeed, the magnitude of such cost "savings" has led some government officials to argue that prison labor is indispensable.[67] In California, because of the state's reliance on prison labor, officials resisted a Supreme Court mandate to reduce the state's prison population. In 2011, the U.S. Supreme Court ruled that overcrowding in California state prisons violated prisoners' right to be free from cruel and unusual punishment; as a remedy, the Court ordered state prison officials to grant early parole to all minimum-security prisoners.[68] Three years later, however, California prisons were once again on trial, this time for not adhering to the Court's mandate. In their defense, prison officials argued that because California depended on prisoners' low-cost labor in the fire camps, they needed to reserve early parole exclusively for those who "volunteered" for firefighting jobs. Otherwise, state officials argued, prisoners "would choose to participate in [other work programs] rather than endure strenuous physical activities and risk injury in fire camps," and so "fire camp beds [would be] even more difficult to fill."[69] In short, state officials were willing to forgo prisoners' Eighth Amendment rights in order to continue coercing them into "choosing" the difficult and dangerous work of fighting fires.[70]

The third brand of immorality that incarcerated labor is said to curb is prisoners' criminality itself.[71] For instance, just as the director of Colorado's prison industry program said that there should be "no rest for the wicked," at the start of this chapter,[72] economist Robert Atkinson writes that "prisoners don't get vacations, that's why they are in prison."[73] Critics of prison labor, Atkinson goes on to explain, "miss the fundamental point: These are criminals who are serving time in prison for illegal activity and, as such, are deprived of some of the rights free people enjoy."[74] As this statement suggests, in order to justify the compulsion of prisoners' labor and exclusion from employment rights, Atkinson repeatedly underscores their criminality: they are *criminals* in *prison* for *illegal* activity.

Most often, this particular immorality narrative is used to argue that labor is the antidote to prisoners' *future* criminality, whether by cultivating their moral compass or by increasing their skills and thereby reducing their recidivism.[75] Prison labor "isn't about making money," argues the director of Washington's Correctional Industries. "It's about making better people."[76] "Think about how much it costs to incarcerate someone," says John Ensign, then senator of Nevada. "Do we want them just sitting in prison, lifting weights, becoming violent and thinking about the next crime? Or do we want them having a little purpose in life and learning a skill?"[77] The "whole impetus behind Federal Prison Industries is not about business," assert federal prison officials, but about transforming offenders into "law-abiding, contributing members of society."[78] Thus, in this rhetoric prison officials explicitly—and perhaps strategically—point away from the profits of prison labor (it "isn't about making money") to argue that prisoners' low- or no-wage labor makes them "better people" by giving them "purpose" and "skill."

One Massachusetts sheriff has taken this argument even further by claiming that prison labor can prevent criminality in general. In 2017, Sheriff Thomas Hodgson made headlines when he offered the free labor of the prisoners in his county jail to help build then president-elect Donald Trump's controversial wall on the U.S.-Mexico border. Such incarcerated labor, Sheriff Hodgson xenophobically proclaimed, would "prevent crime in communities around the country" by precluding Mexican migrants from entering the United States.[79] Through compulsory labor, the sheriff seemed to be saying, prisoners would symbolically remedy their own criminality by the forestalling the alleged (though unfounded) criminality of others.

As such rhetoric reveals, the immorality narratives that are used to characterize prisoners and their labor in America today are the same ones that were applied to poor, indigenous, and enslaved people in the 19th century. It was argued that slavery, a ruthlessly violent system of forced labor, would remedy slaves' purported laziness and ignorance about work, teaching them "habits of regular and patient industry." For paupers, compulsory labor was also said to remedy, as well as punish, their laziness and moral laxity. The same is true of prisoners today. "No rest for the wicked," it is said. "Prisoners don't get vacations." Because of their immorality, they must be required to work and are therefore not rights-bearing workers. But through such compulsory labor, it is asserted, they will become "better people" and "contributing members of society." Work is discursively cast as both punishment and cure for prisoners' purported immorality.

Workfare Workers

Of the four groups analyzed in this book, workfare workers have been the most thoroughly examined in the scholarly literature, and so cultural rhetoric about this labor regime is relatively well-traveled territory.[80] Yet it is worth exploring again, if only briefly, to highlight the discursive parallels between such rhetoric and that of the other workers I examine in this book. In point of fact, much like that of prisoners, narratives of immorality dominate cultural discussions of poverty, welfare, and workfare, similarly echoing 19th-century descriptions of poor, indigenous, and enslaved people.

Immorality rhetoric about welfare recipients was particularly pervasive in the 1980s and 1990s,[81] culminating in then president Bill Clinton's 1996 passage of the Personal Responsibility and Work Opportunity Reconciliation Act. Popularly known as "welfare reform," this legislation prioritized work for welfare recipients, both institutionalizing and expanding compulsory workfare programs. In subsequent years, as welfare reform was periodically renewed or revised, debates about poverty, welfare, and work would erupt anew and narratives of poor people's supposed immorality would once again take center stage. This is what happened in New York City in 2014, for example, when recently elected mayor Bill de Blasio pledged to back away from the city's embrace of work-first poverty policies and phase out its primary workfare program, WEP (Work Experience Program). Many argued vehemently against de Blasio's proposal by revitalizing long-standing arguments that compulsory labor was the key to rehabilitating welfare recipients' alleged immorality. Indeed, they argued that work would cure the same three strands of immorality as for prisoners—indolence, dependence, and criminality—along with a fourth, irresponsibility.

In the first case, workfare proponents argued that compulsory labor reduces welfare recipients' purported indolence by forestalling idleness and promoting an ethic of work.[82] As conservative pundit Heather Mac Donald's writes,

> The rollback of welfare reform under New York City's mayor, Bill de Blasio, has begun in earnest. The city's Human Resources Administration just informed able-bodied, childless adults that they no longer need to do anything in exchange for their food stamps. Sitting at home and watching TV while you collect your benefits is just fine with de Blasio and his new welfare chief.[83]

Without work requirements, Mac Donald claims, welfare recipients will remain idle—"sitting at home and watching TV"—and their presumed laziness will remain unchecked.

Much like prisoners (and the enslaved), moreover, it is argued that compulsory labor will teach welfare recipients *how* to work. As Jason Turner, then commissioner of New York City's Human Resources Administration, proclaimed, workfare is a "learning tool" that teaches "personal accountability, attendance and the importance of following directions."[84] Underlying such statements, of course, is the assertion that welfare recipients do not already know how to follow directions, show up for work, and act responsibly. They must be compelled to work in order to learn such lessons.

Perhaps it is not surprising, then, that welfare critics argue that work requirements should be expanded to more public assistance programs— such as SNAP benefits and Medicaid—rather than contracted as under de Blasio's policies. As a 2016 Heritage Foundation report states,

> Traditional welfare programs such as food stamps and subsidized housing provide one-way handouts; they give aid to able-bodied non-elderly recipients without any requirement to work or engage in other constructive behavior in exchange. By offering income without labor, these programs encourage idleness and reduce the incentives to work.[85]

Such rhetoric rests on the unsubstantiated two-part claim that people who receive public assistance, including those who only receive SNAP benefits, are (1) not already working and (2) will not do so unless compelled. Despite numerous studies showing both claims to be untrue,[86] this rhetoric of indolence, and compulsory labor as its remedy, continues to be a remarkably stalwart tool used to govern welfare recipients, as it is revived again and again to chastise them and extract their unpaid labor.[87]

Dependence is the second strand of welfare recipients' immorality that work is said to cure, in contrast to welfare benefits, which are said to foster it.[88] Indeed, the very language of the 1996 welfare reform bill, along with Bill Clinton's speech on signing it, repeatedly conflated welfare receipt with "dependence" and work with "independence" and "responsibility."[89] Since then, these tropes have continually resurfaced in debates about welfare and workfare, in which the 1996 law is often hailed as the prototype for eradicating this strand of immorality.[90] As avowed in a *New York Post* editorial, for example, welfare reform "took a giant step toward ending the decades-old cycle of long-term dependency that old-school welfare had caused" by "moving welfare recipients into the workforce, giving them a real sense of self-respect and financial independence."[91] But with New York's new policies, critics argue, welfare reform's "epic advance" against dependence is at risk of being undone:

> [New York's new] "no questions asked" approach recalls the come-and-get-it welfare mentality of the [1960s'] John Lindsay era. That, too, ended in disaster, both for taxpayers and for welfare recipients who lost any reason to support themselves. The government check would always arrive on time, even if it afforded only a subsistence existence. The problem was compounded until welfare reform was passed at the federal level, an epic advance that recently celebrated its 20th anniversary. All the talk of doom and gloom was wrong, with millions of Americans moving from welfare to work because they had to. That was an example of tough love that helped downtrodden, dependent people build better lives for themselves.[92]

In addition to asserting (falsely) that welfare recipients will not work unless required to do so (only "moving from welfare to work because they had to"), this passage construes compulsory labor as a means of paternalist uplift: "tough love" that has helped "millions" of "downtrodden, dependent people."[93] Likewise, another workfare proponent proclaims that this system of compulsory labor is "compassionate . . . not heartless," for it allows welfare recipients to "[break] free of their destructive cycles . . . have self-worth and a purpose."[94] Thus, like 19th-century justifications of slavery, such portrayals paint workfare as being for welfare recipients' own good, helping these "downtrodden" people build "better lives for themselves," though there is little evidence to support such claims.[95]

Criminality is the third strand of welfare recipients' immorality that work will purportedly remedy. This is less common than the others, at least in contemporary welfare discourse, but it is notable because unlike prisoners, who have in fact been convicted of crimes (rightly or not), welfare recipients are not criminals. Nonetheless, their criminality is alleged in two ways. First, they are construed as *potential* criminals, for without having to work, it is (unfoundedly) argued, they are likely to engage in criminal behavior.[96] Second, and more common, they are cast as *already* criminally suspect due to the presumption of their fraudulence. Rhetoric about welfare fraud was particularly widespread in the 1980s, stemming from Ronald Reagan's 1976 and 1980 political campaigns, in which he repeatedly recounted an only partially true tale of one woman's extensive welfare fraud.[97] By vastly overstating the breadth and depth of such fraud, Reagan's claims became a central focus of popular and political concern.[98] Accordingly, former New York City mayor Rudy Giuliani was widely applauded for his stringent work-first welfare programs, which supposedly helped "end then-rampant fraud,"[99] while Mayor de Blasio's rollback of those programs has been accused of "deliberately undoing reforms that weeded out fraud."[100] Thus, although the causal mechanisms remain unexplained, compulsory labor is construed as somehow reducing welfare recipients' fraudulence, and without such labor their presumed criminality is expected to abound.

Bad decision-making—or irresponsibility—is the last strand of welfare recipients' alleged immorality that work will allegedly fix. Once again, this argument was particularly pervasive in the 1980s when "out of wedlock" pregnancy and "family breakdown" were seen as the primary causes of poverty and welfare receipt.[101] Such claims had been given legitimacy by the 1965 "Moynihan Report," which argued that many Black families were enmeshed in a "tangle of pathology" caused by "weakness of the family structure," leading to persistent poverty, unemployment, and crime.[102] With such rhetoric, the Moynihan Report put the onus of poverty on the individual, paving the way for neoconservatives' focus on poor people's role in creating and perpetuating a "culture of poverty."

Though such arguments are less pervasive today, they periodically resurface in debates about welfare and work.[103] For instance, as Heather Mac Donald writes in an article titled "De Blasio's New Welfare Plan: Anything to Stop People from Getting a Job,"

> The overwhelming cause of poverty in America today is family breakdown, not inadequate government spending on welfare programs or low wages. . . . And an adult can avoid poverty by taking just three simple steps: graduate from high school, work full-time, and wait until marriage to have children.[104]

Likewise, another welfare critic contends, "The problems afflicting many poor people are often of their own making, at least in part. Having children before getting married, dropping out of high school, etc., are transparently bad choices that millions of people make."[105] In this construal, poverty and welfare receipt are the result of "bad choices," which any implicitly responsible "adult can avoid" with "just three simple steps." For those who behave irresponsibly, compulsory labor is both consequence and cure.

Thus, as with prisoners, work is cast as the corrective for multiple strands of welfare recipients' supposed immorality—idleness and indolence, dependence, criminality, and irresponsibility. Indeed, the overlap in the rhetoric about these two groups is remarkable, as is the extent to which they echo that about 19th-century poor, enslaved, and indigenous people. Yet such overlap is not coincidental: all of these groups are disadvantaged by race and class. As scholar Kathi Weeks writes, rhetorics of work and morality "serve as a respectable vehicle for what would otherwise be exposed as publicly unacceptable claims about racial difference" and, I would add, class difference.[106] The work ethic in particular, Weeks argues, has long been "a deep discursive reservoir" used to "obscure and legitimate" logics of social inequality and socioeconomic marginalization.[107] Such logics were perhaps most apparent in the charges of indolence lodged against freed slaves who sought to work for themselves rather than their former owners. Today such logics are found in the many analogous allegations against welfare recipients and prisoners.

College Athletes

Whereas cultural discourse of welfare recipients and prisoners is dominated by narratives of immorality, and labor as its antidote, that of college athletes and graduate students is dominated by narratives of privilege and how such privilege precludes their labor from being "work." Thus, while prisoners and workfare workers are broadly understood to be performing labor (even if it is not rights-bearing work), college athletes and PhD students are not. Instead, privilege narratives are used to construct their labor as something else: an "avocation," an "adventure." They are said to be lucky, "blessed," to be able to pursue such "opportunities," and when they argue otherwise, they are told to stop "whining."

In the case of college athletes, again and again NCAA officials, university representatives, sports writers, and fans describe them as "privileged,"[108] "lucky,"[109] and "blessed."[110] They are said to be pursuing their "dream"[111] or "avocation,"[112] motivated by "love"[113] and "passion"[114] for their sport rather than money. Athletes "play college athletics . . . for the love of their sport—not to be paid a salary," asserts NCAA president Mark Emmert.[115] College athletes are driven by "a passion for their sport . . . that can't be equated to punching a time clock," argues the NCAA's chief legal officer.[116] Being a college athlete is thus construed as a labor of love, not work, and athletes are lucky to be able to follow their dreams.

To buttress such claims, officials frequently tout the "benefits" and "opportunities" that college athletics provide for athletes.[117] "A college education is the most rewarding benefit of your student-athlete experience," avow NCAA officials in their *Guide for the College-Bound Student-Athlete.*[118] Likewise, Villanova University's president says of college athletes, "These are 18- to 22-year-olds that have come to an institution first and foremost, I hope, to get an education. And that scholarship provides them that opportunity."[119] Despite the pervasiveness of this rhetoric, *Sports Illustrated* writer Stewart Mandel argues that NCAA officials have not always emphasized such "opportunities" enough. Mandel argues that when defending the organization against litigation about the unremunerated use of athletes' likenesses in video games,[120] NCAA lawyers should have underscored even more the "opportunities" that the NCAA gives to athletes,

> painting a picture for [the Judge] of a noble-minded enterprise in which thousands of young men—many from disadvantaged families who couldn't afford college otherwise—leverage their athletic talents into life-changing opportunities, preparing for careers after sports and forming lasting bonds within a community.[121]

In Mandel's view, then, the NCAA should have deployed a more explicitly paternalistic discourse, casting itself as a beneficent patron—"a noble-minded enterprise"—bestowing "life-changing opportunities" upon "thousands" of poor "disadvantaged" "young men." Thus, echoing present and past rhetoric of "downtrodden" welfare recipients, slaves, and paupers who have been portrayed as needing (white upper-class) help and guidance, college athletes are portrayed as the (implicitly nonwhite) needy but lucky beneficiaries of (implicitly white) paternalist uplift.

Coaches deploy such language of opportunity as well. However, in their 2013 team handbook at least, Northwestern University football coaches did not use such benevolent overtones in doing so.[122] For example, this handbook features a decidedly nonbenevolent list of 50 "Twitter tips for student-athletes" ("Read them all and follow them!"). Tip number 10 states,

> Don't use Twitter as an outlet to complain about how rough your life is. You are getting a college education, traveling to interesting places, getting free athletic shoes and apparel and more. Thousands of people would crawl over glass for the chance to enjoy the opportunities you have.[123]

Rather aggressively, then, Northwestern football players are told that they are privileged: they get "opportunities" (and shoes) for which "thousands . . . would crawl over glass." They should not "complain."

This message is central to another strand of privilege discourse directed at college athletes: if they "complain"—a word which is often used to refer to them discussing exploitation and making rights claims—athletes are said to be "entitled," "pampered," and "coddled."[124] Consider, for example, the online commentary on a 2013 NBC Sports article in which NFL football player Arian Foster critiques NCAA college athletics and its principle of amateurism, that is, the nonpayment of athletes.[125] In the article, Foster recalls not having enough food to eat as a college athlete and so having to get "money on the side" in violation of NCAA rules. But he says he felt justified in doing so because of the revenue his university and coach seemed to be making from his and his team's athletic success. He argues that college athletes should be paid for their athletic labor. "I'm a firm believer that an employee should get paid for his work," he says. "And, 100 percent, I see student-athletes as employees." At the time of this writing, there were 95 online comments on this article, a majority of which censure Foster in some way, often using narratives of privilege to do so. As one commenter writes, "Employee? You put pads on and hit people. Get over yourself. I'm so sick of these pampered athletes and their entitlement." Two others write, "Foster just needs to quit crying" and "what a whiny twit." A fourth avows,

> I am so tired of these men complaining that they have to either pay rent or buy food. You are there on a scholarship that includes housing, food, and stipends. if [sic] you can't manage on everything being free . . . that is your

problem. Don't blame the NCAA. You knew what you were getting going in. There are plenty of athletes out there that pay their way through school, while working, and you don't see this issue. And they don't act like entitled jerks![126]

In this construal, college athletes who make rights claims are "entitled jerks," unduly privileged as well as ungrateful for their privilege. "Get over yourself," they are told. And in terms of disrespect usually reserved for misbehaving children, they are disparaged as being "pampered" and irresponsible ("if you can't manage on everything being free . . . that is your problem"), and they are chastised for "whining" and "crying."[127]

This use of privilege discourse recalls Phoebe Maltz Bovy's analysis in her book *The Perils of "Privilege."* In the realm of identity politics, Maltz Bovy argues, accusations of privilege—for instance, "your privilege is showing"—are often used to shame and silence people as well as call attention to the advantages of their social location. For college athletes, I find, such rhetoric serves a similar silencing purpose. "Don't . . . complain," athletes are told. "You knew what you were getting going in." "Thousands of people would crawl over glass for the chance to enjoy the opportunities you have." "Just . . . quit crying."

Yet even as athletes are portrayed as privileged (whether overly "entitled" or simply "blessed"), they are also characterized as being vulnerable and in need of protection.[128] In particular, they are said to need protection from two sources of possible corruption: their own poor choices and commercial exploitation. In both cases, as we will see, the possibility of such corruption is used to justify policing their behavior, similar to the way that charges of indolence, criminality, or irresponsibility are used to justify policing prisoners' and welfare recipients' behavior.

In the first case, recalling rhetoric of welfare recipients' irresponsibility, athletes are said to need protection from their own bad decision-making. Such rhetoric is used, for example, to warn them against alcohol and gambling, to which they are said to be "particularly vulnerable."[129] Yet even more often it is directed at athletes' use of social media. The start of Northwestern football's "Social Networking Policy," for example, is replete with "concern" for athletes' "safety" and "well being" [*sic*]. And in truth, its initial guidelines are at least somewhat protective in nature (e.g., "*Do not post your home address*"[130]). But this "concern" quickly takes on a more punitive tone, even as it is still incongruously framed as protective. For instance, Northwestern's list of "Twitter tips" mentioned above is often overtly aggressive (as well as micromanaging in its exhaustive detail). "Don't craft useless Tweets," instructs tip 2. "Don't Tweet the worthless stuff," tip 24 advises. "Don't Tweet about how much you hate school," says tip 14. "You chose to become a college student-athlete. If you hate school so much you should have joined the Marines."[131] Tip 36 states, "Know the type of Tweets that are boring and painfully unoriginal. They include such gems as A) Just got a great workout in; B) I'm up early, finna get this money; C) Wattup Twitter??" This list of 50 "tips" is full of such directives. Toward the end of the list, tip 45 reminds athletes that all of this advice is in their "long-term best interest":

> If you feel like the Twitter guidelines your coaching staff and/or athletic administrators expect you to comply with prevent you from "keeping it real," then that should probably be your cue to re-evaluate your definition of "keeping it real." Your team support staff has your long-term best interest in mind.[132]

In order to protect athletes' "best interest," moreover, Northwestern officials repeatedly make clear that they are surveilling athletes' social media accounts and will impose severe consequences for any rule breaking.[133] As the university's athletics handbook states,

> Sanctions may be imposed if [social media] sites are used improperly or depict inappropriate, embarrassing or dangerous behaviors. Those sanctions can include, but are not limited to, public or private reprimand, suspension from practice or competition, dismissal from the program, and loss of athletics aid, if applicable.[134]

Though such policing is discursively justified by the need to protect athletes, a close reading of Northwestern's policies suggests that team officials are more concerned with how athletes' behavior might negatively reflect on themselves than with athletes' well-being.[135] "You, as Northwestern Football Players," the team handbook states, "are expected to hold yourselves to a higher standard that will best represent the team & the University. All it takes is one bad tweet to create a problem."[136] Later, the handbook warns, "If you embarrass our team you will be suspended for one game. If it happens a second time you'll be suspended for one year."[137]

In addition to needing protection from their own bad choices (particularly bad tweets), officials assert that athletes need protection from commercial "exploitation."[138] "Student participation in intercollegiate athletics is an avocation," the NCAA 2015–16 Division I manual states, "and student-athletes should be protected from exploitation by professional and commercial enterprises."[139] Such rhetoric usually refers to sports agents, who are characterized as unethically enticing college athletes into professional sports and other commercial activities, thereby jeopardizing their amateur status and NCAA eligibility.[140] As University of Alabama's football coach says of sports agents, "I hate to say this, but how are they any better than a pimp? I have no respect for people who do that to young people. None."[141] Yet despite this construal of athletes as vulnerable "young people" who need protection from such corrupting influences, athletes themselves face harsh consequences for any commercial activity—including any dealings with sports agents—often losing their ability to compete in college athletics altogether.[142]

Ultimately, this rhetoric of protection casts college athletes as childlike figures who require safeguarding, oversight, regulation, and sometimes punishment, while framing their coaches and NCAA officials as parent-like figures who must shelter, guide, monitor, and discipline them.[143] Such rhetoric thus recalls the rhetoric about 19th-century white middle-class housewives, who were similarly construed as vulnerable and childlike, in need of protection and extra regulation. As with housewives, this rhetoric capitalizes on its targets' mix of privilege and disadvantage. This is particularly true of Division I football and basketball players, for whom paternalist narratives of benevolence, opportunity, protection, and uplift trade on their (real or perceived) race and class disadvantage. These "disadvantaged" "young men" are being bestowed "life-changing opportunities." At the same time, narratives of privilege, opportunity, and entitlement capitalize on their (real or perceived) advantages as elite athletes. They are said to be living their "dream," playing the sport they "love," and should therefore be "grateful for that opportunity." Taken together, such narratives delegitimize athletes' labor as *work* and their claims to rights *as workers*. Indeed, when they make such claims, they are shamed and silenced with accusations of undue entitlement: "Get over yourself." "What a whiny twit."

Graduate Students

Narratives of privilege also dominate cultural rhetoric of graduate student labor, though without the added notes of paternalist protection. Much like athletic labor, graduate student work is characterized as a privileged pursuit, a "labor of love" and a "life of the mind," undertaken out of "passion" and rewarded with "opportunity" and "experience" rather than money.[144] The online manual for graduate students *Becoming a Historian* proclaims that despite the "financial and emotional stresses" of graduate school, "being a full-time graduate student is a privilege and a unique opportunity for intellectual reflection, stimulation, and community. . . . Think of every stage as a great adventure," the site advises, "and enjoy your life as a graduate student."[145] An even more quixotic view of graduate student work can be found in an online forum addressing the question, "Why do graduate students allow themselves to be exploited like cheap labor?" In response, a professor— a former graduate student—writes, "Let me explain how graduate school seemed to me":

- I got to study more and more of a subject that I loved.
- I got to read several amazing papers, some of which were so beautiful I still get tremors of joy at the thought of them.
- I got to talk to people who were astoundingly smart and willing to share their knowledge with me.
- I got to work on problems I was really, really passionate about. (I'm still working on some of them—indeed, redoubling my efforts—over twenty years later.)
- I got to work on these problems with those astoundingly smart people! . . .
- Find me the *exploitation* in what I've written above. . . . Graduate school was not exploitation; it was pure joy.[146]

For this commenter, graduate work was characterized by erudite exchange with "astoundingly smart people" and by reading "amazing papers" that continued to spark "tremors of joy." It was "pure joy" fueled by "passion." Though, of course, I do not question this writer's experience, as for all of the sources in this book I seek to analyze the cultural work that their discursive strategies accomplish. In this case, by construing graduate student work as a labor of love, this commenter draws a stark and impassable line between such "joy" and the world of work with its profit-driven economic "exploitation."

In fact, this distinction is often explicit in such rhetoric, as the implicitly class-privileged "ivory tower" and "scholar" are set in opposition to the implicitly class-disadvantaged "factory floor" and "worker."[147] The two are cast as incongruous and incompatible, particularly in debates over graduate student unionization.[148] "The rough and tumble of collective bargaining cannot be imposed on that [student-university] relationship without doing irreparable damage," write Ivy League (and other elite) university officials in an amici curiae brief against graduate student unionization.[149] And as representatives of the Higher Education Council argue, "The very nature of such an adversarial, economic relationship could undermine the fundamentally academic nature of the relationship between faculty and their graduate students."[150] In short, the erudite exchange of the ivory tower would be debased if students were to unionize—that is, if they were to be recognized as "employees" under labor law.

To underscore this point, university officials often deploy another strand of privilege discourse: that much like college athletics, graduate school is an "opportunity"—not work—which provides "training," "expertise," "knowledge," and other "intangible" rewards rather than money.[151] As Brown University officials state, "Graduate education is an educational opportunity that, if successfully completed, leads to an academic degree; graduate education is not a job."[152] Likewise, Columbia University officials contend that "unlike university employees, graduate students who serve as teaching or research assistants come to this institution first and foremost to acquire through that work the knowledge and expertise that are essential to their becoming future scholars and teachers."[153] And as argued by the National Right to Work Legal Defense Foundation, "the primary reward for [graduate student] efforts as teaching assistants is not money":

> Indeed, any monetary remuneration pales compared to the intangible remuneration of academic credits, grades, training, and practical experience in their field. It is highly unlikely graduate or undergraduate students become teaching assistants primarily to earn a living. Consequently, they

should be treated as the students they are, and not as employees whom labor unions wish to control.[154]

Tautologically, then, it is argued that graduate students are not workers—despite working as teaching or research assistants—because they are not paid as such, and because they are not paid as such, they should not be legally deemed workers. (As the reader will recall, similar circular arguments have been applied to athletes and prisoners as well.)

When graduate students make rights claims, much like college athletes they are characterized as overly privileged and ungrateful, "entitled" and "whiny" in the face of their good fortune—or, as one observer described them, "ungrateful brats."[155] "You could argue that there is no one more privileged than the graduate students," declared a former critic of graduate student unionization.[156] "So privileged graduate students at harvard [*sic*] want to unionize?" another critic rhetorically asked. "Are they demanding safe spaces, or demanding a list of trigger words?"[157] In this construal, graduate students who seek worker rights are overly sensitive, perhaps even puerile, as well as unduly demanding. They too are whiny and entitled.

Thus, as with college athletes, narratives of privilege dominate cultural rhetoric of graduate students and their labor. Indeed, the parallels between the two are remarkable. In both cases, their labor is cast as a privileged pursuit: graduate work as an intellectual endeavor and labor of love, college athletics as a calling and a blessing, both driven by passion rather than desire for money. In both cases, moreover, it is argued that the purity of the enterprise would be tainted by becoming an "economic relationship," causing "irreparable damage" to the ivory tower and student-faculty relationships, "pimping" athletes and corrupting college sports. And in both cases, the students who make worker rights claims are portrayed as childishly complaining in the face of their privilege and are variously called "ungrateful brats," "whiny twits," and "entitled jerks." Yet unlike athletes (and 19th-century housewives), graduate students are not portrayed as vulnerable and in need of protection. In fact, their lack of vulnerability is sometimes used to argue against their status as workers. As one Harvard graduate student proclaims in bold type, "*We are not a vulnerable group, and Harvard is not an exploitative employer.*"[158] In short, graduate students' (presumed) privilege precludes them from exploitation because it precludes them from being workers.

·   ·   ·   ·   ·

By unpacking the cultural narratives of immorality and privilege, this chapter reveals their shared artificiality as well as their shared purpose. In American culture, such narratives have been deployed again and again, over time and across groups, to govern workers and control marginalized groups. There are important differences between them, of course, particularly in how they capitalize on logics of race, class, and gender, and therefore how much damage they do to their targets. Despite such differences, both narratives serve the same two goals. First, they cast their targets as something other than rights-bearing workers. For instance, though incarcerated and workfare workers are understood to be performing labor, narratives of immorality are used to justify why they must be forced to work and, therefore, why they are not independent, productive rights-bearing workers. Meanwhile, narratives of privilege are used to construct college athletes' and graduate students' labor as something other than "work" altogether. They are said to love what they do and to be lucky to get to do it. They are described as getting opportunities and adventure, not remuneration. In this way, privilege narratives are used to justify why theirs is not "real" work and so why they too are not rights-bearing workers.

The second purpose of these narratives is to justify workers' need for extra regulation, surveillance, and discipline. They accomplish this by casting their targets as childlike figures: ignorant, irresponsible, immature, and puerile. Such discursive strategies are effective because as research in the sociology of childhood has shown, children are culturally constructed as inferior to adults—unknowing, even naughty and disruptive—so that it is culturally appropriate to relate to them in ways that would be disrespectful of adults.[159] As we have seen, this same construal is pervasive in cultural rhetoric surrounding the four groups of workers in this book, who are portrayed as dependent, unknowing, irresponsible, immature, vulnerable, demanding, coddled, or complaining—that is, much like popular portrayals of children. Incarcerated and workfare workers, for example, are said to be different from "you and I" (who are implicitly adults), "dependent" on (adult) "taxpayers," and ignorant of, or averse to, the (adult) world of work. As a result, they are said to need "tough love," a parent-like figure to whip them into shape. College athletes are also portrayed as needing such a figure. Described as young, vulnerable, and immature, likely to behave poorly and "whine" unnecessarily, athletes are told to "quit crying" and follow the advice of those (adults) who have their "best interest in mind." Meanwhile, though graduate students are depicted as the least childlike of the four groups, they too are described as "whiny" "ungrateful brats," fatuously "demanding safe spaces" and "a list of trigger words."

By framing these groups as childlike and inferior, in need of supervision and even discipline, narratives of privilege and immorality serve as the cultural scaffolding for their bosses' expansive punitive power over them; that is, their status coercion. In the next chapter, I move from the realm of culture to that of the individual, examining workers' experiences of status coercion across these diverse labor regimes.

2 "Either You Do It or You're Going to the Box"

COERCION AND COMPLIANCE

I have a two-year-old child and I tell him, "You can be whatever you want to be, but you will not get a PhD, because I don't want anyone else to have that much control over your future. You can do anything. You can be a doctor, you can be a lawyer, you can do anything. But you will not get a PhD, absolutely not." Because it's not about what you do, it's about your mentor and what he decides or she decides, where she wants you to go, or what she wants you to do.

—Kimberly Mays, former graduate student in biology

It's hard. You're always in fear of being kicked out. That's really what it is. Every day you think, "Is this the day someone is going to walk in and tell me, *You're leaving with a master's.*"

—Laine, former graduate student in chemistry

Kimberly Mays and Laine recently completed their PhD in the sciences. Though they were in different disciplines and at different universities, they both characterized their graduate school experiences as difficult, even oppressive. Laine called hers "the worst time of [her] life," and Kimberly said that graduate school "destroyed [her] ambitions to become an academic scientist." They both endured harassment from faculty members in their departments, though Kimberly described hers as more severe and persistent. They both suffered mental and physical health problems because of their graduate-school work environments, and because of those environments, they both left the academy after finishing their degrees.

Though Kimberly's and Laine's experiences were not unique, they were at the worse end of the spectrum among the graduate students I interviewed, whose experiences ranged from "terrible" to "fantastic." In fact, a similar spread characterized the experiences of all four groups of workers in this study, though with markedly different upper limits, as no incarcerated or workfare workers described their jobs as "fantastic." Even still, it is worth emphasizing that in these labor relations—as in all jobs—workers do not always experience bad labor conditions, overt exploitation, or abuse. Nor do they always interpret the power dynamics at their workplaces as coercive, just as "regular" workers do not always feel or see the economic compulsion undergirding their own employment relations. In part, this is a matter of ideology and interpretation, for the cultural narratives analyzed in the previous chapter inform how these workers experience and interpret their labor. Many simply accept that this is how things are done.

Yet variation in their experiences and understandings of status coercion is not only due to individual differences in interpretation. It is also because in these jobs, as in others, there is a range of bosses—some are kind, some are strict, some are abusive—whose dispositions invariably affect the tenor of the workplace. In fact, in these labor relations bosses' dispositions are particularly important because they have unusually broad discretion in shaping workplace dynamics. As Suzanne, a former biochemistry graduate student, said,

> The problem with the whole sciences right now is that there's no common standard or rules, so it's a bit like *The Wild Wild West*. It really depends— like, how much you learn and how you're treated—all these things depend a hundred percent on who your advisor is.

Indeed, all of the labor relations in this book are "a bit like *The Wild Wild West*" in this way. Because they are not sociolegally constructed as rights-bearing "work," they are not governed by typical workplace norms and regulations. Therefore, the workers who labor within them do so in the absence of many (if not all) employment protections, without recourse to union representatives and human resources departments, and without the basic expectations and privileges of other "workers." Meanwhile, their

bosses' actions *as overseers of their labor* are not closely monitored or regulated by higher-ups, and so such powers often remain unchecked. As a
consequence, while a good boss in these jobs can be quite good, a bad one
can be really bad.

But even when such bosses are at their best, these labor relations are
still predicated on status coercion. Because their coercive power does not
reside in their disposition but, rather, in their institutionalized capacity to
wield punitive power, whether or not they choose to do so. Indeed, even
when they do not, workers are acutely aware of their ability to wield such
power, and this awareness shapes their experiences and interpretations of
their labor.

In the sections below, I examine these experiences and interpretations,
moving from the least severely coercive labor relation to the most. Yet for all
of them, as we will see, workers' awareness of their bosses' coercive power
usually produces their acquiescence. They are sure to "follow instructions"
and remain "compliant." They act like "good soldiers" and "walk on eggshells." Thus, I argue, the coercion at the heart of these labor relations creates and sustains "a relation of docility-utility," as Michel Foucault said of
another context,[1] producing and enforcing "good soldier" worker subjectivities. Yet such subjectivities are not likely to remain confined to these particular labor regimes. Because these regimes often prime workers for precarious employment in the mainstream economy, the coercion at their core
also produces the vulnerable and compliant workers on whom neoliberal
precarity relies.

GRADUATE STUDENTS: "YOUR PROFESSOR IS TRYING TO SQUEEZE EVERY LAST EXPERIMENT OUT OF YOU"

Emily recently earned her PhD in chemistry from a top-tier research university. Echoing Kimberly Mays, the 30-year-old white woman argued
that faculty advisors in the life sciences have too much control over too
many dimensions of graduate students' lives.

> They have a frightening amount of power, I think, because they sort of have
> unchecked dominion, like, over multiple aspects of your life. I think this is
> one of the reasons that some groups of graduate students have tried to

unionize. Because [advisors] can dictate the hours that you work without any sort of check on that, they can demand any sort of product, whether it's reasonable or not, they can terminate you at will,[2] because they're providing your funding. . . . And, in most cases, they have total discretion over when you can graduate and whether you can graduate. . . . And nobody is going to give you a job unless you have a good letter from your advisor. . . . Your advisor has total power over your life. I mean, *in what job setting is that okay?*

In Emily's view, faculty advisors have expansive "unchecked" power over not only graduate students' work lives but also their education and future employment—or, as she said, their "whole life."

At first glance, such power may seem both reasonable and expected. University faculty are experts in their fields and must train graduate students according to the high standards of PhD-level work. Therefore, it makes sense that they have the authority to determine whether students have met such standards, as well as the authority to assess the caliber of students' work for future employers. In specialized fields, in fact, faculty advisors may be among a very small handful of people with the expertise necessary to do so. In isolation, then, faculty advisors' authority as teachers and mentors does not render graduate student labor inherently coercive. It is the broader organization of work in the academic sciences that does so.

In the sciences, faculty advisors not only oversee their students' research; they also oversee their students' labor. They are the "bosses" of their labs, and the graduate students who work in those labs are learning and pursuing their degrees at the same time as they are performing labor for their advisors. As Henry, who is now a chemistry professor, said, "It is complicated in our field, because working in the lab as a job and working in the lab as a student overlap almost one hundred percent." These students are not performing just any labor, moreover. They are conducting their advisors' research.[3] For although graduate students typically choose a lab based on their own interests, once they are a member of that lab their research agendas, and often their particular research questions, are determined by the faculty member in charge of it—their "boss," "PI" (principal investigator), or "advisor"—who owns any resulting findings, publications, inventions, and patents. As Elizabeth, another former chemistry PhD student, explained, though faculty advisors are "usually not in the lab doing the research themselves . . . they're guiding the research, and the research is their idea. The grad students are the hands that execute the experiments." Thus, graduate student "hands" produce not only their own PhD dissertations but also their faculty advisors' CVs, tenure dossiers, grant applications, and professional reputations.

The result is a pressure-filled power structure with high stakes for students and faculty alike. However, because faculty hold nearly all of the power in this labor relation, graduate students are in a vulnerable position.[4] But they are not just any vulnerable worker. Because their advisors have power over their ability to finish their degrees and obtain employment in their fields—that is, power over their status as PhD candidates and future scientists—their vulnerability stems from status coercion.

The most basic power that science faculty have over graduate students is their ability to dismiss students from the lab, which usually means being dismissed from graduate school without a PhD. As Laine explained, "Your advisor basically will tell you your work is either good enough, or not good enough. And if they ever make that decision where they're no longer going to support you, meaning that you can no longer work in the lab, that is a big black X on you." To explain why, the 30-year-old white woman continued,

> I'm an inorganic chemist. So if [I] was asked to leave, it was highly unlikely that another inorganic chemistry advisor would take me on. I would probably have to switch to analytical, or organic, or a different subdivision, and then go through the entire process again. And so, usually if that happens, people leave with a master's and they're done forever. . . . And it's unfortunate, because maybe your advisor isn't the nicest person, or maybe they have emotional security issues. Or, you know, they're all socially awkward. These are brilliant, brilliant people. And so, if you don't get along with your advisor for whatever reason, they can just walk in, and kick you out.

Ron, who is now a chemistry professor, said that although "kicking [students] out" is not common, he has seen it happen. "The most underhanded way that I've seen it handled," the midthirties white man said, "is when [students] come up to get into candidacy, the advisor speaks to the committee ahead of time, and just says to them, 'Hey I don't want this person to pass.' And [the student] will then be failed from their candidacy and, if you fail your candidacy, you're out of the PhD program."

Yet because of faculty reliance on graduate student labor, Ron said that there is often a disincentive for them to dismiss students, even those whose work is not satisfactory. In fact, because of this reliance, he said that there is also a disincentive for faculty to allow good graduate students to finish their degrees and leave the lab. Faculty need their labor. Thus, in addition to being kicked out, graduate students feared the opposite: not being allowed to leave graduate school. As Ron bluntly explained,

> The thing with the graduate students is, they're terrible, right? They're crap. They're awful in lab usually until their final year. And then, in their final year, that's when they suddenly learn skills like time management, and they learn, "Oh wait, if I do two things at once, that will actually speed up the research." So I've *absolutely* heard tell of advisors who have essentially prevented their students from coming up for their PhD defense, because out of nowhere they suddenly became productive, and [advisors] want to keep them on longer to get more production out of them.

Nearly all of the former graduate students I interviewed were familiar with this practice, though a majority of them had not experienced it firsthand. Laine did, however. In fact, she said it was common practice across the labs in her department. "I haven't talked to anybody where that's *not* the case," she said.

> You're trying to leave, you're trying to set up your career, you're going on job interviews, you're writing your dissertation, you're wrapping up your research, and all the while your professor is trying to squeeze every last experiment out of you. . . . Because they've spent so much time trying to get their lab up and running, and now here you are after five years, you're finally a student that can produce work for them. So letting you leave is a detriment to their promotion.

To get around this issue, Laine said, the students in her department developed a "trick": they would request a defense date one or two semesters before they actually wanted to defend their dissertations. Laine used this trick herself. "I pushed, and pushed, and pushed" for a defense date in the fall, she said, even though she really wanted to defend her dissertation in the spring. "Finally [my advisor] was like, 'No, no, no, you just can't, like, it's not going to happen. But spring will happen, spring will happen,' and I got it in writing, and then I was done."

Scott encountered a similar obstacle, but such tricks did not work for him. Near the end of his tenure in graduate school, the 32-year-old white man said that his advisor repeatedly delayed the date of his dissertation defense. At the same time, his advisor made clear that Scott would be dismissed from the lab when his funding expired, whether or not he had defended his dissertation. Scott was "incredibly worried" that he would be pushed out of the program without a degree. "I don't know if he was actually going to do it," he said, "but that's what he told me multiple, multiple, multiple times." Though Scott could not fully explain his advisor's behavior, he believed that it was largely due to his productivity in the lab. "A lot of it had to do with the fact that I was used as labor," he said. "I was used more as labor than as a student." In the end, after multiple defense date cancellations, Scott said he went to his department's director of graduate studies—though anonymously because he feared "blowback"—who helped him set and keep a defense date. Because he did so, however, he felt that he could not rely on his advisor for job recommendations. "To this day, if I'd asked him for a letter of recommendation, I don't know what would have happened." His fear, Scott explained, was that his advisor "would write a bad letter . . . to try to, you know, sabotage my future efforts."

In terms of recommendation letters, Kimberly Mays was in a similar predicament. Because her advisor was not only her boss but also her harasser, she felt that she could not rely on him for a letter of recommendation. "I can't use him," the 37-year-old African American woman said.

> I can't get a letter from him. I wouldn't *want* to get a letter from him. So, I would have to get a letter from someone else, which would be automatically flagged, like, "Wow, why is she not getting endorsed by her PhD advisor? There must be some problems there." And automatically, *I* am assumed to be the problem.

In the end, though Scott was able to get a letter of recommendation from a visiting professor instead of his advisor, Kimberly did not have that option. She left academia, and though she is relatively happy in her current position, she still "craves" being a scientist.

> I still want to be in the lab. I still want to explore some of the scientific problems that are conundrums in the African American community. . . . That's

why I got into this, that's why I wanted to do this. I wanted to save lives, I wanted to impact lives of women who look like me. And, I kind of feel like, I let him win. Because I'm not doing it.

Then her voice choked, and we sat in silence.

Kimberly's and Scott's experiences highlight another way that graduate students experience their advisors' power: control over their future employment through letters of recommendation. As Henry, an early-forties white man, explained,

> Without a doubt, the most profound way an advisor can wield power is in writing a letter of recommendation. . . . Virtually any employer, academic or not academic, is going to give very, very strong weight to the graduate advisor, who probably has seen more of that person's work and development than anybody else.

In this way, graduate work in the sciences differs little from other academic disciplines, as faculty recommendations across the academy are considered essential to PhD students' future employment. Yet not all faculty advisors are also the bosses of their students' labor. When they are, such recommendation letters become a mechanism for this form of labor coercion.[5]

Publications are another means by which graduate students experience their advisors' coercive power. Because the quality and quantity of their published articles affect students' ability to secure academic employment and, in some departments, complete their degrees, publications are crucial to students' academic success. Yet in the sciences, faculty advisors wield substantial power over students' publications. They are nearly always coauthors—typically listed last to indicate ownership of the lab and the project—and they control if, when, and where a paper is submitted for publication. Even more, faculty decide who is included as an author and in what order, signifying the relative importance of each author's contribution.

A substantial minority of the former graduate students I interviewed had experienced some kind of publication problem with their advisor. Henry, for example, recalled a major paper on which he was not included as an author, even though he believed he had contributed to it in a "significant, intellectual way." Not being an author on such an important publication from one's lab, Henry explained, could affect more than one's résumé. If the paper was at all related to that student's research, he said that it could render the student's entire research agenda redundant, making it "questionable whether that person's other works could ever be published."

Henry and the other former graduate students I interviewed described a variety of reasons why their advisors might impede their publications, ranging from what they saw as innocent but mismanaged efforts to distribute credit for the research to outright punitive retribution. Emily described yet another way that advisors might do so: by assigning them "high-risk research." At her top-tier university, she explained, faculty "are willing to engage in pretty high-risk research . . . because they want to advance their careers."

> If [that research] doesn't pan out, they'll just move on to their next project, or they have some backup projects running that will keep their funding going. But the students who are working on high-risk projects, if those don't come to anything, then they might finish and not have any publications, because nothing worked. That's how you end up in situations where somebody finishes grad school [without publications] or quits grad school after five years because they don't have anything, and they're not going to graduate.

In the sciences, as Emily implied, failed projects often do not yield publications, and without publications graduate students in her department would not be allowed to graduate, let alone be hired as postdocs or professors. In her view, most of the risks of high-risk research are borne by graduate students. "That's the consequence," she said, "of that sort of mentality that people want to advance their careers at whatever cost, and they just have peons to do the work for them."

Emily's account highlights the status coercion at the crux of this labor relation: those at the bottom of this power structure feel that those at the top have overly expansive—even punitive—power over them, controlling not only their labor in the lab but also their education, academic credentials, and future careers. Indeed, because of the very real pressure that many faculty members themselves are under, this lopsided labor system allows—and sometimes even seems to expect—faculty to deploy such levers of coercion in order to transfer at least some of this pressure to their subordinates. Of course, not all faculty advisors do so, and even when they do, it is not always considered problematic by graduate students. Overall, five of the twenty former graduate students I interviewed characterized their experiences as highly positive, while an equal number characterized theirs as intensely negative. Yet even when they had positive experiences, these students also had a deep and abiding sense of what their advisors could do for them, or to them.

COLLEGE ATHLETES: "IF THEY WANT YOU TO PLAY, AND YOU'RE INJURED, THEN YOU'RE PLAYING"

In terms of power dynamics, college athletes' labor is similar to that of graduate students in the sciences. In both cases, for example, their bosses' jobs seem to be unusually dependent on their labor; just as science faculty careers are built on graduate students' labor in the lab, coaches' careers are built (or broken) by athletes' labor in the stadium. As basketball player Kate said, a coach's job is "contingent upon the win." Because of this dynamic, she believed that coaches often "lose sight of the human beings, lose sight of the fact that these are young women who are trying to find their way." The result, the 24-year-old Black woman argued, is athletes' "exploitation."

> Instead of, like, guiding them, and mentoring them through that stage, it's more of an exploitation, where [coaches are] like, "Okay, they play basketball for me. I'm going to, you know, play them till they drop. Or push things [like mental health issues] under the rug because I need them to score twenty points." Or, you know, "I'm going to make every decision I need to make in order for us to get a win."

In Kate's view, coaches "lose sight of all morality because money and job are on the line," echoing Emily's critique of faculty who "advance their careers at whatever cost" to graduate students.

While some athletes, like Kate, held their coaches responsible for their sense of exploitation, others blamed the NCAA. For instance, according to Zachary Lane, the NCAA is "just a business that uses the cheapest product"—college athletes—"to generate revenue." To emphasize his point, the 29-year-old African American man developed an extended analogy between Division I college athletics and "pimps," on the one hand, and college athletes and prostitutes on the other. In both cases, this former football player argued, those with power "sell a dream" and promise "glamour" in order to recruit and ultimately exploit their targets. As Zachary explained, a pimp might recruit prostitutes by saying,

> "Oh, we're going to bring you over here, we're going to make you look nice, we're going to get you all dressed up. You like wearing that nice stuff, don't you? Yeah, you look good. You look really good." . . . And what do the college coaches tell you? "Oh, man, I think you should come and play right away for us. Don't you look good in this jersey? Look at our facilities, this is real nice here, right? Look at our lockers, look at our cleats." For an eighteen-year-old kid, you're like, "Oh yeah, I like this, this is nice." [But] when you get there, it's *work*, just like the woman. She might like to have sex already. If she [does] that's even better because . . . I don't have to break your mind now. You're going to do this anyways. . . . Like, for me, I'm going to play football anyways. I might do it for free. . . . [But really] I'm paying for my education, just like the woman is having sex with these men, getting this money, bring-ing it back to the pimp, to the NCAA, or to the university, right? . . . She's bringing the money back to daddy, she's getting taken care of, and it looks all good. "That's my favorite employee," [the pimp says]. "I love you. I'm going to take care of you. I'm going to make sure everything is good. You're hurt? Okay, I'll take care of your doctor's bill. You go to jail? I'm going to bail you out. I'm going to take care of you."

Yet both prostitutes and college athletes, Zachary said, are at risk of "get-ting used up": "If they're done with you, they're done with you." He was able to avoid this fate, he explained, because his older brother, who was also a college football player, warned him against getting "pimped." "The one thing he told me," Zachary said, "was 'don't get pimped.'" And so Zachary made sure to get what he needed out of college football: "to get to the NFL . . . and leave with my education."

As Zachary's analogy suggests, Division I athletics—much like graduate student labor in the sciences—is not only a high-pressure, high-stakes labor relation; it is one in which its subordinates understand their bosses as having expansive power over them. In fact, they experience this power in similar ways. Like graduate students, athletes understand their coaches as having control over their education and future employment, as well as the much-sought-after chance to play their sport at the elite collegiate level. These are the levers of status coercion under which college athletes labor.

For example, just as Laine described graduate students as "always in fear of being kicked out" of graduate school, athletes described their constant awareness of their coaches' power to revoke their scholarships and therefore their dual status as college athletes and college students. "The thing about scholarships is," former football player M. Max said,

> They can literally take your scholarship from you if they want to, if you're not performing.[6] That's what a lot of people don't know. You have to re-sign for your scholarship every year. It's not like you sign on a dotted line and you get four years of college for free. You sign on a dotted line [and] you have to do everything they say or they can take your scholarship anytime they want.

Molly, a former college basketball player, made the same point. In fact, she said that her coach would explicitly threaten to revoke the athletes' scholarships. "Our coach would sometimes say, when she's mad, like, 'You guys are playing horrible,' blah, blah, blah, 'I'm going to take your scholarship away.'" Though Molly believed that it was unlikely that her coach would actually do so ("you have to do something pretty bad"), "technically speaking," the 23-year-old African American woman explained, "if you're not holding yourself up to the standard of the coach, or your grades aren't good, or whatever, your scholarship can get taken."

For most of the athletes I interviewed, however, the more tangible threat was losing playing time. As Zachary explained, "If you do something really egregious, they'll take your scholarship away. If you do something just stupid, then they'll cut your playing time." Coaches' power to cut athletes' playing time is simply "a given," former basketball player Tom Vine said—so much so that most of the athletes I interviewed did not mention it without being asked. Coaches' power to do so was taken for granted. "If you're not performing well in practice," Mike Smith, another basketball player, said, "if you're complaining, or you're just an issue, *you're just not going to play.*"

Although coaches' power to "bench" athletes might not initially seem to be a lever of status coercion, closer analysis reveals its punitive dimensions for athletes, which make it so. Foremost, athletes repeatedly told me, losing playing time means losing something they deeply love. "By not playing," Zachary said, "they've just taken away what you love to do. That's the most ramification right there. That's the biggest effect on you, is like, you're not able to do what you love to do." Football player Bill Murdock agreed. "I felt like all my dreams were on the line every single day at practice. And I better do well, or else." Yet playing their sport in college is not just something they love to do; it is also something they have worked exhaustively to attain. "You came in loving this game," Molly said, "and didn't work for a scholarship just to sit on the bench." This sense of their "work" and "dreams" being "on the line" is intensified by the fact that for the vast majority of these athletes, college sports will be the apex of their athletic career. Most of them will not go on to compete professionally, and they are repeatedly reminded of this fact by NCAA and university officials alike.[7] Therefore, losing playing time means missing out on their athletic acme. This pressure is further intensified by the finite number of games and years they can compete. Per NCAA regulations, athletes have five years to play four seasons. Their eligibility "clock," as the NCAA calls it, starts ticking when they enroll as a full-time student and does not stop even if they do not compete for an entire season.[8] As a result, for these athletes every game felt important, and their ability to play in any given game was controlled by their coach.

Losing playing time not only affects athletes' current athletic careers; it also affects their future careers as well. Foremost, this is because not playing decreases their chances for professional recruitment. As Zachary explained, "You've got to understand this: the thing with the NFL is, they have scouts that come around to watch people play. So, if you're not playing, then you don't have a chance at all." Likewise, basketball player Lindsay said, "If you're not playing, you know, people are going to be wondering why and, like, they're not going to get to see you on the court. So they won't get to scout you as much. They won't see how good you are." Moreover, athletes being "benched" suggests that they are a problem in some way, and just as graduate students rely on their advisors' letters of recommendation for future jobs, athletes rely on their coaches' evaluations of them to professional recruiters. As Lindsay explained, "Your coach is going to be talking to the coaches of the WNBA," and they are going to be asked, "'What's this kid like on your team? Like, does she get along with everybody? Is she a trouble-maker? Does she cause problems? Or does she fall in line?'" The primary risk, Lindsay and the other athletes told me, is that their coaches would characterize them as "uncoachable." "That's a big thing for coaches," the 25-year-old Black woman said. "'Yeah, she's uncoachable, she doesn't really listen, she talks back.'" JohnJohn agreed. "Remember," the 34-year-old Black football player said, "we are all trying to get to the League."

> I don't need this college scout coming to my coaches and the coach is like, "Yeah, he's not coachable, you know, he doesn't really follow instructions well, he doesn't take coaching well." Because that's the biggest thing, that's the biggest problem you could have as an athlete, is you're not coachable. That you're hot-headed, and that you're all for yourself, you're selfish. That's not what you want.

Again and again, these athletes said they needed to be "coachable"—that is, follow their coaches' instructions—in order to keep their playing time and retain their status as elite athletes.

Athletes' constrained mobility only increased their sense of their coaches' power over them. For unlike many more traditional workers, who can quit their jobs and seek comparable work,[9] Division I athletes (along with the other workers in this book) cannot. The NCAA limits their ability to transfer to other Division I sports teams,[10] and their coaches can impose additional constraints.[11] For instance, athletes are not allowed to communicate with other teams' coaches to determine if transferring is even possible without their own coach's written consent.[12] Simply requesting such a "release" can damage their relationship with their coach and lead to loss of playing time.[13] Then, if they are allowed to transfer, athletes cannot compete the following season, losing a year of their already-limited NCAA eligibility.[14] As football player Jayce explained, "If you go in and you don't click with the coach, you can't just get out of that and transfer to another Division I school. Well, you *can*," the white 29-year-old man allowed, "but you'll sit out for a year. I mean, you don't really have much you can do. . . . You literally miss years. . . . So, if you don't get along with one of your coaches, then you're kind of SOL." This sense of being "SOL" is even worse for those athletes who have already lost playing time, such as those who have been "red-shirted," that is, kept out of competition for a season in order to develop their skills or recover from an injury while preserving that season of eligibility. After doing so, however, they have only four years—not five—to play their four-season allotment, so any additional loss of playing time (such as that required by transferring) results in a substantial deficit. This is called "handcuffing a red-shirt kid," basketball player Mike Smith said. "They kind of have them by the balls."

All of these dynamics led college athletes to believe that their coaches had expansive power over their athletic careers and their education—their "dreams"—which is qualitatively different from how most "regular" workers experience their bosses' power. Of course, not all coaches deploy these levers of coercion, and even when they do, athletes do not always experience them as overly punitive or coercive. Indeed, like the graduate students, the athletes I interviewed reported a range of experiences; six of the eighteen characterized their college careers as "good" or "great," while five described theirs as at least somewhat negative. Among the latter, Bruce's experience was the worst. In his view, being a college football player was "terrible," even ruinous. Although his experience is not representative of those I interviewed, it is worth describing in detail because it reveals some of the ways that athletes negatively experience their coaches' coercive powers.

Bruce is white, now in his early thirties. When he went to college, he did not have support from his parents, financial or otherwise, so he started off at a junior college hoping to be recruited (and offered a scholarship) by a Division I team the following year. He worked hard to make this happen, he said, waking up at four o'clock every morning for speed training. His work paid off: at an NFL scouting combine, he ran one of the fastest times in the country; so Bruce assumed that Division I coaches would contact him with recruiting offers. But he did not hear from any coaches. As an assistant coach told him later, however, recruiters had indeed tried to contact him, but his head coach had turned them away because he did not want Bruce to leave. As Bruce explained, "My junior college was turning into a four-year school, and he wanted me to stay . . . [but] I was so upset that this guy ruined opportunities for me to go play somewhere else that there's no way I was going to stay and play for him." So even though recruiting season had ended and scholarships were no longer available, Bruce left his junior college to "walk on" at a state university.[15]

The next year at his new school Bruce played well—so well, he said, that his coach offered him a scholarship for the following year. "'Wow,'" Bruce remembered his coach saying, "'we've never had a walk-on come and contribute the way that you have. We're going to give you the first scholarship that opens up.'" Bruce was overjoyed.

> I'm crying, and I called my mom. That was like the greatest day ever. I was, like, finally now I don't have to work on the side and, you know, I can kind of relax, and focus on what I'm doing here in school, spend more time studying than on my part-time job. It was the greatest moment.

The following fall, Bruce remembered arriving on campus and asking his coach about the scholarship. "Hey, I don't know how this scholarship thing works," he recalled saying. "I mean, how do I get my books? Like, what do I need to do for this?" "'Oh, I'm sorry,'" he remembered his coach saying. "'We never had a scholarship open up.'" Though he did not quite know what to think at the time, Bruce came to believe that the coach "could have given [him] one if he wanted to." But he did not, Bruce said, because

> he just knew that, in the NCAA, you can't transfer without sitting out a year, and if you transfer your senior year, you're done. So, he knew he had me there no matter what. He could use that scholarship to bring in another player. . . . So, it was more about him and that program, than it was about me. . . . I was a starting player, [but] like, I was asking other kids to borrow their meal cards. That's pathetic, that should never be that way.

Not getting that scholarship, Bruce said, "ruined my whole career and my whole experience in college."

Then he injured his shoulder. If it had been treated right away, Bruce said, he would have required only minor surgery, and with a medical redshirt he could have preserved that year of eligibility. But he felt pressured to play.[16] "They kept trying to get me to play and telling me I was going to be okay," he said.

> You're always trying to make them happy, I guess. And if they want you to play, and you're injured, then you're playing. Because you don't want to say "no" . . . because then you think, "Oh well, [the coach] is in control, and he can just not play me ever again. And if I have to transfer, then I have to sit

out a year." There are just so many variables, like, your education, your schooling, where you're at. There are so many things where you just don't want to mess it up.

In the end, his shoulder got too bad to play; he needed major surgery. Bruce left the team. In fact, he left school altogether. "The coach acted like I like quit on him," Bruce recalled, "like I quit on the team and stuff. And I was like . . . *I did everything for you.* I hurt myself. And now my career is over and I really wanted to play NFL. . . . And now I have all these student loans." "I look back at it," Bruce said later in the interview, "there is no way that I should have been set back, like, that behind in life, and have to catch up so much."

For Bruce, being a college athlete was an almost entirely negative experience, and he has continued to feel deeply misused by his former coaches. Yet even when the athletes I interviewed had positive experiences, they—much like the graduate students—were always aware of the power their coaches could wield. Haley is a case in point. Even as she proclaimed that playing college basketball was "the best experience of [her] life," she also described having to "stay on [her] toes" in order to manage her coach's verbal outbursts and negotiate her less-than-secure status as a walk-on. Kate's perspective is perhaps even more telling. Although her experience was less positive than Haley's, her college basketball career was neither particularly negative nor out of the ordinary. Yet she said that talking to me about her experience made her feel "absolutely" nervous. Even though she is no longer in the basketball world—and has not been for several years—she was worried about retribution. "You don't want to burn bridges," she explained. "You don't want to, you know, say bad about this program because of how it's going to affect you. It's kind of like, if I don't speak on it, and I just leave it where it's going to be, then it doesn't harm me in any way." For Kate, a deep sense of her coach's power remained, even after leaving the sport.[17]

WORKFARE WORKERS: "YOU DON'T HAVE A CHOICE, UNLESS YOU WANT THE BENEFITS TO GET CUT OFF"

Although Kate, Haley, Bruce, and all of the former athletes and graduate students I interviewed could have left their positions had they really needed to—and some of them did—the consequences for doing so could be severe. Such decisions were thus more of a Hobson's choice, an only-ostensibly "free" decision between equally intolerable alternatives. This dynamic is significantly starker for workfare and incarcerated workers, for whom the consequences of any form of noncompliance—including job exit—can be dire.

For workfare workers, the primary consequence is being sanctioned: losing access to public assistance programs, including cash benefits, rent and utility subsidies, Medicaid, childcare and transportation assistance, or SNAP benefits.[18] Though such sanctions are usually temporary—lasting one to six months among the workers I interviewed—they permanently reduce welfare recipients' lifetime allotment of public assistance under TANF (Temporary Assistance for Needy Families). In fact, just as NCAA athletes have a five-year eligibility "clock" that keeps ticking even if they do not compete, TANF recipients have a 60-month benefits "clock" that keeps ticking even when they are sanctioned.[19] Thus, welfare sanctions are not only a lever of economic coercion, revoking cash assistance from the poor. They are also a lever of status coercion, removing the poor from the status of "welfare recipient in good standing" and the meager but much-needed benefits which that status confers.

Nearly half of the 43 workfare workers I interviewed had been sanctioned at least once, and a significant minority had been sanctioned multiple times. Yet all of them described the seemingly ubiquitous threat of sanctions. As 30-year-old Shara White said, "That's their favorite. Yeah, that's their favorite. . . . They're always trying to throw [that] they're going to sanction you in your face." While many often-minor misdeeds (or simply accusations of such) could provoke sanctions, failure to comply with one's assigned "work activities" was a common cause among those I interviewed and, studies show, among welfare recipients in general.[20] As workfare worker Kierra Ross explained, "You got to do [the work]. They don't ask if you want to do it, you *got* to do it. . . . You don't have a choice, unless you want the benefits to get cut off."

Yet these workers were sanctioned not because they did not *want* to work. Indeed, like most Americans, the workfare workers I interviewed believed deeply in the value of productive labor. They wanted to work. Instead, they were sanctioned for two work-related reasons: first, when external circumstances interfered with their (inflexible) jobs, and second, when they challenged problems at work. In the first case, for example, Kathy Johnson described being threatened with sanctions when her child's health crisis prevented her from going to work. Although at the time of our interview the 45-year-old white woman was the director of a women's shelter, she was once an unemployed, newly divorced mother of three assigned to work 25 hours a week in order to receive public assistance. She complied with her workfare assignment, she said, until one of her sons became gravely ill. She apprised both her caseworker and workfare supervisor of the situation and stopped going to work in order to stay in the hospital with her son. As a result, Kathy recalled, her caseworker threatened to terminate her public assistance.

> I still remember feeling that way, like they're going to cut me off. Because I was sleeping in a hospital chair while my son was there [in the hospital] when his lung collapsed, and then the other lung collapsed. . . . He went into a partial coma, which turned to be a drug-induced coma. He was nonresponsive to medication. I remember them coming in and telling me to pray for the best, but prepare for the worst. And I'm sitting there on a chair, and I'm in a chaplain at the hospital on my knees praying he wake up. And they're telling me, "We're going to cut your food stamps off." Well, [I said,] "You do what you have to do, because *I'm* doing what *I* have to do, and I will not be there. I'm telling you, I will not be there."

Ultimately, however, Kathy said that her caseworker's threats did not materialize, but only because her workfare supervisor began lying for her, claiming that she was at work even as she remained in the hospital with her son. "I wasn't doing anything I shouldn't have been doing," Kathy told me. "*I was being a mom.* So they covered for me. They would say, 'Yeah, she was here eight hours today,' when they hadn't seen me in three days." Yet it must be noted that the perception of Kathy as a "good mother," especially while not working, has historically been a privilege accorded only to white women, both in the welfare system and in American culture more broadly.[21] Although we cannot know for sure, it is possible that Kathy's whiteness informed her supervisor's sympathy and willingness to lie—that is, commit fraud—in order to protect her benefits. Kathy, meanwhile, was deeply thankful for her supervisor's sympathy, while also frustrated by the fact that her ability to be a good mother while receiving public assistance seemed entirely dependent on her caseworker and supervisor, each of whom had the power to rescind or sustain her family support.[22]

James Pondos recounted a similar story of workfare impinging on his ability to be a good parent, but in his case no one lied to protect his benefits. For his workfare assignment, the 52-year-old African American single father did building maintenance work at a nonprofit agency. He worked for a year without incident, he said, until his schedule abruptly changed "with no regard for my son and things that I have to do." Instead of starting at nine o'clock and ending at 2:30 in the afternoon, he was told—with only one day's warning—that his new (longer) shift would be from 8:30 A.M. to 4 P.M. He told both his caseworker and workfare supervisor that he could not comply with the new schedule because his young son did not get on the school bus until 8 A.M. and, because he lived across town, he could not get to work by 8:30 via city buses. In response, James remembered them saying, "'Either you show or you're sanctioned.'" He came to work late the first week but then received a "termination letter" stating that he was dismissed from the job and sanctioned from public assistance. "I got a four-months' sanction," James said, "which meant no cash assistance, food stamps, and eventually I ended up getting evicted out of my house. Me and my son had to go stay in the shelter." For James and his son, the penalty for not being able to comply with his new work schedule was severe indeed.

The second work-related reason they were sanctioned, these workfare workers said, was that they challenged problems in the workplace. This was most often an issue for those who had been assigned to one workfare site in particular—one of a national chain of nonprofit thrift stores—where they had to sort donations in a large warehouse reportedly rife with heavy dust, bedbugs, and other environmental hazards. "That was *horrible*," 26-year-old Sasha Reed said. "They want you to work with old dirty clothes and bedbugs and stuff. That was the worst site." So, this young African American woman explained, "I did something to not have to go there no more. . . . I left the site, I just left." To her surprise (and my own), she was not sanctioned as a result but was simply assigned to another worksite. April Smith, however, said that she was sanctioned when after just one day in that warehouse, she could no longer work because of her allergic reaction to the dust. As the 30-year-old African American woman recalled, "It's like, a lot of dust. I just sneezed all day, uncontrollably, and I was like, 'Is there something else I could do, like clean around the building, *anything*?'" They would not accommodate her request. "'You have to do this,'" she recalled her supervisor saying. "So I walked off," April said, and was sanctioned for "a good month or two" as a result.

Though Tara Collins had not (yet) been assigned to that particular site, she was well aware of its bad reputation. In fact, she said that her current workfare supervisor would threaten reassigning the workfare workers to that site if they were at all defiant. (Though in point of fact, only caseworkers—not workfare supervisors—can formally make such decisions, Tara and the other workfare workers I interviewed fully believed that their supervisors could prevail on their caseworkers to do so.) "If she gets mad at you," the 38-year-old Black woman said of her workfare supervisor, "she'll send you [to that warehouse]. She has control to do that." Tara then told me about several of her coworkers who had recently talked back to that supervisor and had then "disappeared," either sent to the warehouse or sanctioned from public assistance altogether. "She brags about stuff like that," Tara said.

> Like, "Oh okay, you want to keep talking mess? You want to keep talking mess? You'll be sanctioned." Or, like the boy who just cussed her out last week . . . now he got the [thrift store warehouse]. She was like, "Now let's see how he talks over there."

For these workfare workers, then, there was an overriding belief—borne out by experience—that they would be sanctioned if they did not comply with any workplace directive, including untenable work schedules and working conditions.

For Pauline Wilson, it was this pervasive (and very real) threat of sanctions in combination with persistent mistreatment that led her to defy her supervisor and relinquish her right to public assistance altogether. Although at the time of our interview the 57-year-old African American woman worked with Kathy Johnson overseeing the women's shelter, several years ago she too was a workfare worker, first cleaning at a nonprofit organization and then picking up trash on the highway. Pauline said that she did not mind the work. Indeed, she believed that she had an "obliga-tion" to work for her public assistance. But she detested the ill-treatment that seemed to come along with it. As Pauline explained,

> Some people didn't make it after the first week because they couldn't take it. They said, "You let them *talk* to you like that?" And then some people, they would cry, "Well, I need this money." But if you're not cut out for that kind of stuff—that kind of *humiliation*—it's not going to work. And there's *nobody* cut out for that.

Nonetheless, Pauline lasted two years on workfare, until she finally got fed up one hot summer day while picking up garbage on the highway when her supervisor would not let her get a drink of water. As Pauline remem-bered the incident, she asked her supervisor for a water break but he declined, saying, "It ain't break time yet." Pauline persisted. "I'm hot, I feel I'm going to faint," she recalled saying. "They even give water to thirsty dogs. Can I just have a little bit of water?" He would not allow it, she said; break time was not for another 15 minutes. She went to the van to get a drink of water anyway, Pauline said, which her supervisor saw, of course. He told her to sit down for ten minutes, she recalled, and she did. After the time had passed, however, Pauline said that she went back to work because if she did not perform the labor, regardless of the reason, she believed that she would be marked as "noncompliant," which would result in a sanction. And because it would be her second offense, the sanc-tion would last 90 days. (The first, she said, was for missing work without a written "doctor's excuse.") As she got up to go back to work, Pauline said that her supervisor asked angrily, "Did I *tell* you to go back out there?" "It's been past ten minutes," she remembered saying. "You're going to mark down that I didn't do anything. . . . Let me go back out here. I feel better now." He refused. "I didn't tell you [that] you can go back out," she recalled him saying. By then, Pauline had had enough. "I was speaking my mind," she told me. To her supervisor she said sassily, "I'm sick of you yell-ing at me with your smart mouth." "*I'm* not the one who needs this," she remembered him responding. "*You're* the one who needs this. I *get* a pay-check every month." "You know what?" Pauline said. "You can take that paycheck and stick it up your [ass[23]]."

And so we were back and forth until finally I said, "You know what, you can kiss my ass." So he made me sit in the van for the rest of the day. When we got back to [Social Services], I didn't even go upstairs. I didn't go sign out or nothing. I just said, "Y'all can have this," and I walked off.

In so doing, Pauline said that she lost all of her cash benefits, food stamps, and Medicaid. She was unemployed for eight or nine months until she found what she considered to be a disreputable job in a bar. As she told me with disgust,

> I would rather work in a *bar* than go through that. Even though I wasn't making that much money, I wasn't being *disrespected* like that or treated like I'm a common piece of trash. Because I'm not. I'm not.

Though Pauline ultimately relinquished her benefits rather than be sanctioned, her experience reveals at least one way that status coercion operates in workfare. For Pauline, the threat of sanctions loomed over her whether she did the work or not: had she performed the requisite labor, she would not have been following her supervisor's orders to sit down, and had she followed his orders, she would not have performed the requisite labor. Either way, she believed her supervisor could (and would) mark her as "noncompliant" and trigger a sanction.

But while such sanctions are routine,[24] their consequences are not. In Pauline's case, not only did she lose access to the social safety net, so did her two young children. Her family lost their home, though they were able to stay with her sister. "My sister would help me," Pauline recalled. "And thank God for that. I would have been messed up." For James Pondos, being sanctioned pushed him and his son into a homeless shelter, a not uncommon occurrence among welfare recipients.[25] Meanwhile, New York City workfare worker DiMaggio, who was already living in a homeless shelter, said that had he been sanctioned, he would have been evicted from the shelter.[26] "I could lose everything," the 51-year-old white man said. "If I got sanctioned, I could get thrown out [of the shelter]. That's not a misconception, that's not a scare tactic. They really did it. Plenty of guys I knew personally I helped carry their crap out to the sidewalk." Thus, for workfare workers, sanctions have expansive repercussions for themselves and their families. By cutting off their access to financial, food, utilities, housing, and medical support, sanctions have severe and lasting consequences for their health and well-being, stability and security, home and future.[27]

PRISONERS: "EITHER YOU DO IT OR YOU'RE GOING TO THE BOX"

For incarcerated workers, the consequences of status coercion are broadly similar, though their supervisors have a more diverse array of punitive powers at their disposal. For any form of noncompliance, corrections officers (COs) can put prisoners in solitary confinement, in which they are confined to a segregated cell for 23 hours a day. COs can put them on "keeplock," solitary confinement's less extreme cousin, in which they are confined to their own cells and lose "privileges," such as movement, recreation, exercise, phone use, family visits, commissary purchases, and sentence reductions for good behavior (i.e., parole). Officers can also dispense disciplinary "tickets," which exact fees and, when serious enough, prevent prisoners' parole. And in more extreme cases, they can press new criminal charges, which incur additional prison sentences.[28] For incarcerated workers, then, these technologies of coercion entail much more than the loss of wages and work. They entail the loss of basic human claims such as physical freedom, family relationships, and social connection—both within prison (through internal segregation) and from prison (through loss of parole and added sentences)—all of which has severe long-term effects on the health and well-being of prisoners and their families.[29]

Prisoners' awareness of such consequences permeates their labor and lives behind bars. As 31-year-old Qwon explained,

> We know that they got the power of the ticket, we don't want our privileges gone. We don't want to be locked in our cell twenty-four hours a day. We don't want to not be able to go to commissary and eat what we want to eat, or use the phone to contact our loved ones when we want to. So, we tuck our tail, you know, grown men, you got to handle it . . . because they got the say-so. We don't have no union, so we subject to tolerate a lot more.

For C. Parks, it was the constant threat of such consequences, especially from the more punitive officers, that made prison labor objectionable.

Otherwise, he did not mind the work. For most of his time in prison, the 27-year-old African American man worked in the "mess hall," waking at five o'clock in the morning and "fixing food, serving food, cleaning tables" from 5:30 until 9:30 or 10 A.M. The work, he said, was relatively easy and he earned enough money to "buy peanut butter and jelly for late night." The only problem, C. Parks explained, was the "negativity that came with the work."

> You got certain officers that's on your back, "Do this, do this, do this." You might walk off for one minute to just take a breather and he's on your back, "Do this or I'm sending you back to your block with a ticket."

"But I never caught a ticket for working in the mess hall," C. Parks said. "No, no. Let me take that back. I *did* catch a ticket once." The reason, he explained, was a dispute with the officer who woke him up in the morning. As C. Parks recalled, he relied on the sound of his gate "popping" open as his alarm clock each morning. "So, one day it didn't open."

> So, you know, I'm still laying. I figured it's nowhere near five o'clock. So, it finally opens and I come out, and [the CO is] like, "Hurry up, you're late." I'm like, "I'm late?" And I look at the clock, it's five twenty-five. So I'm like, "I only got five minutes to get ready. Why is my gate just being popped?" So he was like, "Don't worry about that, get dressed."

C. Parks said that he did so, but he refused to rush. "I got to brush my teeth, wash my face, you know what I'm saying? I'm going to an area where we set our food out. I'm not going to rush." As he got ready, C. Parks said that the officer went to the mess hall and then returned, telling him,

> "They don't need you anymore. You can stay." So, I'm like, "Are you sure?" He's like, "Yeah, they said they don't need you, you can stay for the day." So, I'm like, "Alright." So, I closed my gate, I go back to sleep.

Later that day, however, C. Parks learned that he had been punished for the incident; he was put on keeplock for 15 days. "I'm like, *Keeplock*?" he recalled. "Then I get the ticket that says that I was disrespectful . . . that I cussed at him a few times." But "I *didn't* slam my gate," he told me indignantly. "I *didn't* cuss at him. All I said was, 'I'm not rushing, because you opened my gate late.'" He requested a hearing to review the incident, asking that the prisoner in the adjacent cell act as a witness. But his request was denied.

> They said, "We don't need him [as a witness]. There's no sufficient reason why he should be here. Just take this fifteen days' keeplock." So, I settled with having fifteen days on keeplock for that. . . . It was a lose-lose situation. . . . The fact that now I got that on my disciplinary history, [and] I had to pay off five dollars [for the ticket]. I also didn't get to work for those fifteen days. Nor go to program for the fifteen days, [which] I had to make it up later. . . . So, that was the worst thing about it. The negativity.

In C. Parks's view, it was the many punishments that officers could wield—and some officers' propensity to do so—rather than the labor itself that rendered prison labor problematic. By being put on keeplock, he lost half a month's wages, plus another week's wages because of the ticket. He lost the human entitlements that become "privileges" in prison, including freedom of movement (however restricted), exercise and recreation, much-needed food from the commissary, and social connection with fellow prisoners and family members. He also gained a demerit on his "disciplinary history," which could have prevented his parole but ultimately did not, he explained, only because he did not "catch" any more tickets.

Brenda Smith did indeed lose her parole date when she refused to work shortly before her scheduled release from prison. Initially, the 53-year-old African American woman recalled, "I did everything I had to do. I worked. I worked in a kitchen, I work on a unit. I did everything I had to do to make the [parole] board." But once she got her "outdate," Brenda said that she refused to work because she would not be paid for her labor.

> My job was to clean the gallery, the unit, to mop and clean the unit. So I told them I wasn't cleaning it, because you're not paying me. And I'm getting ready to go home Tuesday, and this was a Sunday, so why should I have to mop and I'm not getting paid?

As a consequence, Brenda said that she was put on keeplock for 15 days and lost her parole date—or, as she described it, "They locked me up and they snatched my outdate."

Though Brenda and C. Parks did not disclose any concern about solitary confinement in those instances, the former prisoners I interviewed frequently described the ubiquitous threat of "the box." As Santos said, "Always somebody's 'going to the box'" (echoing Shara White's description of welfare sanction threats). Because of such threats, the Black 28-year-old man explained, he "knew when to shut up" while he was in prison.

> Because I know there it's like the little slightest thing you can go to the box for. Having a newspaper, you know, you go to the box; or having pornography, you can go to the box. Taking a cookie from the mess hall, you can go to the box. . . . You can't look at females, [or] you're going to the box.

Garcia agreed, and because this threat of solitary confinement was used to compel prisoners' labor compliance, he viewed incarcerated labor as deeply troubling. As the 27-year-old Black and Hispanic man explained, "The worst thing about working while incarcerated, I would have to say, is, well, pretty much being forced."

> You're *forced* to do that work. It's up to you whether you don't look at it as that . . . but, at the end of the day—and at the beginning of the day—you're forced to do all of that. Like, you have no say-so. Either you do it or you're going to the box. Either you do it, or you get your ass whooped and *then* go to the box. So, it's really like, they rule with an iron fist. . . . You *can* rebel, but there's still going to be the same result.

In Garcia's and Santos's understanding, any form of noncompliance or misdeed could land prisoners in solitary confinement, and many of the former prisoners I interviewed had experienced it firsthand. O.T.I. recounted several instances in which he was put in the box because he would not clean bodily fluids. He refused to do such jobs, he explained to me, because he had not been trained in biohazard cleanup, though other prisoners had. "I was asked to clean urine and feces off of a floor," the 27-year-old African American man said.

> I found that inappropriate and I suggested that they find someone that's in that area [of biohazard cleanup]. You know what I'm saying? Because of the HIV. Sometimes, they ask us to clean up blood from another inmate, which is very hazardous, and they just give us some tissue and some infector and say, "Here, clean this up."

Because he refused an officer's direct order, O.T.I. said that he got a five-dollar ticket and was put in solitary confinement. "If you refuse an order," he explained, "you can go to the box. So, I got a ticket for refusing an order and I went to the box in that situation. But, I guess they've seen the situation, they let me out in a week. They gave me a break. I could have been in there for thirty days."

Unlike O.T.I., Bruce W. did not get such a "break" when he refused to clean feces as part of his porter job. "I mean we're just talking about *feces*," the 23-year-old African American man said with disgust. "I'm not going to clean no feces. I don't care what gloves you give me." As a consequence, Bruce said that he was put in solitary confinement for 30 days, as he was on another occasion when he refused to clean the chewing tobacco an officer had spit on the floor. "The other incident I didn't want to clean," he recalled, was in "a robostation that oversees the unit. The CO [who worked there] was nasty. He used to chew snuff and he spit on the floor and he expects people to clean it. I wasn't cleaning that stuff." Once again, Bruce said, he "went to the box" for a month.

Like sanctions for workfare workers, solitary confinement is a relatively common consequence for incarcerated workers. Twelve of the forty-one ex-prisoners I interviewed said that they had been put in "the box" at least once (and a significant minority had been in solitary confinement multiple times), broadly reflecting New York State trends.[30] Yet those numbers alone do not capture their experiences. James D., for example, spent two uninterrupted years in solitary confinement, and that was just one of his several stints in the box. Moreover, though the "torture" of solitary confinement was the worst part of it for these ex-prisoners,[31] they also said that going to "the box" was usually accompanied by physical violence. Recall, for instance, how Garcia described prison labor: "Either you do it, or you get your ass whooped and *then* go to the box." Physical abuse is a central component of solitary confinement for many prisoners, and I examine it in more detail in the next chapter. For now, it is important to note that the combination of corporal violence with such a severe *and common* mechanism of status coercion renders "the box" particularly damaging for prisoners.

In addition to solitary confinement, keeplock, and disciplinary tickets, incarcerated workers labored under the threat of another punishment: new criminal charges and more prison time. Although there was a sense among my informants that this consequence was reserved for extreme cases of misconduct or insubordination (such as reporting on or testifying against officers), Tim Jones recalled an incident in which an officer casually made such a threat. Tim said that he was working as a "rec aide," organizing the prison's recreation area, when an officer asked him to do something unusual—something he deemed unacceptable—though at the time of the interview he could not remember what it was. In describing the request, the 28-year-old African American man said,

> It was just like, some things you ask people to do outside their job description, it's like, "Okay, I'll do it, no problem. I'm not doing too much out here anyway." But it was something he asked me that just seemed like, "Huh?" Like, *"Excuse me?"* . . . And I told him—I forgot exactly what it was, but I told him it's out of my job description, my [job] title. He said, "No, it's a direct order." I said, "But I'm here at work though, right?" And he was like, "Yeah, you're at work, but I'm telling you to do it."

In response, Tim remembered saying, "But say, what if I refuse, due to the fact it's not on my job title, and I'm supposed to be technically at work?" As Tim recalled, the officer replied, "'I'll put you on the wall.'"

> And I said, "You put me on the wall, then what? . . . What's the outcome?" He said, "If I put you on the wall and you even flinch, you're not going to make your date." I said, "I'm not gonna have no good time regardless, so what are you trying to say to me?" He said, "You *know* what I just said."

Because "not going to make your date" means not getting out of prison as scheduled, Tim's understanding was that the officer was threatening him with more prison time if he did not comply with the command. Yet as Tim made clear, the threat was not losing parole ("good time"), though that was a commonly reported coercive technique among the ex-prisoners I interviewed and one that is explicitly endorsed in New York State prison guidelines.[32] Because Tim was incarcerated for a parole violation, he was not eligible for "good time" and so it could not be taken away. Instead, Tim believed the officer's threat was an *additional* prison sentence. In order to understand why, some explanation is required. In New York State prisons, officers put prisoners "on the wall" in order to retain or regain control over them. When "on the wall," prisoners must lean against it at a 45-degree angle with their arms and legs outspread, and they are not allowed to move.[33] Any movement can be construed as a threat to the officer, and such threats are countered with swift force—even outright violence—as well as solitary confinement and, in more extreme cases, criminal charges. (As O.T.I. explained, if a prisoner is understood to be threatening an officer, "they have the *right* to take you down to the box and beat you.") In Tim's understanding, then, the officer insinuated that he would deliberately construe any "flinch" as a threat, which would lead to Tim's physical beating, solitary confinement, additional charges, and more prison time. Perhaps not surprisingly, Tim said that he complied with the officer's order, though he later requested a job change and asked the officer why he had threatened Tim in this way. (The CO's response: he had been testing Tim's temper.) Thus, similar to Pauline's experience in workfare, Bruce's in college football, and Scott's in graduate school, Tim's experience behind bars highlights some of the more punitive technologies of status coercion under which prisoners labor.

COERCION AND COMPLIANCE: "I DIDN'T WANT THE CONSEQUENCE"

As Tim's story suggests, the primary product of status coercion is compliance. Even though these workers regularly engage in acts of resistance, they generally acquiesce. This is not surprising, of course. As Frances Fox Piven and Richard Cloward observed in their landmark study of social movements and social marginalization, "People usually remain acquiescent, conforming to the accustomed patterns of daily life in their community, and believing those patterns to be both inevitable and just."[34]

In these labor regimes, acquiescence is not only a matter of cultural hegemony and human inertia. It is also actively produced and enforced by technologies of status coercion. The penalties for defiance are too severe. And so, as Qwon said, prisoners "tuck" their "tails." "You got to handle it . . . because they got the say-so." "You have to train yourself immensely to deal with it," O.T.I. explained, "because you can't really talk back to a superior officer, because then you put your life in jeopardy or—you know what I'm saying—your well-being. So you kind of have to take it in stride. I mean, you don't *have* to ignore it," he allowed, you *can* file a grievance. But every action comes with a reaction. You file a grievance and then they might try to set you up or beat you up on the walkway. So, you just kind of have to take the slaps on the face and turn the left cheek. . . . You got to really walk on eggshells, because you don't want to get placed in that situation where you're risking your freedom and extra time, when you're trying to make it home.

All they wanted to do, these ex-prisoners said again and again, was to "make it home," and so they did whatever they needed to do.

Workfare workers took a similar approach. "I just do my job, you know, whatever I need to, I do it," Tasha Love said. "It aggravates me inside, but what can I do when I feel like they're just taking control of my life?" James Pondos agreed. After sanctions left him and his son homeless, he said that he became extra compliant, doing whatever he had to do even though he considered the work to be unfair and unsafe. "I'm a single parent," he explained, "so I'm already struggling, that's why I'm here in this situation. . . . It's just not worth it [to resist]. So you comply." In fact, when James Griggs was a workfare worker, he said that "compliance" became a kind of mantra. "*You have to be compliant,* is what I kept thinking," the 50-year-old Afro-American[35] man recalled.

> *You have to comply or you're going to be sanctioned.* That's the whole mindset of it. "You have to be compliant or you're going to be sanctioned," you know, like a parent telling a child, "You have to do this or this is going to happen."

Meanwhile, although college athletes and graduate students differed from these workers in many ways, they generally felt the same way. Even though they had more leeway to resist bad bosses and leave their positions— than prisoners and welfare recipients at least—they too said that they usually complied, even with work and working conditions they deemed unjust or abusive. In their view, the stakes were simply too high. As basketball player Shevontae explained,

> [If] you have a complaint or a grievance [with your coaches] . . . you have more to lose than they do. . . . And if something happens to them, they can continue on and find a new job or do something. [But] for you, if something happens to you, everything can be tarnished.

As a result, the Black 26-year-old woman said, "Me personally, I didn't [complain]. I was more like a good soldier. I just wanted to keep the peace." Complaining would have been "unproductive," she said. Instead of solving the problem, it would have "caused unnecessary tension in the relationship."

> Because even when someone says, like, "Open door policy, tell me what you want," we're humans. So, it's impossible to fully filter out if you dislike some-one's criticism. . . . [I] was like, I don't want them to ever hold it against me or resent me. . . . Some [coaches] really do take things out on you . . . and all of a sudden, your minutes decrease. . . . I felt like, if I caused tension, or if I speak up, or I'm kind of like a rebellious one . . . *will I still be in the coach's favor?*

Staying in the "coach's favor" is the "main pillar" of college sports, Shevontae said. JohnJohn agreed. "In any sport," he explained, "you're going to not agree totally with what your coach does or says. But they're the coach. And you're there to be coachable, [so] you follow instructions." For those who have "conflict with coaches," he went on, "there's usually some kind of consequence involved with that. I didn't need the conse-quence. I didn't *want* the consequence."

Likewise, in graduate school, Suzanne said that if a student has a prob-lem with her advisor, "there's not a whole lot you can do."

> I don't even know where you *would* complain. I mean, I think there's usually a person they can go to . . . but it depends. In my case, the graduate student advisors were still acting in the best interest of the university and of the PIs. . . . The PIs are pretty well protected by the universities. I don't think there's a lot that can be done. I mean, as a graduate student, you're sort of the lowest part of the whole.

Emily made a similar point. Employees in more traditional workplaces "can appeal to their boss's boss or to HR for some sort of intervention," she said,

> but your best solution in grad school, if you're experiencing that sort of thing, is to leave your group [lab]—and not just your best solution but in many cases your *only* solution. So, having no recourse at all is what really turns it into some kind of like—like, it's hard to believe that people can have

that much control over your life in a country where otherwise, you know, you're protected by all kinds of labor laws. But those don't apply, because you're a "student," not an "employee."

Because of this power dynamic, athletes and graduate students emphasized the importance of "keeping doors open" and not "burning bridges" with their bosses, echoing prisoners' descriptions of the need to "walk on eggshells," "turn the left cheek," and "tuck [their] tail." As Lindsay said, athletes have to "swallow" any problems with their coaches "because they want to keep that door open." Kate said that she did not want to "burn bridges" and was therefore nervous about being interviewed. And Laine said of graduate school, "You can never burn that bridge. It's very stupid to do that in this field." To emphasize her point, she explained that even though one of the faculty members of her dissertation committee was "mean" and "nasty," she "would have never spoken out against him in a million years, *never*, no matter what he did, said, anything." "*And he was really bad*," she emphasized again and again. "But . . . there's nothing he could have said or done that I would have reported. . . . If you don't have clout, and if you're not protected, if you don't have that PhD . . . you're just so vulnerable."

The centrality of compliance in these labor regimes is underscored by the fact that they all have narratives of noncompliance, that is, negative labels for those who do not dutifully acquiesce with their bosses' directives. Behind bars, noncompliant prisoners are often dubbed "knuckleheads,"[36] whom Paul D. defined as "someone who doesn't want to do anything, goofs off." In workfare, they are more straightforwardly labeled "noncompliant," a label which carries considerable cultural power because of the narratives of indolence and dependence that dominate welfare rhetoric. "They label people like they're useless, lazy," Pauline Wilson said, "like *they're* better than them, like it can't happen to them. [But] it can." Meanwhile, noncompliant college athletes are deemed "uncoachable," which means that "you won't fall in line," Lindsay said, "you talk back." "That's the biggest problem you could have as an athlete," JohnJohn said. In graduate school, such narratives of noncompliance are usually less explicit, but, similar to athletes, the noncompliant are seen as "not teachable" or not able to "handle it," because they are deemed not smart enough or not willing to work hard enough. Take, for example, D.N., who uncomplainingly claimed that he worked one hundred hours a week (and more) as a graduate student. In his view, many students who did not complete their PhDs were simply "lazy." "They'll quit," he said.

> I mean, some don't want to stay one hundred hours a week in a lab, right? ... Now, why do people get fired? Yes, there have been so many people who got fired in my last month. Basically they're just too lazy, they just don't get the job done. And then, the supervisor can't be wasting the limited resource of money on that person, right?

In order to "get the job done," D.N. maintained, graduate students must be "self-motivated" and "self-driven." Nik agreed. Many students are too "immature," he explained. They are still "trying to figure out their lives" and are therefore unable or unwilling to "commit" to science. "They're just, like, too young," he said.

> They haven't quite figured out that this is *science*. ... Maybe this is just my idea of it, but science should be self-directed, you know, a choice. If you're going to make a choice about what to do with your life, and you don't really want to do science and so you're not really sure that that's how you want to spend sixty or more hours a week ... then I don't know that you should be there.

In Nik's construal, science is an all-encompassing endeavor, one to which students must "commit" after deciding that it is what they want "to do with [their] life." Those who are not willing to make such a commitment, Nik and D.N. variously argued, are often "immature" or "lazy."

In each of these labor regimes, then, a premium is placed on worker compliance, and those deemed noncompliant are stigmatized as such. Yet these labor regimes do not produce compliant subjects for the regimes alone. They also produce such subjects for devalued jobs in the mainstream economy, because in fact they actively prime workers to embrace precarious employment. For instance, graduate school grooms newly minted PhDs to accept undervalued and insecure positions as adjuncts and postdocs. Indeed, in the sciences postdocs have become apparent prerequisites for tenure-track jobs, while at the same time their duration has increased significantly.[37] As Suzanne said, "There's a lot of bitterness in

the field right now, because you end up staying in your postdoc forever."
(Hers lasted eight years.) Sunny, another former graduate student, voiced
such "bitterness." "Now that [postdocs] have become five years, six
years . . . and you don't know if you're even going to get a [faculty] position, it's not worth it."

Workfare and incarcerated workers are also conditioned for compliance in the mainstream economy, most often for low-wage, unstable work
in construction, fast food, and the "temp economy."[38] In fact, four workers
I interviewed—C. Parks, Qwon, Jarome W., and Pauline Wilson—made
this point explicitly. As C. Parks said,

> If you can get through work in prison, when you come home you can do
> anything. There's a lot of stuff that shouldn't bother you . . . even work at
> McDonald's. . . . If you can get through working in prison, working out in
> the free world shouldn't be that much harder.

Likewise, Qwon said that the "bare minimum, nothing" he earned in
prison made him willing to accept low wages outside of prison. As he
asked rhetorically,

> How can I come out here and *not* appreciate a job in society, in the real
> world, where it matters, when I was just working for thirty-eight cents, or
> fourteen cents, or twelve cents? You know what I mean? How can I *not*
> come out here and appreciate it, even if it had to be a minimum wage or, you
> know, a stepping-stone [to a better job]?

It is not just that these workers are primed to accept "anything," "any
kind of job," as Jarome and Pauline said of their respective job searches
after prison and welfare. Their embrace of low-wage, precarious work is
often mandated by the state. In the case of welfare recipients, for example,
most families receiving public assistance have at least one adult working,
usually in low-wage jobs.[39] According to New York State welfare policy,
those workers will be sanctioned—that is, they will lose their public
assistance—if they quit or lose their job "without good cause,"[40] an ill-
defined stipulation that, among my informants at least, usually worked
against them. Thus, when Sasha Reed quit her job at McDonald's after a
dispute with a manager, she said that she was sanctioned for six months,
losing both cash benefits and food stamps. "Once they found out I quit,"

she said, "they're like, *Oh, you don't want the money?* ... So [Social Services] fired me, gave me six months off." As welfare recipients experience it, their compliance with seemingly any aspect of their job in the low-wage economy is enforced by sanctions. As in workfare, they understand that they need to comply with their bosses' directives in order to retain access to the social safety net.

Likewise, as legal scholar Noah Zatz and colleagues have shown, the criminal justice system uses the threat of incarceration to compel the labor compliance of both former and potential prisoners (i.e., parolees and probationers).[41] Parole and probation requirements typically mandate that their charges maintain employment as a condition of their non-imprisonment, just as courts can do for those who cannot afford to pay child support or criminal justice debts. As a result, the authors argue, this vast population of Americans who are not incarcerated but fall under the ambit of the criminal justice system are effectively forced to accept and comply with low-wage, precarious, and even dangerous work, for they "cannot afford to refuse a job, quit a job, or challenge their employers."[42] Workers in these forms of "carceral labor"—much like workers behind bars—understand that they must submit to their bosses' directives in order to avoid (further) confinement.[43]

Among the workers I studied, college athletes were the only exception. They are not directly primed for "bad jobs" in the mainstream economy. Nonetheless, according to some of my informants, their college athletic careers could exert downward pressure on their future employment prospects. Inasmuch as their sport is expected to take precedence over their education, for example, athletes may not graduate as prepared for the workforce as they might otherwise. Football player Zachary Lane said that he and his teammates felt pressured to stay away from academic majors that were more time-consuming or time-constrained than others but which usually led to higher wages.[44] "So, a lot of kids want to go there and become business majors ... or engineers," Zachary said. "But guess what?"

> The engineering schedule wants you to have the classes only at three o'clock in the afternoon, which interferes with practice time. So, what do they do? [Coaches and athletic academic advisors] steer you back to whatever schedule works for them. "Oh, sociology, we'll put everybody in sociology." ... Or, you know, this kid wants to be a kinesiology major, but the classes he needs

to take are during the football practice. "Okay, we can't have him do that, try to force him into something else. Try to get him to go over here."

Furthermore, inasmuch as their sport dominates athletes' time, experience, and aspirations, they often feel significant pressure—both internal and external—to play professionally. But although top-tier professional athletes earn high (even astronomical) wages, others do not. Professional football players in the Arena Football League earn less than $15,000 a year, for example, and basketball players in the NBA's D-League earn $18,000–$30,000 a year.[45] Such jobs are thus roughly parallel to postdocs in the sciences: underpaid and uncertain stepping-stones to high-wage, high-status employment.

· · · · · ·

In all of these labor regimes, supervisors can wield considerable punitive power over their subordinates. Not all of them do so, but doing so is par for the course in these regimes. It is simply expected that officers will put prisoners in solitary confinement for not following their orders, regardless of the content of those orders. It is expected that caseworkers will sanction workfare workers for not following their supervisors' directives at work. It is expected that coaches will dock athletes' playing time for not doing what they say. And it is expected that advisors will not grant PhDs, or write positive letters of recommendation at least, for graduate students who do not follow their instruction.

Though the severity of these punishments varies widely across these groups, all of them are severe enough to produce workers' compliance, the consequences of which extend well beyond these particular labor regimes. Athletes, for example, know that they need to be "coachable." They need to follow directions, which may include playing while injured or choosing "easy" majors that do not conflict with practice times, regardless of their interests or job prospects. Graduate students believe science to be an all-encompassing endeavor, requiring long hours in the lab throughout graduate school and then again through long years of postdocs, all with uncertain job returns. Workfare workers—and welfare recipients in general— know that compliance is their key to retaining access to essential elements of the social safety net, even after they obtain "real" jobs. Because such jobs rarely pull them all the way out of poverty, they often continue to rely on public assistance, but in order to keep it, they have to hang on to their low-wage, insecure jobs. And so the welfare system's "sticks" of status coercion continue to enforce their labor compliance. The same is true of prisoners. All prisoners know that compliance behind bars is of paramount importance. But even after they leave prison, the criminal justice system's coercive "sticks" follow them: they must comply with the many (often stringent) requirements of parole, including maintaining employment, which is no small feat for the formerly incarcerated.[46] If they do not, they may be sent back to prison.

The coercion in these labor regimes has a far-reaching effect, producing compliant yet productive workers not only for the regimes themselves but also for the low-wage "precariat."[47] In this way, my analysis underscores Michel Foucault's emphasis on the state's production of docile yet productive bodies.[48] This modern mode of governance, Foucault argued, is enacted through dispersed forms of state power, including institutional actors, policies, and norms, as well as individuals' embrace of such policies and norms. Such is the case for the workers in this book, whose labor productivity and compliance are enforced by criminal justice, welfare, and education systems' actors, policies, and norms, as well as by their own internalization of those policies and norms. In order to succeed—or simply survive—they know they need to be "good soldiers." Thus this analysis also underscores Karl Marx's argument that the labor process produces worker subjectivities as well as commodities.[49] For as we have seen, these labor regimes not only produce *actions* of compliance; they produce *ideologies* of compliance. Although these workers hold both hegemonic and counter-hegemonic ideologies of work, they generally accept, and often embrace, the importance of being coachable, teachable, and compliant: hardworking, unquestioning, and acquiescent. Perhaps this is not surprising given the severity of the consequences they face if they do otherwise.

3 "They Talk to You in Any Kind of Way"

SUBJUGATION, VULNERABILITY, AND THE BODY

I have to go see this lady [caseworker] every single Wednesday. If I don't go see her, she's going to call my employment counselor. She's going to get me sanctioned because I didn't come. It's like *jail*. . . . That's what it seems like: *my probation hours*. I have to check in at this time. They want me to do this. I have to be there at that. Oh, I better not do this wrong or else I'm going to get sanctioned.

—Jennifer Rose, workfare worker

"I want him to scrub the floor with a toothbrush."

—D.Q., former incarcerated worker, recounting his supervisor's chosen punishment for him falling asleep at work

I worked for, actually, a well-known scientist. . . . He was, let's say, famously demanding . . . [which] translated into very high expectations at our group meetings, which could be everything from, you know, "I was hoping that you'd get more done" to . . . ranting and screaming. . . . [He had] extremely unrealistic expectations about what could be done in a certain amount of time, which I'm not sure was actually so much unrealism as a strategy.

—Henry, former biochemistry graduate student

I played in two All-Star Games. So, when I went, it felt like almost how the slave trades worked. I had a guy that evaluated me mentally as soon as I got there. Then, I walk in a

room, they tell me to strip down to my underwear. . . . I got
guys checking body fat percentage on me, guys looking me
up and down, [asking] my height, my weight. And, if you
think about it, back in the 1800s when they had the slave
trade . . . that was the same thing they did when they were
auctioning people off. . . . I mean, I understand why they're
doing it, because they're investing millions of dollars in the
players. . . . But, on the same parallel, I felt like I was a slave.

—Lawrence, former college football player

As a workfare worker and welfare recipient, Jennifer Rose said that her
schedule was so closely monitored and punitively enforced that she felt
like a convict on probation. "It's like *jail*," she exclaimed. Meanwhile, both
D.Q. and Henry recounted degrading punishments for what their supervisors deemed to be inadequate work performance. In prison, D.Q. said
that his boss ordered him to "'scrub the floor with a toothbrush'" because
he had fallen asleep at work. In graduate school, Henry said that his faculty boss was prone to "ranting and screaming" at the students—a deliberate "strategy," he speculated, to compel them to work longer and harder.
As a college football player, Lawrence said that his body was so meticu-
lously appraised that he felt like a "slave" on an 1800s auction block.

   In this chapter, I conceptualize these experiences as ones of worker
subjugation: strategies deployed by employers to dominate and control
workers and facilitate the exploitation of their labor. Though these strategies often overlap, here I categorize and analyze them as three distinct
modes of subjugation: (1) bodily surveillance and regulation, such as
Jennifer Rose experienced as a workfare worker; (2) degradation and
abuse, both verbal and physical, as recounted by D.Q. and Henry in prison
and in graduate school; and (3) "othering" and dehumanization, such as
Lawrence's experience of corporal commodification as a college football
player.

   These modes of subjugation are not unique to these labor relations, of
course. As work and labor scholars have shown, workplace surveillance is

a long-established—and by many accounts expanding—mechanism of labor control.[1] Likewise, worker degradation, abuse, and dehumanization (though not always articulated as such) are pervasive in the workplace, as evidenced by the many studies documenting worker harassment and mistreatment, demeaning and "dirty" work, job deskilling and routinization, and exploitative labor practices.[2] In short, such modes of worker subjugation are both routine and widespread.

In labor regimes in which employers have access to the punitive powers of status coercion, however, they take on new shape and intensity. In these regimes, such modes of subjugation intersect with employers' coercive "sticks," iteratively reinforcing each other's effects and amplifying both employer power and worker vulnerability. For example, labor surveillance—the rigorous regulation and monitoring of workers' actions and bodies—both creates and catches worker missteps to be punished, and in these labor regimes at least, such punishments are the same technologies of coercion used to compel worker compliance: solitary confinement for prisoners, sanctions for workfare workers, loss of playing time for athletes, and loss of faculty support for publishing, degree conferral, and future employment for graduate students. In this way, surveillance and regulation—as relatively routine forms of worker subjugation—can quickly lead to the more expansive and severe punishments of status coercion.

Degradation, the second type of worker subjugation I analyze, interacts with status coercion in similar ways. Inasmuch as degrading treatment prompts worker resistance, for example, it can also trigger coercive punishments. This is what happened to D.Q. when his refusal to comply with a punishment he believed to be overly degrading (cleaning the floor with a toothbrush) landed him in "the box." Degradation also intersects with the third type of worker subjugation I analyze: othering and dehumanization. For these workers, degrading treatment on the job creates a sense of "othering," making them feel like "animals," "slaves," "criminals," or "commodities." At the same time, othering can be used as justification for these workers' subjugation and coercion. For when they are seen as something less than rights-bearing workers—bodies to perform in the stadium, hands to produce results in the lab, defrauders to be disciplined in welfare offices, or criminals to be punished behind bars—their surveillance and degradation may seem warranted, and their supervisors' ability to impinge on their well-being, futures, and families may seem less consequential.

Not surprisingly, these modes of subjugation are enacted differently across the four labor regimes I examine in this book. In large part this is due to variation in the scope and severity of these bosses' punitive power— but not entirely so. As Marxian analysts would argue, the goal of such subjugation is twofold: domination (worker control) and exploitation (extracting surplus value from workers' labor).[3] Yet across the four labor regimes in this book, these interrelated goals are not equally accessible or desirable. For example, because prisoners and welfare recipients are seen as surplus (and highly racialized) populations to be regulated and punished,[4] I find that *domination* rather than exploitation is most often the primary goal of their subjugation. They are surveilled and regulated, they are degraded and abused, and they are routinely dehumanized in an effort to exert (racist) disciplinary control over them. To be sure, their labor is also exploited—its surplus value extracted by power-holders—but as these workers' experiences reveal, the central goal of such subjugation is their domination: the punitive regulation of their bodies, even as they work.[5] For college athletes and graduate students, the inverse is true. Rather than surplus populations, they are seen as creators of capital and therefore the primary goal of their subjugation is their *exploitation* rather than domination. They too are surveilled and regulated, degraded, and sometimes abused and dehumanized. But for them, such modes of subjugation are primarily deployed to increase their labor output in order to gain maximum profit from it—though, to be sure, their bodies are also disciplined and controlled in the process.

Yet for all of these workers, the underlying objective of such subjugation is the same: the production and preservation of their vulnerability to employer power. Surveillance, degradation, and othering are strategies through which their supervisors exert power over them, continually making and remaking these workers into vulnerable subjects. In many ways, this is true of all workers, but as we will see, when such supervisors have access to the "sticks" of status coercion, workers' vulnerability is amplified.

SURVEILLANCE AND CONTROL: "I NEVER FELT
AUTONOMOUS OVER MY OWN TIME, MY OWN BODY"

For Michel Foucault and his contemporary interpreters, corporal surveillance and control are the central mechanisms by which the modern state
exerts disciplinary power over individuals. From analysis of Bentham's
panopticon to the concepts of "governmentality" and "biopower," this
scholarship has shown how the state uses surveillance to regulate people's
bodies, particularly through self-monitoring and the internalization of
state power.[6] Conceptualized in this way, surveillance and control do not
have to be deployed in a direct or overtly degrading manner to be understood as a mechanism of subjugation. For regardless of its particular technique, this mode of subjugation is predicated on the exercise of power:
higher-ups surveilling and regulating their subordinates in an effort to
govern and discipline them.

Among the workers I interviewed, however, bodily surveillance and
control was the type of subjugation they least often spontaneously dis-
cussed. This was not because such corporal policing was absent or unim-
portant in their work lives but, as their stories below suggest, because it
was often normalized for them—routine rather than remarkable—and so
they often experienced it as less degrading than the other mechanisms of
subjugation.

Nonetheless, like many workers in more traditional workplaces, those I
interviewed were subject to pervasive surveillance and regulation. In prison,
as one might expect, this mode of subjugation is both explicit and extreme—
and for F. Gordon was the reason that prison labor felt like "slavery." "In the
kitchen, I was a slave," the 25-year-old African American man said.

> Because I'm serving you, but the CO's behind me looking over my shoulder
> making sure I'm giving you the right proportion. . . . Like, you're not letting
> me perform my job. I know what to do. But the minute you [the worker],
> like, go overboard with something, they pull you to the side, cuss you out,
> make you go wash dishes. Like, I done wash dishes plenty of times, passing
> on too many cookies to one person.

Like many more-traditional workers, F. Gordon felt that high levels of
surveillance and regulation diminished his autonomy as a worker, "not

letting [him] perform [his] job" in the way he deemed appropriate—in the way that he knew how to do—even if that entailed occasionally breaking the rules by "passing on too many cookies."

Though such surveillance and regulation were unremarkable for most of the other ex-prisoners I interviewed,[7] this was not the case for workfare workers. In their view, the intensive surveillance and regulation they experienced were highly degrading, in large part *because* of their normalization for prisoners. As the reader will recall, for example, Pauline Wilson described with frustration her workfare boss monitoring and restricting her labor and bodily movements as she picked up trash on the side of the highway, similar to the way that F. Gordon described his boss in the prison mess hall. Like F. Gordon, Pauline interpreted such corporal policing as unnecessarily punitive, but even more so. For her, its excessiveness left her feeling outraged because, in her view, such overtly punitive policing only made sense if its target were a convicted criminal. "It's like you did something [wrong]," Pauline said. *"It's like they convicted you for not having a job."* As her experience suggests, moreover, the primary goal of such bodily control was not her labor output; indeed, her productivity would likely have increased had she been allowed to get a drink of water. Rather, in her understanding at least, the goal was her domination. Her supervisor was exercising his ability to control her bodily movements, even impinging on her bodily needs, in order to wield his power over her. For Pauline, the punitive surveillance and control of workfare workers' bodies, combined with their degrading and dehumanizing treatment (described below), was how she experienced on a daily basis what scholars call the "criminalization of poverty."[8]

Johnny Dominoes and Jennifer Rose felt the same way, though in general the bodily surveillance and control they recounted was the more dispersed and routine—though nonetheless punitive—type of corporal governance to which all American welfare recipients are subjected: the persistent monitoring and regulation of their labor as well as their efforts to find employment, of their income and spending, their household occupants and relationship status, their parenting and children's behavior, their sexual activity, drug use, and more.[9] For instance, Johnny recalled a common occurrence among New York City welfare recipients. After waiting eight hours in the social services office for his appointment—itself a form of bodily regulation and subjugation—the 54-year-old Hispanic man had the following interaction with his caseworker:

> The lady asked me for documents, a proof of residence, who I am, birth certificate, the rental lease from the landlord, if in fact I owed back rent, which I did, and then members of the household, which at the time was just me and my daughter. Oh, and if you have any bank statements or loans outstanding of your own property, cars or vehicles, driver's license. . . . And then they fingerprint you.

"This process," Johnny explained, made him feel "like a second-class citizen. As if they were doing me a favor, not that I earned it [as a veteran] or that American citizens have the right to get help. So, I felt almost as if I'm a criminal. I felt like a criminal." Similarly, Jennifer Rose said that the requirement to see her caseworker every week to report on such matters—under threat of being sanctioned—made her feel like a convict on probation. "That's what it seems like," she said, "*my probation hours.* I have to check in at this time. They want me to do this. I have to be there at that. Oh, I better not do this wrong or else I'm going to get sanctioned."

According to workfare worker Phil Jackson, such "vigilance is misguided." Though it secured workfare workers' cheap labor, he argued, it did not help them gain full-time employment. "I see that it's a leverage," the 48-year-old African American man said, a way to control workfare workers and exploit their labor.

> [They] need us, [they] need this work done. They can't afford to pay the county workers, because it's not in the budget. So, for that little eight hundred dollars or seven hundred and seven dollars they give you a month, they need you to do this. . . . There's no future, there's no goals. They don't have no goal-setting practices in workfare, [such as,] "Well, last week you did twelve applications. Has anything come up, is there anything we can help you with? Can we get a letter from somebody, is there some special reference or something we could write for you?" . . . No, there's nothing like that. There's no encouragement, no positive reinforcement. It's all, "You were late, you missed a day, da, da, da. *You owe me.*"

In Phil's view, the surveillance and control of workfare workers facilitated the exploitation of their labor while impeding their transition to permanent employment and out of poverty.

College athletes also experienced pervasive surveillance and control, though they said that this mode of subjugation was more often construed as protection rather than punishment. When Lindsay wanted to put a pink triangle on her basketball shoe as a symbol of gay pride, for example, she said that her coaches framed their arguments against it in terms of protecting her personal "brand." As the Black 25-year-old recalled,

> So, they called me in their office and they're trying to make it about, like, "We don't want you to, like, hurt your brand." And it was my senior year and they're like, "You're going to get job interviews and so, we don't want it to be negative on you." And I'm like, "I have a fucking crew cut so, like, I don't really think it's any surprise."

Independent from her success on the basketball court, then, Lindsay said that her bodily displays were monitored and regulated; not because the coaches actually cared about her brand, she speculated, but because they cared about their team's reputation. Lindsay believed that they did not want to be seen as a "gay program."

Athletes' social media accounts were also surveilled and controlled, not only by their coaches but also by their fellow athletes through mandatory peer surveillance.[10] As with Lindsay, moreover, such regulations were often framed in terms of protecting athletes' personal reputations. As Kate said,

> In the age of social media ... they definitely told us, like, "Be conscious of what you're saying, or how you're saying it, or the image that you're presenting yourself as." You know, the language was very directed around how was it going to make you look as a person, or as a student-athlete. And then, indirectly, you're also representing the school. Therefore, you have a responsibility to uphold the way in which you present yourself as a person.

Haley recalled her coaches justifying their social media rules in a similar way:

> They just reminded us that, number one, companies and people looking to hire us in the future are going to be looking at our social media. And, like, little girls who looked up to us are also looking [at it]. So, we had a few instances where they're like, "You got to take that picture down."

In fact, that happened to Haley once when she posted a picture of herself playing basketball in her bathing suit. "One of my coaches called me and was so mad," the white 23-year-old recalled. "She was like, '*You look stupid!*'" When I asked Haley if her coach had actually used the word "stupid," she laughed and said, "Yeah . . . or worse." In the end, even though she believed that "there was nothing wrong with [the picture]," she took it down. "What they say goes," she said.

Athletes' bodily displays were thus regulated both on the court (as in Lindsay's experience) and off (as in Haley's). The reason, these athletes explained, is that they were expected to be round-the-clock "representatives" of entities larger than themselves: not just their personal "brands" but also their teams, universities, and the NCAA itself. Indeed, this belief seemed to be deeply ingrained in several of the athletes I interviewed. "As a student-athlete you're not just representing yourself and your family; you're representing the whole school," football player Zachary Lane said. Basketball player Molly agreed, almost verbatim: "As a student-athlete, you're representing not only yourself, but your university." Thus, across different teams, universities, and sports, these athletes had received, internalized, and articulated precisely the same message. In truth, this is not all that surprising given the ubiquity of this message in the many instruction manuals directed at college athletes.[11]

A few athletes did feel unduly constrained by such bodily governance. For instance, even though playing college basketball was her "dream," M.K. also wished that her behavior had been less monitored and controlled while in college—or as she put it, that she had been able to act like a "normal student." In college, the Black 29-year-old woman said, she longed to

> just go to a party and not worry about any repercussions . . . just be able to go out, and be wild and crazy like a normal student, and not have to worry about if it will get back to your coaches. . . . Like, I wasn't able to just enjoy myself.

Kate felt the same way, though for her it was more about wanting control over her "body" and "identity." While she was playing basketball in college, the Black 24-year-old said,

> I never felt autonomous over my own time, my own body, and my own—kind of like—movement through the world. I always felt like, what I did was

very dependent on the crux of the program. Like, your identity was so far ingrained into that of the program that it was hard to separate yourself.

This was especially challenging, Kate explained, because college is a time when "you're learning a lot about yourself." She wished she had had more space to figure out her own sense of self—what was important to her— without having to prioritize basketball, both the implicit and explicit expectations of her coaches and her sport. "That became really difficult," she said, "just moving through the world and feeling like,"

> "Can I say 'no' to this thing, because I would really like to go meet with my professor?" Like, "No, you can't." I mean theoretically, sure, you can, but it's like this unspoken demand that is put on student-athletes that you now have certain requirements that you have to uphold whether they're like in writing or not. . . . You always had to think about the consequences of what you were going to do, and how it was going to affect basketball. . . . They make it very hard to distinguish who you are as a human, and then who you are as a student-athlete, because it all becomes convoluted.

While Kate and M.K. felt that their identities and everyday "movement through the world" were overly controlled, other athletes felt that way about their economic independence. Shevontae, for example, argued strongly against NCAA restrictions on athletes' ability to capitalize on their athletic success, and like Kate, she framed her argument in terms of controlling her body and identity. "If you want to run a camp with your own name, because it's your name," the Black 26-year-old woman said, "and this is the off-season when you have your time, you should be able to do that. And get paid for it. You should be able to do that, because *that's your body and your name, period.*" Jayce agreed. Athletes "should definitely be able to endorse" themselves, the white 29-year-old former football player said. "It's kind of ridiculous that you can't use your own name to go out and make money with. I think that players should be able to use their own name one hundred and ten percent. It's *crazy* not to be able to do that." Being prevented from doing so, Jayce argued, was "hurting [his] future in football": he could not promote his brand. For these athletes, pervasive surveillance and regulation made them feel out of control of their own identities, bodies, and futures.

In comparison, graduate students were the least surveilled and controlled of the four groups of workers in this study. Whereas the other workers described being overtly monitored and regulated both on and off the job, graduate students felt that they had at least some autonomy inside the lab and even more outside of it—except for the fact that they felt they were expected to be in the lab most of the time. "You needed to be there all the time," Iris, a 34-year-old Hispanic woman, said.

> But, you know, [my advisor] wouldn't ever say anything specific. . . . A few times [he] was like, "No, this isn't a nine-to-six job." So you knew for sure nine to six o'clock wasn't enough . . . but you never know how much was enough.

Like Iris, many of the former graduate students I interviewed had a strong but indefinite sense of how much lab time "was enough." At the very least, they said, working in the lab as a graduate student required long weekdays, a significant part of every weekend, and most holidays. And even when their lab bosses did not explicitly regulate their work schedules, the students often told stories about other advisors who did. For instance, Iris said another professor in her department "had people filling in time sheets." Zane told of a faculty member who required graduate students to sign formal contracts promising to be in the lab 8 A.M.–5 P.M. every day. Suzanne described faculty advisors who "would go home with their family and then would call the lab at ten o'clock at night to see who was there." Working long hours "was definitely required," the early-forties white woman explained, "almost like an honor thing."

For Gustavo, however, such long work hours, combined with their uncertain payoff and students' degrading treatment, made graduate school intolerable. In his view, graduate school entailed "work[ing] very, very long hours for very low money under the premise that you will gain in the future. You know, one day, basically your master just signs off, and you're released." Graduate school, the 35-year-old Chicano man said, was akin to "indentured servitude," and he left after three years without a PhD.

Aside from Gustavo, most students simply accepted long work hours as a central, and necessary, component of their graduate work lives. They believed that they needed to work long hours in order to "get results." As D.N. said, for example, working "one hundred hours a week in the lab" was the only way to "get the job done." Likewise, when I asked Sunny how many hours graduate students typically worked in the lab, the 41-year-old Hispanic woman said,

> I mean, whatever needs to be done. As a graduate student, I worked most holidays. It was just like, you just wanted to get your project going. And you know that you're just expected to put everything on hold in your life, and have the lab as your priority. And so, if you can start another project, and get something done through the weekend or a holiday, you will. There is no nine to five. It's kind of amorphous, like, you're just there whenever you need to be. And you can't leave early. . . . They look down on anyone that leaves before six o'clock.

Thus, as Sunny's comments suggest, the expectation that graduate students work long hours in the lab to do "whatever needs to be done" was not entirely related to productivity. Regardless of their results, Sunny said that graduate students would be "looked down on" if they left the lab "early," that is, before six o'clock in the evening. Iris made a similar point when recounting the story of Jake, a fellow graduate student in her lab who was ultimately dismissed from the program. "He was incredibly, incredibly bright," she said, "I mean, just a very, very smart guy." But over time, she said, he was working "fewer and fewer hours" in the lab and so "our boss said, 'I'm not going to graduate you. You're not leaving here with a PhD.'" Although, of course, we cannot know the reality of this incident— as we cannot in any such accounting—Iris's telling of this story reveals what it meant for her. In her view, Jake's dismissal from the lab and the PhD program was due to his resistance to working long hours, not his lack of productivity; because despite his fewer work hours, Iris said, Jake "was producing good results."

> And, honestly, compared to what I had done, he was doing much more than I was. But I think Jake had greater potential than I did. So [our boss] thought that if he was working more hours, and applying himself more, he could do even better than that.

Regardless of his "good results," Iris believed that Jake was expected to work long hours in the lab in order to live up to his "potential." He needed to "apply himself more," "do even better" than he was already doing. By not doing so, Jake was seemingly refusing to comply with the institutionalized expectation of science as an all-encompassing endeavor, and as a result, Iris believed, he was dismissed from graduate school.

For many of these graduate students, then, the expectation that they work a significant but indefinite number of hours created a blanket sense of surveillance and control, one that they often internalized. Though this internalized and diffuse—"amorphous"—sense of bodily governance differed from that of the other workers I interviewed, their day-to-day experience of it was very real. Moreover, as Iris's story of Jake suggests, for these former graduate students, as for the other workers I interviewed, this mode of subjugation was backed by their bosses' powers of status coercion. If they did not work enough—whatever "enough" was—they would be kicked out of graduate school.

DEGRADATION: "THEY WILL DISRESPECT YOU TO THE POINT UNTIL YOU'RE READY TO FIGHT THEM"

From disdain and aggression to bullying and sexual harassment, workplace degradation and abuse are widespread.[12] It is thus not surprising that this mode of subjugation is also prevalent, and sometimes severe, in the labor regimes I examine here, particularly in prison labor and workfare. In prison, John S. said, corrections officers "talk to you like you're the scum of the earth." When I asked for an example, the 24-year-old white man said that COs would yell at prisoners, "You little shithead, hurry up!'" while they were working. "They will call you niggers, spicks, crackers, whatever your race," Mike Russ said of officers.

> They will disrespect you to the point until you're ready to fight them, so disrespectful . . . and then, once you fight them—which is dumb—once you fight the COs, you get a whole 'nother charge added onto you. And then they all come in and beat the crap out of you, like six, eight, ten, fifteen [of them], all beating you.

In this single quote, the Hispanic and Black 19-year-old man highlighted many of the themes I analyzed earlier: the coercive threat of additional criminal charges and more prison time, the apparent futility of fighting back, and prisoners' sense of impending physical violence, which I also examine in more detail below. Here, however, I want to draw attention to Mike's emphasis of officers' (often racialized) "disrespect" of prisoners. "They will disrespect you to the point until you're ready to fight them," he said, even though fighting back is "dumb." For Mike, the degradation levied on prisoners was so intense that against all reason they became willing to risk officers' many powers of status coercion as well as physical violence.

Jarome Wilks gave a nearly identical account of COs' verbal abuse of prisoners, which was often characterized by racist overtones and was so intensely degrading that it frequently provoked prisoners to fight back, for which they faced violent consequences. At the "shock" prison where he was incarcerated,[13] the 20-year-old Black African American man said, officers—who were called "drill instructors"—would "call us out on our names" (which I learned means being called racist or homophobic slurs and other highly derogatory insults). As Jarome recalled,

> Sometimes some drill instructors say some racist stuff to us. And, like, there was nothing we could do about it, because we're inmates. So, we got to accept everything they do. But there would be times, like, the inmates go at the drill instructors, like, they get to tussling with the drill instructors. But if you do that—remind you, it's the drill instructor that provoked it—they'll call for backup and they beat the brakes off you.

Sal Winter experienced firsthand a similar sequence of events when an officer called him "cocksucker."[14] "Now, in prison that's serious," the 24-year-old white man explained to me.

> Because, you know, there's a lot of weird shit going on in there, so you don't want to be affiliated with something like that. So, he's just calling people names like that. . . . So, I called him something [i.e., cocksucker] back. You know, just like, not even caring.

As a consequence, Sal recalled, "about three o'clock in the morning . . . like six cops came into my space and they were like, 'Come on with us.' So, they took me into the showers and, you know, they took their turns [punching and kicking] me." He was bruised and "sore," he said, though "they stay away from your face" so that the abuse cannot be detected.

Although Sal said that he returned the officer's slur in that incident, most prisoners unequivocally warned against doing so. Regardless of their treatment, they said, prisoners must perform deference. "We got to accept everything they do," Jarome said. "You're really not even supposed to voice your opinion," O.T.I. said. When I asked the 27-year-old African American man what "voicing" one's "opinion" meant—did it mean saying, "Excuse me, sir, please don't talk to me that way," or did it mean "Fuck you"?—he replied, *"Any way!"*

> You can be polite *or* you can be rude. It doesn't matter. Because I can say, "I'm sorry and I apologize" and they'll still say, "Shut the fuck up" or "Suck a dick." You know what I mean? "Who do you think you're talking to?" "Don't get sass with me." "Don't eyeball me."

To explain the latter, O.T.I. said, "If you look them straight in the eye, they don't like that. They want you to look down."

> Because [if] you look someone in the eye and talk to them, they'll take it like, "Oh, you're staring me down. That's a threatening motion," and then they have the right to take you down to the box and beat you. Because it's like showing an aggressive motion when you look at someone. . . . So, when you talk to them, you have to look down—no eye contact—because you don't want to show any threatening motion. You really are not supposed to say anything.

Thus, prisoners strongly believed that they needed to demonstrate their deference—look down and not speak—even (and perhaps especially) in the face of intense degradation: "Suck a dick," "You little shithead," "Cocksucker," "Nigger," "Shut the fuck up." For they believed that any form of resistance, however mild (such as not looking down), could lead to corporal violence and solitary confinement, along with officers' other technologies of status coercion behind bars.

Workfare workers also recounted pervasive verbal abuse, though it seemed more likely to involve disdain and condescension than outright name-calling. But for them, as for prisoners, such degradation was buttressed by the threat of coercive punishments. As Tara Collins explained, in addition to having to do "dirty" and "ignorant" work that prevented them from getting "real" jobs, workfare workers "got to deal with the attitudes of [their] superiors."

And they talk real ignorant to you. They don't take into consideration that you have kids, health issues, you know. You miss a day, they're going to sanction you, they're going to cut you off, they're going to kick you out the program.

For the Black 38-year-old woman, the combination of such disrespectful ("ignorant") treatment, demeaning ("dirty" and "ignorant") work, and the seemingly ubiquitous threat of sanctions rendered workfare deeply degrading.

Lisa Williams agreed, particularly in terms of workfare workers' disrespectful treatment. In describing her former supervisor, for example, Lisa repeatedly emphasized how "nasty" she spoke to the workfare workers. "She just had a nasty mouth," the 26-year-old African American woman said.

> She used to talk to us *real* nasty: "Y'all all be on welfare, all y'all like, you ain't going to never be nothing." . . . I would just be telling her, like, "You shouldn't talk to people like that, like we're your kids. You got your own kids to talk to like that. We're grown people." [But the supervisor would respond with] the same stuff, just, "You're not going to be nothing, you're going to be on welfare your whole life." Just the same stuff all the time. It's always *disgusting* words coming out of her mouth, nothing nice to say.

As Lisa's account suggests, some workfare workers said that they could sometimes mildly push back against such verbal abuse without facing harsh consequences. But Steven Rodriguez did not agree. Recalling O.T.I.'s description of prisoners, Steven argued that workfare workers always needed to perform deference in the face of their subjugation in order to avoid their supervisors' sticks of status coercion. "Sometimes they get really nasty at the mouth," the 35-year-old Hispanic man said of workfare supervisors, "and you got to be quiet, and you can't say nothing or they'll send you downtown to your employment counselor and you'll get sanctioned." Pauline Wilson agreed. Over and again, she said that workfare workers would "lose" (be sanctioned) if they pushed back against what seemed to be their incessant degradation. "You still lose, you still lose," the 57-year-old African American woman said. "You can get hot-headed or whatever, you're still going to lose. You're still going to lose."

Thus, like prisoners, workfare workers often felt deeply degraded by their bosses. But instead of the racist, homophobic, and gender-policing abuse ex-prisoners most often recounted, the verbal abuse workfare workers described usually centered on accusations of laziness and worthlessness—they "'ain't going to never be nothing.'" Yet for both groups, the underlying message was the same: they had failed to fulfill hegemonic notions of (white, male) productive citizenship. Like prisoners, moreover, workfare workers generally believed that if they did not demonstrate their deference when treated this way, they were at risk of their bosses' powers of status coercion.

For athletes and graduate students, such degradation was both less severe and less pervasive, though they too recounted relatively common incidents of verbal abuse. In fact, Lindsay argued that "verbal abuse is one of the biggest under-written-about, under-known things in college sports."[15] As the 25-year-old Black basketball player explained,

> Because, like, [in sports] it's okay to yell and scream in people's face . . . or, like, shaming them, or making them [feel] so horrible. . . . They would call them, like, "weak" or a "girl." . . . Like, "You need to push through." Like, "You need to be better." If you're hurt, you're "weak." Like that whole like danger-ous dynamic that pushes players to not speak up for injuries, and/or pres-sures them to play through injuries when they probably shouldn't.

As Lindsay described it, verbal abuse in the sports world tends to focus on athletes' perceived failure to attain (gendered) hegemonic notions of strength and toughness—a narrower critique than that levied against workfare and incarcerated workers, but still cut from the same cloth.

However, while Lindsay argued strongly against such degradation, most of the other athletes I interviewed seemed to accept it as a relatively routine and unremarkable aspect of elite sports. "I mean, everybody gets yelled at," Haley said. "You just learn to, like, take it and move on." In fact, several times during our interview, Haley pointed to the lessons she felt she had learned from such "yelling," which included "being able to take a lot of heat" without "immediately yelling back" and "parsing out what [she] needed to hear versus what [she] needed to let go." "It was pretty hard," the white 23-year-old woman said.

> I felt like I got told things that were unfair. And, like, when coaches were angry, sometimes it would fall on me. And that's fine. Like, that was part of my role [as a walk-on]. It was hard, but I learned how to make it into some-thing that was productive for me.

For example, Haley recalled, her coach once asked her how she would improve the basketball program. Haley responded honestly but carefully, suggesting that "the assistant coaches could be more positive." "We weren't soft, or anything," Haley said, reassuring me that the athletes on her team were not in fact failing to comply with (masculinized) expectations of physical strength and mental toughness.

> Like, we knew it was going to be hard, we knew the coaches could be a-holes sometimes. But, like, there's a point where, when you're trying to teach somebody, like, positivity is the way to go. . . . So, I was having that conversa-tion with Coach, and she just did not hear it the way that—I must have done a bad job of verbalizing it, or something happened, but, you know, a switch flipped and she went off on me . . . yelling, cussing. . . . "Who the fuck do you think you are? . . . You don't even play. Why do you think you could say things like that?" And it just turned into, like, a forty-five-minute rant of, like, yelling at me, and just going off about everything. . . . [Afterward] I was like, "Okay, well, now I know what *not* to say."

Playing basketball in college, Haley went on to say, "was a great experi-ence, I'm never going to take that away. But, there are definitely some questions about people being treated with respect the way they should have been. . . . But," she conceded, "you get that everywhere." Thus, while Haley (mildly) objected to her coaches' lack of "positivity," she also repeat-edly qualified her critique, variously emphasizing the lessons she learned from it, her own responsibility for not "verbalizing" it well enough, and her belief that such mistreatment is "everywhere." Though it could be "unfair," Haley seemed to believe, verbal abuse was par for the course.

Football player M. Max also considered coaches' "yelling" at athletes to be "normal." And like Haley, he generally deemed it routine and unre-markable, except for one incident which he described as "real bad." "Not the normal kind [of yelling] which I was used to," M. Max said, "because I was never the type of guy that did things to get the coach to yell at you. . . . But the way he yelled at me was kind of like—he called me out on my name," echoing prisoners' descriptions of officers' slurs. "I just wasn't hav-ing it," the 37-year-old Black man said, and he started tussling with the coach on the sidelines. Yet even in that incident, M. Max later rationalized his coach's mistreatment, at least in part, by explaining that it had come from "the heat of the moment." Haley did the same. Her coach's "yelling" and "cussing," she explained, "wasn't like a personal attack on me. It was like, heat of the moment. She's angry, you got to take it out." Both Haley and M. Max thus legitimized their coaches' verbal abuse—which at times could be extreme—as almost unavoidably arising from the emotion of the sport, which had to be released. As Haley said, "You got to take it out."

Graduate students, by contrast, tended to categorize their faculty advisors' verbal degradation as either a purposeful teaching and management tool or a "personal attack," to use Haley's words. In the first case, for example, Laine argued that graduate students getting "ripped apart" and their "egos shot" by faculty members was an effective and necessary pedagogical strategy. As the 30-year-old white woman explained,

> I think that, in theory, graduate school does what it's supposed to do: where you go in, you think you know everything, because you're a hotshot in college, but it turns out you know nothing. And when it comes to actually doing lab work, it's really difficult to transition from book smart to lab smart. . . . So, it's necessary, you need to go through this. You need to have your ego shot, you need to have people rip you apart, and show you that, "You don't know everything, but here's how you do learn things, this is how you approach these problems." You need to go through the experience where you're presenting your research in front of everyone, and they rip you apart. And if you do that five times . . . you can do anything.

At the same time, Laine believed that such degradation could become overly destructive and inappropriate. She recounted the story of another graduate student whose advisor was notoriously abusive: bullying and pressuring students to work long hours and "get results." (In fact, six of the twenty graduate students I interviewed described their own lab bosses as "abusive," "toxic," and/or a "bully.") In that case, Laine said, the student ultimately fabricated results "because she didn't have time to run the experiment," and she was therefore dismissed from the graduate program. Laine made a point of not condoning the student's actions. Fabricating results, she said, "is the biggest flaw you could possibly—you just don't do that, *you can't*. Our word is everything here in chemistry, and so if you make up results, that's not okay." Even still, Laine believed that most of the blame for this "nasty" situation fell on the faculty advisor.

It's one of those things where you just—you know exactly what happened. This guy is notorious for being mean, breathing down your neck, yelling at you if you don't come in on a Saturday just because you went to church or something.

"It's hard," Laine went on.

I mean, I went to a top-ten school, and so . . . we're relatively smart people, and we're relatively driven people. And we're working incredibly hard. And when you are doing everything you can, and giving everything you've got, literally everything—your social life, all of your friendships, [your health]—I mean, I cannot stress enough how bad [graduate school] is in general. . . . It really takes a toll.

For Laine herself, the "toll" was recurring panic attacks, which were severe enough to require daily medication. But "as soon as I was out of graduate school," she said, "I stopped having panic attacks. Like, it all, everything just got better. I gained weight again. Like, it was just—it was bad. [Graduate school] was bad." Laine thus espoused two somewhat-conflicting views of verbal abuse in graduate school. On the one hand, she described it as both routine and "necessary." Students "need" to have their "ego shot." On the other hand, she told of the harsh consequences that might result from more extreme cases of abuse, all the while emphasizing how "bad"—stressful, harmful—her graduate school work environment had been.

Unlike Laine, Henry did not talk about internalizing the pressure of graduate school in this way, though he did describe his advisor—similar to that of Laine's friend—as "famously demanding." Moreover, he too believed that his advisor's "ranting and screaming" was a calculated "strategy," in this case to push students to meet "unrealistic expectations." When I asked Henry how common such behavior was among faculty advisors in the sciences, the 42-year-old white man replied, "I wouldn't say it's common, but . . . it's certainly not outside the realm of normal experience in how groups are run in the sciences." In his current capacity as director of graduate studies, he said, "I have grad students who come into my office in my program, to tell me about things that are probably borderline abusive, verbally abusive behavior, and things like that. Not every day, luckily, but it does happen."

For other graduate students, their bosses' abusive behavior seemed to be driven more by personal characteristics than management strategy. For instance, Sunny attributed her advisor's "abusive," "caustic," and "toxic" behavior to being "overprotective and insecure," a "control freak." "She had this kind of very protective, very suspicious of everybody, negative way of being," Sunny explained. "Like, she's really nice and then, all of a sudden, she would just lash out for no reason." Sunny said that she and the other lab members witnessed their boss's "dangerous" behavior firsthand when she "sabotaged" a postdoc working there. "There was a guy there who had done so well, he helped her so much," Sunny said. "She sabotaged him. Everyone saw it."

> He had been there like seven or eight years [as a postdoc], and he wanted to apply for his own K22, and then eventually his own R01 [grant]. . . . He wanted to become independent. . . . So, he went and interviewed. He tried to get letters of recommendation to do his own R01, [but the lab boss] called people, and badmouthed him behind his back. And even for interviews for private companies, she would call them, and say that he wasn't to be trusted, or hired. I mean it was really crazy, because he was a great person. He was a great—he was a better scientist than she was.

Because of this experience, Sunny said, she and the other lab members "realized that it was really a lost cause, and people started to leave even if they didn't have everything [i.e., publications] they wanted to have. So, yeah, people are mistreated all the time," Sunny said. "And there's nowhere we can go." The only recourse, Sunny believed, was to leave the lab and therefore leave behind years of work and any publications that might come from it.

Emily also described her lab boss as a "bully, which," the 30-year-old white woman explained, "is one of those things where, like, as an adult, that sounds kind of funny to say. Unless you've been bullied as an adult, and then, you like totally get it." Her boss "just waged psychological warfare on people," Emily said, "and at some point, [she] decided that I was going to be that person." One of the ways her boss did so, Emily explained, was by blocking the students' publications.

> So, she had signed off on [one of my papers] . . . and then she decided, "No, I don't like Emily." And so, she found something in the paper she didn't like, and said, "You need to fix this." So, I fixed it, and then she found something

else, and then she found something else, and then she stopped reading the paper. And, like, six months later, this paper that she had signed off on six months previously, I still wasn't allowed to submit. And it wasn't until I said that I was leaving [the lab] that she said, "Oh, okay, you can go ahead and submit that paper now." . . . It's like, she was waiting for me to leave. But, she had done that to a number of people. She kind of turned her sights on me when the previous person left, [because] she no longer had a target.

Much like Sunny, Emily felt that her only recourse was to leave that "toxic environment" and in so doing forgo all of her research and related publications. In order to complete her PhD, Emily said that she had to switch to a different field of chemistry altogether. "It was a pretty dramatic change," she said, but "I was kind of desperate."

Though verbal abuse was the most common type of degradation that workers reported across the four categories of work, some also cited three types of physical degradation: (1) being required to perform what they deemed to be degrading work, (2) being physically punished in an overtly degrading manner, and (3) being physically abused. In the first case, for example, incarcerated and workfare workers said that some jobs made them feel like "the scum of the earth." And indeed, such jobs often conformed to what scholars call "dirty work."[16] For workfare workers, these degrading jobs included cleaning toilets (Jennifer Rose, Clevelanda, Kierra Ross, Tashia Green, and Kim Hunky) and picking up particularly repugnant trash (April Smith and Shara White). For instance, April Smith described with distaste picking up drug "needles" and "condoms" as "doing what nobody else wants to do."

> They take us to drug neighborhoods, like, you're cleaning up after the drug dealers. . . . We pick everything up: needles, condoms, whatever we see down there, we have to clean up. [And] it's dangerous! . . . A man just got shot and killed in the store, and you got us right over there two days later cleaning this area. We don't get no water, no nothing. *And we're wrong when we complain?* It's not right. How is this preparing us? I *know* how to clean up. I clean my house. How is this preparing me for a *job?* We're supposed to be getting job-ready. This is not job-ready. *This is doing what nobody else wants to do.* And it's not fair.

"But," the 30-year-old African American woman said resignedly, "this is what I have to do to get my benefits." Shara White agreed. Though she believed that welfare recipients should be required to work—"It's just to get you off your feet . . . not going to be in the bed, put your feet up and smoking little cigarettes and collecting my money every two weeks"—she did not think that they should be "going to pick up somebody's trash, used condoms, and stuff out on the floor." "It made me feel like I'm a bum," the 30-year-old African American woman said. "I feel like a bum." Likewise, incarcerated workers described cleaning feces (Bruce W., Ron D., John S., and O.T.I.) and cleaning up after officers (Bruce W. and Apache) as unduly degrading work. As Bruce W. avowed, "I'm not going to clean no feces. I don't care what gloves you give me." John S. agreed. "This one guy . . . took a dump in the shower, and they wanted us to clean it," the 24-year-old white man recalled. "And they didn't want to give us rubber gloves, and so I'm like, 'I'm not doing it. It's not sanitary. *I'm not doing it.*'"

In addition to such "dirty work," incarcerated and workfare workers described having to perform unnecessarily arduous labor—often when labor-saving tools seemed to be readily available but were not supplied to them—as another form of physical degradation. As April Smith said of workfare, "A lot of things they shouldn't have us doing. A lot of things is too much."

> My thing is, I don't have a problem with gardening. I do gardening on my own. They'll have us out there with gloves, [but] they'll have a right-hand glove and no left-hand glove. Like, downstairs at the basement—I kid you not—it's stocked with supplies. *Stocked.* There's no reason why you shouldn't have the things we need. Gloves, that's all we ask. *Gloves.* We picking weeds; they got the little trowels but, no, we have to pick them by hand. There are pricklies [and] we have to pick them by hand.

In a similar vein, Jarome W. believed that having to cut the prison's extensive lawns with Weedwackers, instead of lawnmowers, made the work degrading. "They had lawnmowers and a truck, [but] they make us use the manual Weedwackers, like it's slavery," he said. Mike Harris agreed, but in his case, prisoners were required to use push mowers. "I felt like it was slave labor," the 20-year-old African American man said. "Like I was on some type of plantation when I was out there mowing the grass—a big field, you know—with push lawnmowers . . . [just] to make us suffer."

The second type of physical degradation these workers recounted was punishment whose primary purpose, it seemed, was degradation. In prison, J.D. recalled, "I done seen a cop telling the inmates to, like, get all the way butt naked down to their boxers. . . . Like, why would you ask a man to get all the way naked for no reason? Just to embarrass them," the 22-year-old African American man concluded. Likewise, D.Q. said that his supervisor—who was a civilian, not a corrections officer—wanted him to "'scrub the floor with a toothbrush'" as a punishment. In explaining what happened, the 27-year-old African American man recalled,

> [The supervisor] had a big deal with people falling asleep [at work]. And one day I came in there and I was real sick the past few days. So, [actually] the day before that, he caught me asleep—I'm not going to lie—he caught me asleep. You know, it was what it was. He caught me. I told him, "Man, I'm tired. It won't happen again." And we left it at that. The very next day, we come in early in the morning, and I guess it was how I was sitting that made it look like I was asleep, so when he said something to me about it, he never let me explain myself. He just automatically assumed that I was asleep or whatever. [He] pulls me in the hallway, tells the officer he caught me sleeping for the second time, whatever, whatever, whatever. The officer asks him, "Well, what do you want to do? Do you want to write him a ticket or whatever?" He tells him, "Yeah, I want to write him a ticket and I want him to scrub the floor with a toothbrush." I'm like, "*What?*" It kind of threw me off.

In response, D.Q. "flipped out," he said. When I asked him what that meant—"yelling? cussing?"—he said, "Absolutely, absolutely. The whole nine, you know."

> I was just basically telling him, like, "*What do you mean you want me to scrub the floor? I'm not scrubbing no floor with no toothbrush.*" You know, he's saying whatever he's saying, but I'm talking over, I'm not even listening to him, you know. I just told the officer, I'm like, "Yo, you might as well put the cuffs on me now, because I'm not scrubbing no floor with no toothbrush. He out of his mind." So, I went to the box for thirty days. . . . I wasn't scrubbing no floor with no toothbrush.

For D.Q., this punishment was so overtly degrading that he disobeyed all of the basic rules of prison life, "flipping out" at his boss and, not surprisingly, being put in solitary confinement as a result.

The last form of physical degradation these workers reported was corporal violence. Only incarcerated workers recounted this type of degradation, which they often euphemistically described as officers putting "hands" or "feet on you." As Bruce W. said,

> Sometimes [in solitary] they get in your cell, pop in, and beat you. If you was resisting them, if you had a mouth on you, if you was to do anything aggressive to them, then they would come in there about three in the morning, two in the morning, wee hours in the morning, just to beat on you—so you will be defenseless. And they always handcuff you in the box, so you can't do nothing to them.

But such violence was not only reserved for those prisoners who "had a mouth" on them, Bruce explained. In solitary, he went on, COs "come by your cell and antagonize you. They talk to you. They belittle you or make you feel like you're nothing. To provoke you to react and, once you react, then they come in and they got a *reason* to put their hands on you." For Bruce, as for many ex-prisoners, there seemed to be an exceedingly slippery slope between verbal abuse, resistance (however minor), and physical abuse behind bars.

O.T.I. also recounted corporal violence in solitary confinement, though only in response to my direct questioning. Otherwise, it seems, such treatment—particularly in "the box"—was routine enough as to be unremarkable. "Yes, when I went to the box, they smacked me around a little bit," he said.

> You know what I mean? Because they want to show you who's boss, and that's their way of doing it. Just like, well, like in slavery. If you get out of line, they give you a whooping, you know what I'm saying? They want to show you and instill in you fear on who's boss.

For O.T.I., then, such violence was an instrument of subjugation rather than indiscriminate brutality: "they want to show you who's boss . . . like in slavery."

Yet to be clear, O.T.I.'s account of being "smacked around a little bit" was both common and mild among prisoners' reports of physical abuse. Twenty-two respondents spontaneously described 52 times they experienced or witnessed physical violence, 23 of which were associated with solitary confinement.[17] Among these were cases of extreme violence: a prisoner forced to consume 27 hotdog buns and a gallon of water and then punched in the stomach until he vomited; a prisoner beaten by six COs in the showers in the middle of the night; a prisoner who because he threatened to complain to state officials about mistreatment was severely beaten by multiple officers and then transferred to another facility for a longer sentence.[18]

Though these extreme cases were less common, violence pervaded prison life for most of the male ex-prisoners I interviewed. In fact, according to D.D.G., the threat of being killed by officers at Attica Correctional Facility was explicit.[19] "As soon as you get off the bus," he recalled,

> The COs got their sticks hitting them on their hand with the gloves on. The same gloves that they're not supposed to have at other jails, they got them in here. The same beating-up gloves that they beat inmates on. . . . They supposedly supposed to have banned them, but they got them. And they take the stick and hit them in their hands, so while you're getting off the bus, [they're] intimidating you. . . . They don't say nothing, but they're screwing with you. They want you to look at them, but you're supposed to keep looking down because, if you look at them, they're going to think you're tough. . . . [Then] what happens is the sergeant will give you a speech: "Welcome to Attica. I got two things for you. You don't put your hands on my COs, they won't kill you. Enjoy your stay."

Because of the pervasiveness of such violence, K.H. said, being in Attica was "scary, really scary." "I mean, yes," the 47-year-old African American man allowed,

> I don't negate the fact that we put ourselves in predicaments and we're paying our debt to society, but to be abused along the way isn't right. And yeah, okay fine, some of us abuse officers. Don't get me wrong, because we're not perfect, we're not angels. But the job of a correction officer is to subdue a person, not abuse him. If you need to be subdued, his job is to subdue you, not to abuse you. [But] that's what I'm seeing right now in corrections. . . . I'll be the first one to tell you that as an ex-convict, I wasn't right all the time. I did some things, but I didn't deserve to be abused along the way.

Thus, for K.H., D.D.G., and other former prisoners, the degradation of prison life and prison work was extreme, even life-threatening. Yet while Attica is perhaps an extreme site with an extreme case of coerced labor, degradation—particularly verbal abuse—was prevalent across three of the four labor relations I examined (prison labor, workfare, and athletic labor) and not uncommon in the fourth (graduate student labor). Moreover, because supervisors across all of these labor relations had access to the punitive powers of status coercion, many of these workers felt that there was little they could do to challenge such degradation, causing them to feel a sense of othering and dehumanization.

OTHERING AND DEHUMANIZATION: "NOT REALLY UNDERSTANDING THAT WE ARE HUMAN BEINGS"

"Othering," comparative literature scholar Edward Said wrote in *Orientalism*, entails "disregarding, essentializing, denuding the humanity of another culture, people or geographical region."[20] Such "denuding" of one's "humanity"—or dehumanization—political theorist Hannah Arendt argued in *The Origins of Totalitarianism*, is an essential precursor to genocide.[21] "Othering" and "dehumanization" are thus overlapping phenomena. The former is typically used to describe the processes by which individuals or groups draw symbolic boundaries between themselves and others in a hierarchical way; defining themselves against, and thereby privileging themselves over, "the other." Dehumanization is a particular type of othering: the categorization of the other as less than human.

Both othering and dehumanization recursively intersect with the other mechanisms of subjugation I examine here. For the cultural construction of some groups as an "other" serves to justify the two forms of subjugation that I have already analyzed: corporal control and degradation. By virtue of their difference, their (supposed) inferiority, such groups are said to need to be surveilled, controlled, and disciplined. These are the tools by which othering is enacted and enforced. As a result, not surprisingly, the targets of such tools of subjugation often experience an acute sense of alienation. They *feel* othered.

To varying degrees, workers across all four of the groups articulated a sense of feeling like an "other." In table 1, I organize their descriptors into four categories of othering and dehumanization, which include their sense

Table 1 Themes of "othering" and dehumanization

Othering: Second-class citizen	Dehumanization: Less than human	Dehumanization: Thing/commodity	Dehumanization: Degraded thing
"Child"/"kid"	"Species"	"Asset"	"Footstool"
"Kids in India"	"Alien"	"Commodity"	"Trash"/"garbage"
"Like I was in Ethiopia"	"Animal"	"A coach's paycheck"	"Crap"
"Like immigration"	"Monkey"	"Product"	"Ain't crap"
"Second class"	"Dogs"	"Collection of stats"	"Shit"
"Lower class"	"Like horses to carry things"	"Numbers"	"Less than shit"
"Peasant"	"An animal they don't care about"	"Cheap labor"	
"Poverty"	"Inhumane"	"Free labor"	
"Servant"	"Less than human"	"Lab hands"	
"Indentured servant"/"servitude"	"No human respect"	"Workhorse"	
"Slave"/"slavery"	"Not a human being"	"Property"	
"Peon"	"Not an individual"	"Pawn"	
"Lowlife"	"Amorphous"		
"Bum"	"Nothing"		
"Useless"	"Like we didn't exist"		
"Nobody"			
"Criminal"/"like you're in jail"			
"Inmate"/"you got green on"			
"Gang member"			

of being treated as some kind of second-class person (e.g., a "child" or "peon") as well as various types of dehumanization: feeling as though they were treated as less than human (an "alien" or "animal"), like a thing or commodity ("workhorse"), or like a degraded thing ("shit"). Despite these analytical distinctions, in their usage such categories were not mutually exclusive. In fact, when describing their sense of subjugation, the workers I interviewed often drew on several different categories, even within a single sentence.

Across these groups, distinct patterns emerged as to which types of othering they were more likely to articulate. Incarcerated and workfare workers most often used overtly degrading terms across three of these four categories (second-class, less than human, and degraded thing), while athletes and graduate students usually used less overtly degrading terms and most often from the fourth category (thing/commodity). These differences are likely due to the divergent ways their subjugation is enacted. As mentioned, prisoners and welfare recipients in America are often seen as surplus populations to be controlled and punished. Therefore, the primary goal of these modes of subjugation is their *domination*. Officers, caseworkers, and workfare supervisors surveil, control, and degrade these two groups in order to exert their own dominance—their superiority—over them, which not surprisingly leaves them feeling deeply degraded. And so they draw on such terms to articulate their sense of othering and dehumanization. Conversely, college athletes and graduate students are often seen as creators of capital, and therefore the primary goal of their subjugation is *exploitation*. Coaches and faculty advisors surveil, control, and discipline these two groups primarily to extract surplus value from their labor. These workers often experience this with a sense of commodification, and so they use such terms in articulating their feeling of othering and dehumanization. In the remainder of this section, I examine each of these groups in turn, exploring how they conveyed this aspect of their subjugation.

Among ex-prisoners, for example, Bruce W. used a remarkable number of these themes to describe his view of prisoners' treatment. When I asked him whether he identified as a "worker" or "prisoner" while working behind bars, the 23-year-old African American man said, "I feel more—honestly—like a slave."

> I say "like a slave" because of the way they treat you. It's the human decency they don't really have. No human respect for you. They figure, if you got the state greens on, then you are below them. You are a peasant. They are upper class, you are lower class. You're poverty. You are nothing. They talk to you in any kind of way.[22] Sometimes, they put hands on you, they put feet on you.

Indeed, because prisoners' mistreatment was so extreme and ubiquitous, Bruce argued that this book should focus not on their labor but rather on their "inhumane treatment" and their need for "human equality." "I think you should talk about human equality," he told me, " . . . because they feel our social status gives them authority and power to abuse [their position]."

Ron D. agreed. Again and again, the 24-year-old African American man pointed to prisoners' "inhumane" treatment to argue that I should focus my research on their mistreatment rather than their labor. "I think you should do more about how we get treated in prison instead of work," he said, "because how the people get treated in there is just absolutely crazy." When I asked him for an example, Ron said, "I'll tell you a story about how they spit on people's food in the box. How, in the box, you got to dig—well, this is just in [this one prison]—you got to dig through your food to find your spork. And they only give you five minutes to eat." Ron then went on to describe officers' severe physical abuse of prisoners, ending with the following prescription: "I think Albany just need to send somebody in there undercover and see how people get treated. This is inhumane, how people get treated in there."

Many other prisoners felt a similar sense of dehumanization, often articulating it in terms of being treated like an "animal." "They treat us like we weren't human beings," Jarome said.

> They treat us like we are some kind of animal, like we didn't exist. . . . Like, if an animal chose not to do something, people will beat them animals. That's how we are feeling in there, like some type of animal.

"Let me put it like this," Mike Russ said. "You know how if you had a dog and you abuse it? Like, they will treat you like you're an animal, an animal that they don't care about." "They treat you like you're an animal," Derrick said. "I mean, like, I'm not an animal. I'm a human being just like you. You bleed, I bleed. We shit, everything the same. Just our skin color is different." "We're a species to them," F.E. said. "We are a lower-level, borderline-animal-treatment sort of people." Such mistreatment, the 21-year-old African American man said, shocked him when he went to prison. Before being incarcerated, F.E. recalled, he believed that prisoners would be treated decently if they showed respect to the officers. "I mean, I'm a firm believer [that] you got to give to get respect," he said. "I've always been that type of person, because I always give it. So, to just be disrespected and disvalued so much in prison for no reason is ridiculous, man. It's ridiculous."

Workfare workers also articulated a sense of othering, though instead of being treated like "animals," they usually characterized it as being treated like "criminals" and other types of second-class citizens. "They treat us like slaves," John T. said, "like back in the old days. Or like you're in jail." Felisha Jones agreed. "I feel like this is jail stuff," she said. "I feel like we're supposed to be having our orange suit on and then the ankle bracelet on and something like that. That's how I feel." "We're all second class in here," Will Jones said.

> Everybody, who all work for welfare in this program right now, is second class, because they don't care. . . . It's hot as hell outside today. . . . People can pass out, get dehydrated, and they don't care. Because we work for welfare. And it's not right.

They should "treat us like an employee instead of treating us like we garbage," Will went on, "like we trash in the street." Pauline Wilson agreed. As a workfare worker she felt that she was "treated like . . . a common piece of trash."

Meanwhile, other workfare workers articulated their sense of othering in more paternalistic—though still degrading—terms: they felt as though they were treated like children. Recall, for example, Lisa Williams's description of her workfare supervisor. "She was so disrespectful," Lisa said. "I would just be telling her, like, 'You shouldn't talk to people like that, like we're your kids. You got your own kids to talk to like that. We're grown people.'" Jennifer Rose agreed, and in trying to convey her sense of workfare supervisors' unwarranted and unchecked power, she discursively drew on several tropes of absolute authority: master to slave, God to servant, adult to child. "I felt like a slave," the 27-year-old Black and Hispanic woman said. "I felt like an indentured servant."

> It's like, the people they send us to [workfare supervisors] are like God: they control everything in the palm of their hands. Everything is like, "Don't do this, we're going to tell, we're going to tell, we're going to tell, we're going to tell." It's like, we're all *adults*, [but] you're making it seem like I'm a little kid, constantly telling me that you're going to tell on me.

In fact, at some work sites, Jennifer went on, workfare workers are required to wear red badges, labeling them as "DSS" (Department of Social Services). Evoking Hester Prynne's "A," such badges were thus a physical marker of their otherness. "You have those badges that . . . just put all your business out there," Jennifer said in exasperation and shame. "It *does* get frustrating," she said. "Because it's like, I don't want to be here as much as you don't want me here. . . . If I could find a regular job and work, I would."

By contrast, the public marking of college athletes is more often positive than negative. They tend to be heralded for their accomplishments rather than shamed for their hardships. Even still, Shevontae argued, athletes' humanity is also diminished. But rather than being treated as "criminals" or "an animal they don't care about," she said that athletes are reduced to a set of performance statistics and treated as performing "monkeys." "Honestly, I think that's what people overlook, how your personal life might influence your performance."

> Like, it sounds so common sense, but no one ever wants to think of that. We're so quick to watch a game, we're very much into, "You're doing me a service, *jump, monkey jump! Run monkey, run!*" I hate how we even speak about pro athletes, and you might say something very ignorant like, "Oh, they're terrible, they're a waste," or whatever. . . . And you would never know if my aunt died the day of the game. That wouldn't be released to you. You wouldn't know if I'm a cutter; you wouldn't know that. You wouldn't know if I'm bulimic. Like, the simplest things you would not know. You wouldn't know if my boyfriend just hit me, my girlfriend's hit me. You wouldn't know if my dad died, all of that [kind of] thing. And that's throughout a season. *And you keep going.* Think about it! Think about how many stories you've heard of that happening. You've never heard of it on ESPN. But, needless to say, that happens: someone's lost a parent in college, someone has been to the ER, someone has been an alcoholic, someone's been a drug addict. . . . Just because you have a college scholarship, it doesn't mean you have outside money. You don't know if my phone bill is turned off. You don't know if I'm living the good life at this institution, doing all these great things, [but] my family is getting kicked out of their house and they're homeless. *Imagine that stress.* Like, you're flying to a tournament in a nice plane, you're eating food, you're on TV answering questions, but really all that you're thinking about is the fact that your parents just got kicked out of their house, or your

mom is struggling with addiction. . . . People don't get that we are developing as human beings, like everyone else in college, but with a constant cam-
era, microphone, and expectations. Like, my value is some numbers. You
guys go online and look at my values, some averages of my performance
numbers. . . . We don't treat [athletes] as humans.

Lawrence also felt reduced to a series of "numbers," though his sense of
dehumanization centered on the commodification of his body rather than
his performance on the football field. "I walk in a room, they tell me to strip
down to my underwear," the 31-year-old African American man recalled.

> I got guys checking body fat percentage on me, guys looking me up and
> down, [asking] my height, my weight. And, if you think about it, back in the
> 1800s when they had the slave trade . . . that was the same thing they did
> when they were auctioning people off.

They do this type of bodily appraisal "all the time," Lawrence told me.

> They evaluate you mentally, they evaluate you physically. I mean, I under-
> stand why they're doing it, because, you know, they're investing millions of
> dollars in the players, so they want to make sure, you know, any little possi-
> ble thing, they want to evaluate anything. But, on the same parallel, I felt
> like I was a slave.

Both Lawrence and Shevontae drew on racialized notions of othering to
convey this sense of their subjugation. Shevontae felt like a performing
"monkey." Lawrence felt like a "slave." While the first is a racist trope and
the second is a racist legacy, they are both used to articulate a sense of the
objectification and exploitation of athletes in these predominantly Black
sports.[23]

Other athletes felt similar, though they more often conveyed their sense
of dehumanization in less overtly racialized and degraded terms. Rather
than a "slave," they said that they felt like a "commodity." For some of these
athletes, at least, such differences were likely due to their race and racialized experiences of dehumanization. For example, white 34-year-old Bill
Murdock described athletes not as "monkeys" but as "a coach's paycheck."

> Like, [the coach] sees you as a commodity. And I'm twenty-one—nineteen
> to twenty-one—and just dealing with, like, okay, I'm in a real world, people

don't care about my dreams at all. . . . You're just another guy, you're just another athlete. And if you're not doing the job, there's the next person out there.

Bill recalled once holding the door open for his coach, who then said, "'Stop trying so hard Murdock.'" Bill was taken aback.

I'm like, *are you human?* In no other line of work would that even be okay to talk to your subordinates that way. And we're not really their subordinates. We're who they're supposed to be mentoring and training, right? . . . Now, I'm not saying they're all like that, but there is plenty of them like that: they just give a crap about the players. It's all about winning.

Lindsay agreed, but for her the worst part was not athletes' commodification per se, but coaches' pretense of caring—their rhetoric of "family"—that thinly veiled it. "That's my problem with, like, the whole 'family' thing," the midtwenties Black woman said.

We're assets. We are products. . . . Like, they're giving you a scholarship. That is goods and services, you're exchanging your services to them. Like, they're giving you something in return for something. It's not out of, like, "We just want to help all the kids go to college and play their dream sports."

For Lindsay, the "sham" of such rhetoric was exposed in high relief during a time in college when she was struggling physically and emotionally. She felt that she needed time away from basketball to recover, but her team was heading into a big game, and because she was a top player, her coaches did not want her to take a break. It seemed that they did not care about her well-being. "I ended up talking to the coaches about it and I was just like, 'I need some days off, like, I'm losing my mind. . . . I don't even want to play basketball anymore.' That's how worn out and tired I was," she said to me.

So I tell the coaches and, like, they don't receive it well and they're pressuring me [to play]. . . . [Then, later, the coach] walks by and, like, rolls her eyes [at me]. She's so flippant about what I'm going through. I wanted to punch her in the face. I was like, it's such a sham of, like, "we're a family." Like, you really don't care about me, you just care if I perform or not. You really don't care about my mental state right now. Like, *am I okay? Am I going to hurt myself?* Like, *am I just alive as a human being?*

"I understand that this is a job, this is a business," Lindsay went on. "It's just the whole sham idea that 'we're a family'" that left her feeling both frustrated and dehumanized.

Kate and Bruce felt the same way. They both believed that their coaches did not care about them—their health, their well-being, their humanity—despite rhetoric to the contrary. As Kate said, "The biggest problem I had with our program was that [coaches] lose sight of the human beings, lose sight of the fact that these are young women who are trying to find their way." As this midtwenties Black woman went on to explain,

> I couldn't stand behind the decisions that were being made [ignoring some players' serious mental health issues], because I felt like they were being made out of transaction, out of money, out of business, out of, like, just the crux of college athletics. . . . Because they don't care about you as human. At least that's the way that it comes across. They'll tell you all the time, "Oh no, I care about you," like, "You know, I really care about your well-being, and I want you to be well, and da, da, da." But, if it's between going to see a [mental health] counselor and missing practice, it's like, "Well, you're just going to have to not see that counselor, because I can't have you miss practice." You know what I mean? . . . My health and well-being, particularly my mental health, is incredibly important, and it's like you always have to decide between my human needs versus what I need to do for basketball. And they should never ask you to choose between that. . . . There just wasn't a lot of care for the human being.

For Bruce, this sense of dehumanization became especially clear after he left his football team (and college) because of the shoulder injury. "They never even called me," this late-twenties white man said. "The coach never even called me."

> They never called me to say, "How are you doing?" The coach never even called me to say, "What's going on? I haven't seen you." . . . I was just like their workhorse that they didn't really care about. . . . They didn't care about me as a person at all, or my health. . . . I left there with a terrible taste in my mouth.

For these athletes, then, their sense of dehumanization—particularly commodification—was exacerbated by the pervasive rhetoric of "care" and "family." Though their coaches often used such rhetoric, most of these athletes did not ultimately feel "cared" for. "They don't care about you as human," Kate said. "It's all about winning," said Bill. And for Bruce, whose severe football injury (among other things) "ruined" his career and his education, such treatment left "a terrible taste in [his] mouth."

Some graduate students also felt commodified and overlooked as "human beings," though usually to a lesser degree and without the rhetoric of "family" veiling (and exacerbating) it. Even still, Sunny used several of the same terms to describe her sense of othering as did the other groups of workers in this study. For instance, while explaining the prevalence of verbal shaming in her department, Sunny said, "I think that goes back to not understanding, not having a respect for that person *as a person*. . . . We're all these amorphous postdocs and grad students, you know. Not really understanding that we are human beings after all." Because of this, she said, "So many people are leaving science . . . because they're just sick of being treated like slaves." Yet such treatment is normalized in the sciences, Sunny argued.

> Literally every single PI says, "Well, I had to do it, they have to too." There's no appreciation for life balance, or them being a person. They are *hands* . . . and they're not supposed to complain about it because that's the way it always was.

Sunny thus used multiple descriptors—not "a person," not "human beings," "amorphous," "slaves," "hands"—in an effort to convey her sense of othering. Other former graduate students felt similar. For example, as the reader will recall, Gustavo described graduate school as "indentured servitude," and Emily argued that graduate students are treated like "peons." For these graduate students in the sciences, it seems, it is openly expected that their "humanity" will be "denuded." "You know that you're just expected to put everything on hold in your life," as Sunny said. And they are "not supposed to complain about it because that's the way it always was."

Laine believed that the only way to change this status quo is to abolish tenure for faculty. Because in order to get tenure, she explained, faculty advisors "use fear" to extract work from their graduate students.

> If you do not have strong graduate students, there's no way as a professor you'll get tenure. It's just not going to happen, because you need to rely on

your graduate students' work. . . . And they use fear to [do] that. And I think that if they did not have a secure job position, they'd have to go about it in a different way.

In Laine's view, eliminating faculty advisors' job security—and perceived immunity—"would give [them] more accountability. They would not treat the fragile graduate students like garbage. They would value these people."

Michelle Fisher did not feel dehumanized in this way while she was in graduate school—though her explanation of why is telling. "In my graduate studies," this late-twenties white woman said, "I think it was so valuable, and important, to know that my advisor was on my side. [He] treated me almost like a teammate, or like I mattered to him. I wasn't just a pawn in getting his research done. I mattered to him." Thus, in Michelle's experience, "family" was not empty rhetoric. She believed that her advisor had created a true sense of family among his graduate students. "I think he considers it his family that he has created, and that he has nurtured into all of these different jobs, and he stays connected with all of them because he cares about them." So, for example, when her advisor won a major award, Michelle said, many of his former students "flew [across the country] to celebrate with him. You know, like, it wasn't something that they felt like they had to do. It was something that they wanted to do." But, Michelle conceded, her advisor was "rare." He was not the typical lab boss.

·   ·   ·   ·   ·

As their stories suggest, these workers' experiences of subjugation are not always so different from those of more traditional employees. Indeed, many workers believe that their bosses do not care about them as human beings. Many feel that they are treated like workhorses, garbage, slaves, or criminals.[24] Plenty of workers are talked to with disdain, even yelled at or called names. They may feel shamed and degraded, especially if they are seen as not adhering to hegemonic (heterosexual, white, able-bodied) constructions of masculinity or femininity. They may be targeted and harassed, whether through overt abuse or "psychological warfare." And they may be stringently—sometimes punitively—surveilled and regulated both in and out of the workplace.

For all workers, moreover, these mechanisms of subjugation exploit and reify their vulnerability to employer power. For "regular" workers, such vulnerability is usually produced by economic coercion: they may lose their jobs (and wages) if they challenge their bosses' degrading treatment, harassment, or over-the-top surveillance. Though some might be able to leave their jobs for better ones, for many workers such coercion is enough to mold them into "subjected" yet "productive" workers.[25] And so they endure such forms of subjugation.

For the workers in this book, however, their vulnerability is more likely to be produced by status coercion than economic coercion. Incarcerated workers may be put in solitary confinement and kept in prison longer; workfare workers may lose access to the social safety net; college athletes and graduate students may lose their education and sought-after careers. The punitive and far-reaching character of these consequences is what differentiates the subjugation in these labor regimes from others.

In Michel Foucault's terms, these intersecting mechanisms of subjugation and coercion are "micro-physics of power": ways in which social institutions exert power over individuals.[26] Such exertions of power, Foucault argued, are neither intangible nor inconsequential. They are embedded in the body. As Foucault said, they "have an immediate hold upon it; they invest it, mark it, train it, torture it, force it to carry out tasks, to perform ceremonies, to emit signs."[27]

The subjugation and coercion I examine in this book "land" on the bodies of these workers—and perhaps all workers—in at least two ways. First, as this and the previous chapters have shown, these workers must perform subjugation on the job through labor compliance and acts of subservience. They must work without complaint, picking up used condoms, perhaps, or cleaning urine and feces. They must look down; they cannot appear threatening. They must readily consent to others' censorship of their social media use and bodily displays. They must endure cussing, screaming, or slurs without talking back. They must be good soldiers. If not, they are at risk of punishment.

The second way that subjugation and coercion are embedded in these workers' bodies is that even after these jobs have ended, their corporal consequences remain. The stress of sustained social subordination for all of these workers,[28] but especially for workfare and incarcerated workers, who are already stigmatized and marginalized;[29] the mental and physical consequences of both poverty and prison life (particularly solitary confinement),[30] along with the pervasive fear and reality of violence behind bars;[31] the bodily injuries of athletics;[32] the depression and anxiety of graduate school:[33] all of these, and more, have lasting physiological effects. These workers' bodies are "marked."

Even so, as we will see, they resist.

4 "Stay Out They Way"

AGENCY AND RESISTANCE

He'd call me something like, "Stupid motherfucker, son of a
bitch. Go sit the fuck down!" And I just wasn't having it. . . .
We had a big argument on the sidelines. I was trying to get
at the coach, he was trying to get at me.

—M. Max, former college football player

I gave her a couple of words. She have an issue with respect.

—April Smith, workfare worker

I was one of those slackers. I'll be honest with you. . . . I'm
not going to work ninety hours a week for thirty thousand
dollars a year. . . . Fuck that, I'm going hiking on Sunday.

—Gustavo, former graduate student in neuroscience

I swallowed a lot of things that I really wanted to speak out
on. As a man, I strive my best not to put myself in harm's
way. I know how to get around a few things.

—K.H., former incarcerated worker

Although submissive compliance is the primary objective of the coercion
and subjugation in these labor regimes, workers regularly resist these
"micro-physics of power."[1] In this chapter, I examine their strategies of
agency and resistance, which include the overt defiance described by M.
Max and April above, Gustavo's deliberate underworking, and K.H.'s

strategic avoidance. To be sure, these are widely divergent strategies: M. Max's physical confrontation—"trying to get at the coach"—is dramatically different from Gustavo's "going hiking on Sunday," which itself is dramatically different from K.H.'s tactic of getting "around a few things." In my analysis, however, these are all important modes of worker resistance.

There has been debate among scholars about what worker opposition entails and, therefore, whether all of these strategies are truly *resistance*.[2] While customary forms of worker resistance—strikes and other work stoppages, union organization and collective bargaining—have dominated labor scholarship, many other modes of resistance have long been recognized. In the early 1930s, for instance, Marxist theorist Antonio Gramsci argued that prior to any working-class revolution, an ideological battle over beliefs and ideas—a "war of position"—would be necessary to undermine the power of the ruling classes.[3] In *Manufacturing Consent*, Michael Burawoy brought Gramsci's analysis of hegemony and resistance to the shop floor in an examination of workers' "making out" strategies: their manipulation of output and time in order to maximize their wages.[4] Burawoy found that though such strategies yielded both symbolic and material benefits for the workers (including greater autonomy and higher earnings), they did not produce the revolutionary counter-hegemony that Gramsci had described. To the contrary, such strategies increased workers' productivity and employers' profits, while also ensuring workers' consent and compliance. Thus, Burawoy argued, these "making out" strategies ultimately reified workers' subordination under capitalism.[5]

In political scientist James Scott's conceptualization, however, such strategies should nonetheless be understood as important modes of resistance. Through his analysis of peasant rebellions in the global South, Scott argued that for those without power, resistance does not only take the form of overt rebellion. It also includes an array of more covert "everyday" activities: foot dragging, false compliance, pilfering, slander, sabotage, and more.[6] "Most of the political life of subordinate groups," Scott wrote, "is to be found neither in the overt collective defiance of powerholders nor in complete hegemonic compliance, but in the vast territory between these two polar opposites."[7] And to exclude such covert, quotidian strategies from definitions of resistance, he argued, is to "overlook entirely the vital role of power relations in constraining forms of resistance."[8] By taking such power relations into account, Scott expanded the meaning of resistance to include any actions that "reject subordination."[9]

Though many scholars have since advanced Scott's approach to resistance,[10] there has also been a turn against what is characterized as a tendency to "consider every autonomous act to be an instance of resistance"[11]—or as organization studies scholar Dennis Mumby writes, "seeing [resistance] in every nook and cranny of organizational life."[12] In this vein, geographer Cindi Katz defines "resistance" quite narrowly, for in her view real resistance only stems from oppositional consciousness and leads to emancipatory change.[13] Katz differentiates "resistance" from other more attenuated modes of opposition, which she calls "resilience" and "reworking." She uses "resilience" to refer to survival strategies—"scrappy attempts to make survivable everyday lives and livable futures"—which do not develop from oppositional consciousness and which bolster rather than upend dominant power relations.[14] And she uses "reworking" to refer to pragmatic responses to problems, which may "recalibrate power relations and/or redistribute resources" but which do little to change the overarching power structure.[15]

Although such categories are analytically instructive, Katz's analysis runs the risk of defining resistance out of existence. Foremost, it is unlikely that *any* form of resistance—barring wholesale social and economic revolution—would lead to the broad and deep change that Katz describes. Indeed, even seemingly successful social movements would not meet such criteria.[16] As sociolegal scholars have shown, moreover, even ostensibly *un*successful social movements, which do not produce legal change, can indeed lead to important but hard-to-quantify changes in legal consciousness, thereby laying the foundation for future political mobilization and collective action.[17] Furthermore, as historian Robin D. G. Kelley has argued, acts of apparent accommodation can also be understood as forms of resistance when they give rise to new spaces of oppositional consciousness.[18] In his analysis of Malcolm X's autobiography, for example, Kelley disputes Malcolm's dismissal of his own 1940s zoot-suit-wearing hipster stage as an apolitical and destructive time in which he frivolously embraced "ghetto adornments."[19] By historically contextualizing Black hipster subculture, Kelley argues that this seemingly superficial era of Malcolm's youth "was not a detour on the road to political consciousness but rather an essential element of his radicalization."[20] As Kelley explains,

Seeing oneself and others "dressed up" was enormously important in terms of constructing a collective identity based on something other than wage work, presenting a public challenge to the dominant stereotypes of the black body, and reinforcing a sense of dignity that was perpetually being assaulted.[21]

For Kelley, then, the category of resistance must include those actions that assert and protect one's sense of self from attack.[22]

Thus, while there are obviously limits to resistance—the concept would lose its meaning if it referred to every act—this scholarship suggests that in order to understand what resistance is, it is necessary to understand the context in which it occurs.[23] Rather than narrowing the definition of resistance to unequivocally deliberate, overt, or effectual opposition, this approach broadens it to account for the multiple and mutable power relations that govern social spaces and the people within them. By doing so, it is possible to see that worker resistance may take many shapes: overt defiance against employer demands, to be sure, but also subterranean survival strategies for workers whose bodies and minds are under assault.

As I have shown, the bodies and minds of the workers in this book are indeed under assault, at least to some degree, from the coercion and subjugation that pervade their workplaces. In this chapter, I adopt this more expansive conceptualization of resistance to examine the ways these workers push back against this assault. I identify four interrelated axes by which resistance can be analyzed: its level of action (individual vs. collective), the openness of its defiance (covert vs. overt), the narrative frames used to explain it (e.g., sovereignty vs. rights), and its goal (e.g., "respect" vs. justice). From these analytical dimensions, I construct three broad categories of resistance, which I call "getting by" strategies,[24] "standing up" strategies, and mobilization strategies (see table 2).

In the first case, "getting by" strategies are individual and covert acts of defiance deployed to protect oneself, in these labor regimes, from status coercion and subjugation. Among the workers I interviewed, these strategies were often justified by asserting one's sovereignty as an "adult" or a "man." And for my informants this type of resistance included two particular tactics, which I call "oppositional compliance" and "strategic avoidance." The first is a disengaged form of compliance, such as when workers obey supervisors' mandates but refuse to engage with them in any

Table 2 Resistance strategies in coercive labor regimes

	Level of action	Openness of defiance	Narrative frame	Goal
Getting-by strategies	Individual	Covert: Oppositional compliance Strategic avoidance	Sovereignty, e.g., adulthood masculinity	Self-protection
Standing-up strategies	Individual	Overt: Verbal resistance Labor resistance	Sovereignty, e.g., adulthood slavery masculinity Morality, e.g., religion	Respect
Mobilization strategies	Individual and collective	Overt: Legal mobilization Collective action	Rights, i.e., individual and human rights	Justice

substantial way. The second also entails worker compliance, but its focus is avoidance rather than detachment, such as when workers go out of their way to avoid their supervisors in order to protect themselves from punishment. Yet one might appropriately ask: even within this more expansive conceptualization of resistance, how can *compliance* be categorized as *resistance*? I wondered the same. But from my informants' experiences I learned that these strategies can be used to interrupt—and even destabilize—the coercion and subjugation at the core of these labor regimes. I argue that when deployed to thwart institutional imperatives, compliance and avoidance are indeed forms of resistance.

The second category of resistance in this typology, "standing up" strategies, includes more overt forms of defiance than the first category, though the openness and intensity of such defiance vary substantially. Typically, workers deploy these more overtly defiant strategies in an effort to assert and maintain their sense of self-respect. As with getting-by strategies, they often justify them with narratives of sovereignty and, less often, morality. In some ways, then, this category of resistance is similar to the first. The primary focus of both is the individual worker: both categories entail individual-level acts; they both seek individual-level goals (self-protection and self-respect, respectively); and they are both justified with individual-focused narratives (e.g., self-sovereignty). The differences between them, I find, stem from their goals. When workers feel "disrespected" in these labor regimes, most often because of the technologies of subjugation I have described, they tend to deploy more overtly defiant "standing up" strategies of resistance. But when they are trying to navigate around—and thus protect themselves from—their bosses' sticks of status coercion, they tend to deploy more covert "getting by" strategies.

Meanwhile, as shown in table 2, mobilization strategies—the third category of resistance—are also overtly defiant, but they are usually deployed in an effort to seek justice rather than respect, and are therefore often justified with appeals to rights. Though this category includes both individual and collective action, it tends to be less centered on the individual than the first two categories of resistance. For even though legal mobilization can be an individual-level strategy (e.g., individual rights claims), it still involves mobilizing an entity—law—that extends beyond the individual. Thus, whether through a formal assertion of rights (legal mobilization) or group action (collective mobilization), this third category of resistance is more outwardly focused than the first two.

Though this typology broadly adheres to a progression from "everyday" resistance to more traditional forms of worker organizing, it does not intend to hierarchize these forms of resistance in any way. In fact, I find that there is often overlap and slippage between them. A worker's strategic avoidance of his supervisor to protect himself from punishment can quickly become overt defiance if he feels "disrespected," and the degradation of one worker can prompt others' collective action in the pursuit of "justice." Despite the analytical differences between these strategies, then, there is not such a clear distinction between them in people's everyday lives. Indeed, the same worker is likely to deploy different tactics depending on the situation. Rather than a hierarchy of resistance, this typology highlights the ways context fundamentally shapes the form that resistance takes.

GETTING-BY STRATEGIES: "STAY OUT THEY WAY"

Because bosses in these labor regimes have the power to disrupt workers' personal and familial relations, harm their health and well-being (as well as that of their families), and obstruct their education and future employment, protecting oneself—one's body and mind, one's family and future— against such punitive power is an act of resistance. Moreover, because of the prevalence and depth of subjugation in these regimes, especially in workfare and incarcerated labor, protecting oneself—one's sense of dignity, one's sense of identity—from such subjugation is also an act of resistance. Resistance in this category thus includes efforts to dodge punishment and degradation through "strategic avoidance," as well as efforts to protect one's sense of self through strategically disengaged "oppositional compliance." These are workers' strategies for "getting by" in coercive labor regimes.

Both of these strategies were common among incarcerated workers, though strategic avoidance was their primary tactic. As K.H. said, "As a man, I strive my best not to put myself in harm's way. I know how to get around a few things." For the 47-year-old African American man, this meant usually complying with officers' demands ("I swallowed a lot of things that I really wanted to speak out on"), while also avoiding officers as much as possible. "I'd stay out the way as much as I could," he said. Being able to do so, K.H. asserted, was part of being a "man," thus suggesting his embrace of a more "strategic masculinity"—rather than overtly aggressive hegemonic masculinity—in the face of prisons' many risks.[25]

Twenty-one-year-old F.E. felt the same. "Most of the time I really didn't say too much to the police [COs]," the young African American man said, "because I didn't feel like dealing with their bullshit. I'm not going to deal with all that because, it's a lose-lose." Sal agreed: "I don't really have no conversation for the police," the 24-year-old white man said. "I don't

engage with them at all." Likewise, Dom M. said that his strategy behind
bars "was to move around that, like, stay-out-of-their-face type stuff, don't
say nothing to them." And C. Parks said, "I never really got into alterca-
tions with police."

> I tried to stay *far* from having altercations with the police, because a lot of
> individuals don't even come out [of prison] when it came to police. So, I
> didn't want that. I didn't want that for myself or even my family. So I tried
> my best to, you know, just stay out they way. Stay out they way.

To protect himself and his family, C. Parks—along with many of the other
former prisoners I interviewed—said that he did what he needed to do
while also avoiding officers as much as possible. Not doing so, these incarcerated workers said again and again, would be a "lose-lose": physical violence, solitary confinement, perhaps more prison time, and sometimes
even death.

D.D.G. described his more aggressive version of this strategy. He said
that he would comply with officers' orders, while also refusing to sustain a
façade of friendliness with them. As the 28-year-old Black man explained,
in his view the worst part of his job behind bars was having to deal with
officers who "make jokes and stuff." "I don't want to joke," he said.

> I just want to do my time. . . . I understand my position as: I'm here to do my
> time, because I was doing something wrong in America, I broke the consti-
> tution, etcetera. I did a crime, so I'm here to do my time.

Officers, D.D.G. went on to explain, "are here to get on me in case I get out
of line again." In his view, their job—and their only job—is to discipline
prisoners. Thus, he asked rhetorically,

> So, why would I be friends with you [the officers] when anytime if I do
> something wrong, you're going to jump down my neck? It's like a mother
> and a father to their kid: we're not really friends; this is a business agree-
> ment. You're my dad and my mother, if I need something, I need some help,
> you're going to help me with that. If I get out of line, you're going to give me
> an order. We're not buddy-buddy friends. I'm not going to go to the play-
> ground with you and play, or the jungle gym. It just doesn't go hand in hand.
> And that's what [officers] try to do sometimes. [But,] when they do it, I
> know that it's a trick . . . because you're not my friend and eventually you're

going to remind me of that. [And] you're going to remind me in front of your *real* friends—which is the other fellow COs—and you're going to say some crazy stuff, then I'm going to feel offended. But I did it [to myself] by opening up the door to you, and even let you play with me at the beginning. That's why I don't like it. . . . [So instead] I just walk away, I don't respond. "Did you hear what I said guys?" [an officer might ask, trying to joke.] "Yeah, I heard you" [he would respond in a deadpan manner]. I just keep on walking. I just keep on walking down the company. They say lock it in because they don't like my attitude. Alright, I lock it in, because I'm not going to [joke with you].

D.D.G. refused to act "buddy-buddy" with COs because in his view real friendship was not possible. He was their subordinate, "their kid," and they were in a "business agreement," not a friendship. Had he fallen for their friend "trick," he said, he would have felt hurt—"offended"—when they switched roles to discipline and degrade him by "jumping down his neck" and "saying some crazy stuff" to him. So he protected himself—his feelings, his sense of self—by "just walking away" and refusing to respond to the officers' friendly overtures. As a consequence, he said, he had to return to his cell ("lock it in") because the officers did not "like [his] attitude." But for him, this penalty was worth his self-protection.

As the above passage suggests, D.D.G. discursively used the parent-child relationship to explain his avoidance strategy, but he used it differently from many of the other workers I interviewed. Recall, for example, when Lisa Williams objected to her supervisor's degradation in talking to the workfare workers as if they were her "kids." "We're grown people," Lisa countered indignantly. D.D.G., by contrast, used the same trope not to challenge prisoners' degradation but to justify the hierarchical relationship between officers and prisoners: officers were like his "mother" and "father"; he was like their "kid." His emphasis was thus hierarchy, not sovereignty. And so for him it made sense that COs might discipline and sometimes even degrade him, but he would not "open" himself up to further hurt and indignity by pretending to be their friend.

Workfare workers also deployed strategic avoidance in order to protect themselves and their families. "I just bite my tongue and I sign out and go home," said Will Jones. "Because, for one, I'm not trying to get sanctioned." Although at one point in our interview Will said that he wanted his coworkers to "file a petition" or start some kind of "movement" against their boss for her disrespectful treatment of them, at heart he believed doing so would be counterproductive. "If you do something about it, what's going to happen in the outcome?" the 30-year-old African American man asked rhetorically.

> She's still going to have her job and you're going to be out of a job and you're going to be out of your benefits. . . . So, that's why I bite my tongue and do my job and go home. . . . Bite your tongue and do it. Because if you don't, what's the outcome of it? You're terminated. If you stand up, you're terminated.

Tara Collins also deployed this strategy, particularly since having already been sanctioned once for talking back to her supervisor. "I mean, I'm not a bad person," the 38-year-old Black woman explained.

> I'm grown, I just really don't like people talking to me any type of way. So, like with me and [my supervisor] up here, we argue. Me and her got into it, because she doesn't know how to talk to people. So [now] I don't even talk to her. And it's a shame I have to be uncomfortable. I come here and I sign in, and I stay out of her way, so she doesn't even see me half the time. All she see is my name.

Like Lisa Williams but unlike D.D.G., Tara drew on notions of sovereign adulthood to challenge her supervisor's disparaging treatment. She is a "grown" woman, she argued, and therefore does not "like people talking to [her] any type of way"—disrespectfully, abusively. To protect herself from such mistreatment and, even more, to protect herself and her family from the consequences of challenging it, she took great lengths to avoid her supervisor. "When I say I stay out of the way," Tara went on, "*I stay out of the way*. The only way they know I'm here is because my name is on the piece of paper."

"Getting by" strategies were less common among the athletes and graduate students I interviewed, as were all of the resistance strategies I examine here. This is due to a combination of factors. At the most basic level, I interviewed half as many of these workers, so they are simply less represented among my informants. Yet their relative lack of resistance is likely due to the ways that their labor relations render them less inclined to challenge their supervisors and problems at work, at least in comparison to workfare and incarcerated workers. For example, college athletes and graduate students have a greater degree of choice in both selecting and leaving their labor relations than do workfare and incarcerated workers, even though such "choice" is significantly constrained. This perception of autonomy, in combination with their sense of privilege (stemming from the narratives described in the first chapter), means that many athletes and graduate students feel not only that they have chosen this pursuit but that they are lucky to be there. This dual sense of "choice" and "privilege" makes them more likely to accept workplace conditions, however bad. In addition, as I discuss in more detail below, the mechanisms for filing workplace complaints are substantially less clear for these student workers than they are for incarcerated and workfare workers (at least in New York State). Often these student workers did not know, practically speaking, how they would mount such resistance even if they felt that they could, which for the most part they did not. Unlike workfare and incarcerated workers, moreover, athletes and graduate students rely on their bosses—sometimes long after their jobs have ended—for future employment. Challenging their coaches and advisors might "burn" those much-needed "bridges." As a result of all of these factors, the students who faced significant problems at work tended to endure a great deal until such problems got so bad that they left the job altogether, which itself is a form of resistance, examined below. For the most part, then, these student workers "chose" between submissive compliance and job exit, rather than engaging in on-the-job resistance.

Kate was an exception. Much like Tara, Will, and D.D.G. in workfare and prison labor, she deployed both oppositional compliance and strategic avoidance with her basketball coaches. "Frankly speaking, I wasn't too fond of my coaching staff," the 24-year-old Black woman said.

> So, I mean, I played for them, and I'd do what I needed to do, and I followed the rules. But on the grounds of, like, "Oh, let's have a conversation here," or them asking me, like, "How are you doing today?" There was none of that. It was more of a transaction. Like, you're basically giving me a scholarship, I'm on your team, we understand the transaction, cool.

Just as D.D.G. described prisoner-officer relations as a "business agreement" (albeit a hierarchical one), Kate described athlete-coach relations as a business "transaction." She complied only as much as necessary to sustain that transaction—maintain her scholarship, play basketball, and graduate from an elite university—but like D.D.G., she refused to pretend they were friends. In Sal's words, Kate "didn't really have no conversation for" her coaches.

In a similar way, as described earlier, Zachary Lane said that he made sure to get what he wanted from college athletics while also protecting himself from being "pimped." Unlike Kate, who used both oppositional compliance and strategic avoidance, Zachary primarily used the former. "I knew exactly what I needed to do," the 29-year-old African American man said.

> Because my goal—I didn't come here to be a student, I came here to get to the NFL and be a professional football player. That was my goal. . . . And I knew if I focused on that and did everything I did, everything I could to make sure I got to there, then I'll be fine, and leave with my education.

Zachary resisted being exploited and degraded by college athletics ("getting used up") by maintaining a laser-like focus on achieving his goals.

Sunny adopted a similar strategy as a graduate student in pharmacology. When her faculty boss "sabotaged" the postdoc in her lab, she focused on protecting herself from becoming her boss's new target. "All I thought was 'survival,'" the 41-year-old Hispanic woman said. "I really felt my survival was at stake here, and I couldn't lose it, because it can have really bad repercussions for me. . . . It got down to that point where it was survival mode for everyone." In order to "survive" and protect herself from those "bad repercussions," Sunny—much like Kate, Zachary, Tara, and Will—kept her head down and did what she felt she needed to do, which in her case meant showing up for weekly meetings with her advisor, who insisted on such meetings but who rarely attended. This oppositional compliance was as much as Sunny felt she could do; more overt forms of resistance did not seem possible. "There's nowhere we can go" to complain, she said.

STANDING-UP STRATEGIES: "I DON'T LET NOBODY DISRESPECT ME"

Whereas the workers I interviewed deployed "getting by" strategies to protect themselves in some way, usually from the punitive technologies of

status coercion, they deployed "standing up" strategies in order to preserve their sense of dignity in the face of subjugation or exploitation. They
did so in two ways: (1) verbal resistance, talking back to what they saw as
disrespectful treatment, and (2) labor resistance, including refusing to
work, underworking, and leaving jobs they deemed too degrading or
exploitative. Though these strategies typically involved more overt defiance than "getting by" strategies, they ranged significantly in the intensity
and explicitness of their insubordination.

At the less defiant end of the spectrum, for example, some workers said
that they strategically used kindness and respect in an effort to maintain
their own sense of self-respect. Though at first glance this strategy does
not seem to be a form of resistance, much like the getting-by strategies
described above, I argue that it becomes one when it is deployed to coun-
ter institutionalized subjugation. Recall the example of Malcolm X, whose
so-called ghetto adornments arguably helped him preserve a "sense of dignity" despite it "perpetually being assaulted."[26] Likewise, because the
institutionalized degradation and dehumanization in these labor regimes
renders workers' sense of dignity under assault, I argue that pushing back
against this assault—even with kindness—is a form of resistance. In
prison, for example, Mary said that despite being treated "like a slave and
not valued," she maintained her sense of self-respect by treating the COs
respectfully. "I'm a hard worker," the 52-year-old white woman explained,
"because I work for the Lord."

> I don't work for anybody but [the Lord], you know. That's where I just keep
> my mind-set. . . . It's like, I must have needed to have that [officer who
> treated me disrespectfully] in my life for whatever reason. . . . You know,
> there's people every day, no matter where you are, they just don't like you or
> whatever. But I had a lot of pride in myself. . . . I would say "good morning"
> every morning and "goodbye," and . . . I did what I had to do. I felt good
> about myself.

For Mary, deliberately being kind to an officer who treated her "very
unfair" enabled her to preserve her sense of self-respect and, in so doing,
allowed her to take what she saw as the moral high road (as articulated
through religiosity). Because she worked "for the Lord" and not that
officer, and because she behaved righteously in doing so, she was able to

defend herself against the degradation of prison life in general, and that officer in particular. She could feel "good about [her]self."

K.H. deployed a similar strategy in prison, but rather than using it to sustain his sense of self-respect, he did so to change COs' behavior. "Some people you can kill with kindness," he explained. As a result, K.H. said that he was often able to get the "respect" he knew he deserved. Graduate student Laine did the same. "You want to make [faculty members] think that you think that they're the smartest person," the 30-year-old white woman said. "That's the best way of success. I call everyone 'brilliant.' When I'm talking to them, I work in the word 'brilliant' because it makes our conversations easier . . . especially with the real jerks."

Sunny also described using this killing-with-kindness approach with her "abusive" advisor, though she explicitly requested respectful treatment as well. "I've never let her abuse me," she said.

> I've always been very clear about, you know, "I don't appreciate being treated like this, or being talked to [like this]." And I've tried to be very professional when I talk to her, and not take it personally.

Kimberly Mays adopted a similar approach with her own advisor, at least initially, though she said that she ultimately lost her ability to sustain it. "I normally tried to do my best to have some diplomacy with him," the 37-year-old African American woman said, "because I recognized that he was in a position with power. I knew the kind of control he had. So, I would try to extinguish a lot of hot topics." But when her advisor was overtly disrespectful toward her in front of her coworkers, Kimberly said that she began to push back more forcefully.

> When he decided to have a conversation—like a blow-up conversation— with me in the lab, at my bench, with all of my colleagues looking in and listening on instead of pulling me into his office, like he does with everybody else, that's when—that was it. That's when I was like, *You have no respect for me, so I'm not going to have any for you* . . . I lost all respect for him at that point. I was like, "I don't care." . . . [I said,] "Are you kidding me? You got to have this conversation with me right now like this?" . . . And I said, you know, "The best thing for me to do would be to leave your lab, and finish my dissertation somewhere else, because my ability to maintain any professionalism is fleeting."

Although Kimberly did not leave his lab, because she could not have done so without losing all of her research, she did drop her façade of deference, which ultimately contributed to her belief that she had to leave academia. As the reader will recall, Kimberly could not use her advisor as a reference because in her view he was not a reliable one—largely because she had been openly defiant in this way. It was also true that she did not *want* to use him as a reference, because he had mistreated her and she did not want to remain under his power. Yet without his recommendation, she could not pursue academic jobs.

Workfare workers described a similar process of abandoning their usual performance of deference in response to disrespectful treatment. Like Kimberly, when they felt that such disrespect was extreme, they gave up any expectation of retaining their status—in their case, as welfare recipients in good standing—and became explicitly insubordinate. But most of the time, workfare workers tried to engage in defiance in a way that would not jeopardize their status, walking a very thin tightrope between challenging their mistreatment and minimizing their insubordination. For instance, Sasha Reed said that she could push back "a little bit" against her supervisor's disrespect, "especially," the 26-year-old African American woman said, "because we're all grown here, so you can't just talk to me any kind of way." But if she pushed back too much or too often, "like if it happened every day," she explained, her supervisor "is not going to tolerate it. . . . That's when people get termed [sanctioned]." Felisha Jones said that she too could carefully push back against her supervisor's disrespect. "She'll be having attitudes," the 23-year-old African American woman said of her workfare boss. "She be coming here with attitude, so I'm like, 'Leave that at home, because we didn't do nothing to you.'" Once, Felisha recalled, her supervisor replied, "'I don't got no attitude.'" Felisha insisted otherwise: "I'm like, 'You have attitude.'" But then, Felicia said, she had to let it go. "I have to drop it, because she'll be like, 'Don't make me have to sanction you,' and all this other stuff. I'm like, I ain't got to do that, I got kids. . . . [So] I have to drop it and just do what I got to do." Even still, for both Felisha and Sasha, being able to voice their disapproval of their supervisors' degrading treatment helped them preserve their sense of self-respect. They were able to assert their status as sovereign, respect-worthy adults. "We're all grown here," Sasha said. "We didn't do nothing to you," Felisha said. "Leave that [attitude] at home."

April Smith also used this strategy with her workfare supervisor, and with apparent success. When I asked if she had experienced any problems with her supervisor, she said, "Yeah, I gave her a couple of words. She have an issue with respect. She has a bad attitude sometimes," the 30-year-old African American woman went on to explain.

> Like, if she have a bad day, it's like everybody is a problem. *I* have issues at home from time to time . . . I do, but I come here, you don't know that, because I don't let it be shown. . . . I'm not going to be like, "Oh, I'm having a bad day, so I'm going to talk to you disrespectful, like you're smaller than me."

In response to her supervisor's "bad attitude," April said that she had "demanded [her] respect" by saying,

> "Listen, you're going to talk to me with respect. I talk to you with respect. I understand you're going through things. I'm going through them too, but I don't come off at you. Don't talk to me disrespectful. . . . I don't let my husband disrespect me. I don't let nobody disrespect me. . . . It's not going to happen."

After that, April said, her supervisor began treating her more respectfully. "She just started saying, 'Good morning, good morning,'" a basic level of courtesy that does not seem to be a given in workfare workplaces. April thus felt that she had gotten her "respect" and, in so doing, successfully navigated the tightrope between defiance and deference.

In prison, Larry G. deployed a similar strategy. Although he said that he generally "held [his] tongue" ("when you're in Rome, you got to do what the Romans do"), he also refused to disregard degrading treatment. If an officer spoke to him disrespectfully, the 50-year-old Black American man said, he would look at the officer intently, even though as a prisoner he was supposed to look down. "The way I just *look* at them," he said, and then he would say,

> "*Are you done?*" They say, "Yeah, I'm done." I say, "Okay, have a nice day officer," and I walk away. And then they look at you, like, "I can't get him." See? "You're not going to get no rise out of [Larry]."

In Larry's view, his assertive but controlled response to officers' disrespectful treatment earned him "respect" behind bars.

Derrick made the same point, though he also said that he was willing to get aggressive, even violent, if he deemed it necessary to "get respect." "Like with me, I pretty much did what I wanted" in prison, the 33-year-old African American man proclaimed. "You're not going to tell me nothing that I can't do. You're not my mom. My *mom* doesn't tell me what to do. She *asks* me. So, that was my motto. I made sure I got my respect." Thus, like April and Sasha above (and M. Max below), Derrick asserted his sovereignty: he is an adult, not a child being ordered around by his parents. In order to retain his sense of sovereignty behind bars, Derrick said that he adopted a "nonchalant" attitude. "It's about how you carry yourself," he told me.

> You carry yourself the correct way, you say the right things out of your mouth, you could get a pass for a lot of things. . . . When you respect me, I respect you. You don't respect me, I don't respect you. I'm going to treat you back the same way you treat me.

After detailing his background in martial arts, Derrick said that if a CO treated him disrespectfully, he would indeed "put [his] foot down." "If you put me in that corner where I have to [fight], then I got to do what I got to do. . . . That's the only way you get respect."

Though most of the workers I interviewed did not describe using such violence to challenge their subjugation, there were a few exceptions. For instance, Will Jones said that he punched his former workfare supervisor for calling him a racial slur—"My boss called me the N-word, so I punched him in his mouth"—and he was sanctioned as a result. In addition, M. Max got into a physical altercation with his coach after the coach cursed at him. "I wasn't as humble as I am now," the 37-year-old Black man explained with a laugh.

> I was, you know, just a young kid, from the ghetto, from the hood, come from nothing. . . . I didn't appreciate the way he was talking to me, trying to call me out on my name, or whatever. So, we had a little blowup on the sideline. . . . I was trying to get at the coach, he was trying to get at me. I was a grown man. I guess he didn't understand and wanted to talk to me like I was a kid, and I just wasn't having that. . . . So, you know, I gave him *my* piece of mind. In the long run, it cost me but, right then, I felt good.

The "cost," M. Max said, was that he was suspended for a game and later had to explain the incident to NFL recruiters. But for him, this cost was worth it. He "felt good" asserting his sovereignty: "a grown man" giving the coach "[*his*] piece of mind."

More often than physical aggression, however, workers reported being verbally defiant to their supervisors in an effort to resist their subjugation. In prison, for example, D.Q. said that he "lost [his] cool" and told an officer who was "disrespecting" him "how [he] felt." As the 27-year-old African American man recalled, the officer was upset because D.Q. had been late for work two days in a row, and was going to give him a disciplinary ticket. D.Q. pushed back, arguing that he had not been late the second day, that in fact it had been the officer's fault for not seeing him come to work on time. In response, D.Q. recalled, the officer "makes a big argument about it" and D.Q. "started ignoring him." But then, he said,

> I just felt like he just went overboard. He wanted to keep going with it, you know, I felt like he was disrespecting me, and I just, I lost my cool on him. . . . I didn't put my hands on him, but I told him how I felt.

As a result, D.Q. said that he was put in solitary confinement for 45 days. "It was worth it to me, though," he said, "because I got my point across and I felt good about it." Like M. Max, he felt that he had successfully challenged his "disrespect."

Pauline Wilson and Tara Collins also recounted incidents of overt insubordination in response to their workfare supervisors' disrespectful treatment. Pauline told her supervisor to "kiss [her] ass" after their disagreement about taking a water break. Tara said that she called her supervisor "the B-word." As the 38-year-old Black woman explained,

> I had got into a domestic violence situation and I had a black eye when I came [to work], and I had sunglasses on. And, you know, [the supervisor] asked me what happened, and I told her, I was comfortable with telling her. But [then] she was actually telling the two other participants in the program about my situation. And I was like, "Yo, that's not cool. My business is my business."

In response, Tara's supervisor reportedly said, "'You can't tell me what I can or what I cannot say.'" "So," Tara recalled, "we exchanged a few words.

I called her the B-word, and I left out." Tara said that she was sanctioned as a result, as Pauline almost certainly would have been had she not relinquished her public assistance. Yet despite such negative consequences, like D.Q. and M. Max, they felt it was worth it. As Tara said, she refused to be talked to in "any type of way."

In addition to such verbal (and sometimes physical) resistance, the workers I interviewed engaged in various types of labor resistance, particularly work refusal, underworking, and job exit. Work refusal was the most common, especially among workfare and incarcerated workers, who said that they sometimes refused to perform jobs they deemed overly demanding, degrading, or exploitative. For instance, Tara Collins said that she would not do the more arduous landscaping jobs her workfare crew often did in the city's public parks. "I'm going to tell you something about me," she declared.

> When we go out to this park, I don't mow no grass. I have four sons. I don't mow grass, I don't Weedwack, I don't shovel. So, when they do that, I'll do something else. Like maybe I will sweep up the grass for them, or I will carry the garbage bags for them while they're moving furniture and stuff like that. You see here: I know what [my supervisor] *want* me to do, but I know what I'm *going* to do.

Tara refused to do such work, she explained, because she found it degrading or, as she said, "ignorant." "We don't 'work,'" she asserted,

> we do *other* people's jobs, we do the city's jobs, we do jobs that the mayor's team should be out doing. You know, this is supposed to be a workfare program, which is supposed to help enlighten you and enrich you, to help you learn how to succeed and how to keep a job. [But] it's really a deterrent. We're coming here every day, getting ate up, dirty, mowing grass, shoveling snow, I mean all type of stuff. That's not "work," that's *ignorant*.

In Tara's view, being required to perform such difficult and dirty work without pay ("*other* people's jobs") was unduly degrading. And she refused to do it.

Indeed, a number of workfare and incarcerated workers said that they refused to perform particularly "dirty" jobs. For workfare workers, such jobs usually entailed cleaning bathrooms; for prisoners, cleaning feces and other bodily fluids. As workfare worker Kim Hunky explained, "I don't mind cleaning, but when you're telling me to get down and clean behind the toilet, I'm not going to . . . I'm not a slave." Workfare worker Ambrosia Washington agreed. "I don't want to clean a bathroom, where everybody used [the toilet]. Like, I wipe down the elevator or I vacuum, different duties, or even mop the stairs. But I just don't like doing the bathrooms." Likewise, in prison Derrick said that without being given proper equipment, he refused to clean "an outhouse for the whole prison, like all the feces and urine and all that stuff."

> I'm not cleaning that shit. . . . If you ain't got any special suit for me to wear to clean that, I'm not cleaning that. All you get is some rubber gloves, and you still got your same uniform on, your green uniform. . . . We had to clean up the septic tanks and all that. I'm not cleaning that shit. You give me a special suit to wear, I'd go in there and clean. I ain't got a problem with it. . . . [Otherwise] no, it's not going down.

Meanwhile, James D. said that when he was working in the prison mess hall, he refused to serve pizza that had fallen on the floor, despite being ordered to do so. But had he served such pizza, James believed, he would have degraded not only himself but also the prison population. Although, in retrospect, James said that he might have found "a better way . . . to bring it up," he "still wouldn't do it." "In my character, there are certain things I don't care what the consequences are," the 52-year-old African American man explained, highlighting his sense of morality—his "character"—as the justification for his work refusal. "I'm going to stand up [in that situation]," he said. "I believe that there should be a line or demarcation for some things in life." Apache agreed. His line, he said, was cleaning up after corrections officers.

> One thing that I refused to do—and this is definitely for the record—me, personally, I refuse to clean up anything after a police officer. I'm just, I'm not doing it, because that's really slave labor. I'm not cleaning up after you. No. I clean up after the people that's in here amongst us. I feed us, I cook for us, you know what I'm saying? . . . [But] I never cleaned up *nothing* after a cop.

For this Black American man, cleaning up after "cops" was unduly degrading labor. And to explain why, he drew on rhetoric of slavery. Echoing Kim

Hunky's description of cleaning toilets for workfare, Apache said that he refused to do such "slave labor," thereby asserting his sovereignty as an autonomous being worthy of respect. Or as Derrick said simply, when faced with the prospect of his everyday clothes being smeared with feces, "I'm not cleaning that shit."

While such work refusal was the most common form of resistance for jobs deemed overly degrading, underworking was the most common form of resistance for jobs deemed overly exploitative. Among my informants, however, this was not a common strategy: just 3 of the 121 workers I interviewed said that they had deliberately underworked.[27] C. Parks was one of them. "I didn't overwork," he said of his labor behind bars. "I'm like, I'm not overworking for this little bit of money." Qwon agreed. "I never went over and beyond," he said. Likewise, in graduate school Gustavo said that he decided to be a "slacker," at least by graduate school standards. "My schedule is here [in the lab] from, like, eight in the morning until eight at night, you know, six days a week. . . . I'm not going to work ninety hours a week for thirty thousand dollars a year. Fuck that," he said. "I'm going hiking on Sunday."

Eventually, Gustavo decided to leave graduate school altogether, thus shifting his resistance strategy from underworking to job exit. "I mean I love science, you know, I love scientific research. I like hearing about discoveries," the 35-year-old Chicano man explained. "But it turns out that answering a scientific question takes being in a lab labeling very tiny tubes and getting yelled at while you're doing it." For him, it was not worth it. In order to preserve his sense of self-respect against this double assault—both degradation ("getting yelled at") and exploitation (working "ninety hours a week for thirty thousand dollars a year")—he gave up on his "love" for science. Meanwhile, both Sunny and Emily left what they each described as "toxic" bosses and work environments. Rather than leaving graduate school altogether, however, they joined other labs and eventually completed their degrees, though not without significant costs, which included losing their research and publications, changing subfields, and prolonging their time in graduate school. For these students, job exit was the course of last resort. Even when faced with extremely difficult working conditions, most graduate student workers remained in their labs and completed their degrees.

Job exit was equally rare among the athletes I interviewed. The costs for transferring to another school were simply too great. Football player Bill Murdock was an exception. "If things didn't turn out right, I was pretty quick to leave," the 34-year-old white man said. Though he initially dismissed his inclination for leaving as being "young and dumb," he went on to explain that transferring schools was his strategy for dealing with coaches' unfulfilled promises. "First of all, the coaches make big promises," Bill said. "Like, I was told by one coach, 'Oh, yeah, you're going to come here, you're going to have a chance to start as a freshman.'" But when he arrived on campus that fall, Bill recalled, that coach had already left the team and the new coach had other priorities and promises to keep. So Bill left.

Bruce also transferred to a different university. Though he had previously planned to do so in order to play for a more elite football program, after he lost that opportunity he left out of principle, as a form of resistance. "I was so upset that this guy ruined opportunities for me to go play somewhere else that there's no way I was going to stay and play for him." For Bruce, job exit—despite its costs—was the only way to oppose his coach's ill-treatment.

Jahad also left his job in prison, though because of exploitation rather than degradation. As the 49-year-old African American and American Indian man explained, he was working as a welder in a Corcraft[28] factory, until he compared his meager wages to the company's sizable sales. Then he decided to "quit."

> I quit when the numbers came down for the year that I worked, and our Corcraft [factory] made thirteen point one million dollars. . . . I tallied up all of my pay stubs, and I think I barely made three hundred or four hundred dollars for that year [at $0.33 an hour]. And I said, "It's slave labor," and literally that's what it is. It was slave labor to me. . . . [So] I quit.

In Jahad's view, the difference between his wages and his factory's sales was too extreme, rendering his work "slave labor." In order to "quit," however, Jahad said that he had to submit a request for another job assignment and await its approval by prison officials. Simply walking off the job was not an option.

By contrast, both April Johnson and Sasha Reed said that they walked off their workfare jobs when their complaints about bedbugs in the workplace were ignored. "I'm showing [the supervisor] I'm getting bit by bed-bugs," April recalled.

> And he's saying I still have to work back there. And I didn't understand it. I
> don't want to just walk off, because I have my two kids. I'm thinking about
> [them] at the end of the day. But *come on.* [So] I started not going back
> there.

Sasha Reed recounted a nearly identical story. There were "bedbugs going around," she said, "people coming out from the back with bumps and stuff. And they still want you to work. . . . I left the site, just left." But as all of these workers' stories suggest, job exit was usually reserved for more extreme incidents (if it was available to them at all), instances in which they felt that their subjugation or exploitation was particularly acute. Because of their bosses' sticks of status coercion, job exit usually came with significant costs.

MOBILIZATION STRATEGIES: "I CAN BECOME A SOLDIER FOR HUMAN RIGHTS"

When the workers I interviewed sought justice, rather than "respect" or self-protection, they were more likely to deploy mobilization strategies, which included both rights claims and collective action. In the first case, even though none of these workers had access to traditional human resources departments, all of them could (technically) file a complaint with some kind of authority—though to be sure not without significant fear of retribution. For example, prisoners in New York State can lodge complaints via the prison system's inmate grievance program,[29] and those I interviewed did so with some frequency. Fourteen ex-prisoners said that they had filed at least one, and often multiple, grievances, albeit with mixed success. In their view, grievances were a deeply imperfect apparatus for justice.

C. Parks said that he filed a grievance about the incident in which the officer did not "pop" his gate at the usual time and he refused to rush to get to work. He was charged with insubordination, and as punishment he got a five-dollar ticket and 15 days of keeplock. To dispute these charges, the

27-year-old African American man requested a hearing at which his neighboring prisoner could testify, but, he said, "they denied my witness, [so I] filed a grievance." C. Parks thus mobilized law twice in this incident: first by requesting a hearing and second by filing a grievance when they would not accept his witness at the hearing. Neither of his efforts were successful. "The grievance came back saying there's no real reason for him to be there," C. Parks said.

> But he's a witness! His witnessing was to tell you that I didn't do all those things: I didn't slam my gate, I didn't cuss at him. All I said was I'm not rushing, because you opened my gate late. . . . [But] they wouldn't hear it out.

At that point, C. Parks believed it was a "lose-lose situation." He felt he had no other option but to take the punishment.

Meanwhile, Jahad said that some of his coworkers in the Corcraft factory filed grievances over unexplained fluctuations in their bonuses. Such bonuses were important, Jahad explained, because they could as much as double the workers' pay rate. "Usually we'll get a hundred percent bonus, you know, eighty percent bonus or whatever," he recalled.

> [But] it was a time period where, you know, the bonus just dropped to zero for three, four weeks at a time, without any cause for it. We didn't know why, but we know that we were putting out the same amount of product or even more. . . . So that was a problem. . . . We didn't have any reason [explanation]. So people filed grievances, because that was our only [recourse] or whatever. They file complaints, but [prison officials] said, "Oh, this is not grievable, just something that's a privilege. You're not entitled to the bonus. We just give you the bonus for your good work."

Though Jahad himself had not filed a grievance in this case, it was this seemingly unfair and unexplained decrease in his pay, along with the disparity between his wages and the factory's multimillion-dollar sales, which led him to leave the job. But in doing so, he also lost the higher wages and sense of "normalcy" the factory job had given him.

A.T. said that he filed "many" grievances over the course of his nearly 40-year prison sentence. Once, for example, he filed a grievance about his unpredictable and overly long work hours in the laundry room. As the 64-year-old Black man recalled,

Guys have to leave their laundry bags in the morning in front of the laundry room, and you know, pick them up at the end of the day. [The laundry] is supposed to be done. You know, these were a lot of laundry bags. . . . On the floor I was on, I think we had, like, [only] fifty people. But, you know, these are guys who were working; some work on the outside crews and stuff. They get dirty. They have a lot of stuff [to wash]. But the issue was that our officers always wanted to shut down the laundry room unnecessarily. So, what should have taken from eight to maybe one, would take me sometimes to, like, eight o'clock at night.

"The work is not hard," A.T. went on to explain. The problem was that he was not compensated for the additional time, and the hours were simply too long. "I had no time for myself," he said, "so I filed a grievance about it." But his grievance was not successful. Prison officials said that they had the prerogative to shut down the laundry room at any time. "I kind of knew going in that I wasn't going to be successful," A.T. recalled. In fact, whenever prisoners file grievances, he explained, "You're grieving the same people who grieved you. It doesn't really change much. All it does is let them know what you're thinking. . . . But I had to try."

Workfare workers felt the same way about "fair hearings," procedures they could request to dispute workfare problems and other public assistance concerns, including unwarranted sanctions.[30] "But," Tasha Love said, "I don't think that works." Take, for example, Pauline Wilson's water-break incident. After she left social services that day, there was in fact a hearing about the incident. But as she recalled, the supervisor in question did not attend, and when Pauline asked why he was not there, she was told, "Well, we got his side of the story." But when she asked to read his version of the events, her request was denied. Pauline said that she then recounted her version of the story, including when she told her supervisor to "kiss [her] ass." As she remembered it,

> They said, "Well, you know you can't disrespect him." I said, "Well, what about him disrespecting me?" And the lady was like, "Well, actually, like he said, he doesn't need the job that you're doing. He *has* a job." . . . I was like, *whatever.* I said, "Y'all can have this." So, for months I was out without a job.

In Pauline's view, the hearing was almost a rerun of the original incident: she was chastised for not respecting her supervisor, while his disrespectful treatment of her was dismissed, even normalized. "'He *has* a job,'" Pauline remembered them telling her, a statement that was seemingly meant to justify her supervisor's authority to discipline—and even degrade—her.

Though for Pauline such legal mobilization seemed to be a futile attempt for justice, a few workfare workers said that this process did indeed allow them to claim their rights. In fact, Gail Cornwall said that she was able to get several sanctions overturned through fair hearings, though she also believed that her success provoked additional sanctions on her. "I think they just found a reason to take their money from me," Gail said, "because I was that one that fight them. I would go for the fair hearings." Yet for the 56-year-old African American woman, the extra sanctions were worth it. By filing the complaints and winning, her sense of justice was affirmed. "They didn't think I was smart enough. But I *was* smart enough," Gail declared.

> I got receipts from them when I brought the paperwork in. I would ask downstairs—because you have to drop everything off on the first floor—I will say, "I need a receipt." The receipt is my way of saying, "If you don't have what you're supposed to have from me, then you're telling a lie, because I have the receipt."

And so when Gail arrived at the hearing with all of her receipts in hand, showing that she had filed the requisite paperwork and therefore should not have been sanctioned, the judge ruled in her favor. As she went on to explain,

> I don't know if they were doing it [imposing sanctions] because they were going to make me feel the pain in some kind of way, which they didn't make me feel the pain, because God works in all ways, you know. So, everything that [they] were trying to do to me, it was like hitting [them] back, you know. It wasn't really hurting me. It was just that I knew I was right and I knew I had the paperwork. So they started treating me a little different, which didn't matter, because I knew I still had to be who I am.

Ultimately, even though Gail got better treatment as a result of her legal mobilization, such treatment had not been her goal. For her, the goal was justice. "It was just that I knew I was right," she said.

Johnny Dominoes also filed a workfare grievance, though in his case it was to recoup unpaid earnings rather than challenge a sanction. As the

54-year-old Hispanic man recalled, one of his workfare assignments was somewhat unusual. Instead of "volunteering" at a typical workfare site, he was assigned to work as a truck driver as part of New York City's "Back to Work" program. The trucking employer was supposed to pay him hourly wages, which the city would subsidize. But like any workfare assignment, if Johnny did not comply with the job's requirements, he would be sanctioned. "The problem," Johnny explained, "was I was supposed to get paid, but the employer held back my wages."

> He was not paying me. He explained to me that it's not incumbent upon him to pay me, that I have to wait to get paid by the state, the social services, so [I should] speak to my caseworker. So, I kept getting the run along, but, in the meantime, in order not to have my case closed for failure to comply, I kept working for free. That lasted like a month and half, and then I finally got a paycheck, but it was only a meager check. [The boss] claimed that it was because after everything else was paid for, like, uniforms, gas, truck expense—all kinds of stuff—tolls, tickets, and everything. But I told him nobody ever told me I had to pay for gasoline tax and all this other stuff, and I never got a ticket. So, I said, "No, I think you're doing something illegal here." . . . So, I went back and I filed the Attorney General's office to investigate, and they forced them to pay me back what they owe. . . . I finally got paid after like eight months after the fact.

In the end, Johnny attained some sense of justice, and not only because he recouped his own wages but because his grievance—along with others'— prompted the closing of that workfare site. "They actually investigated," he said, "and they found that there were a lot of illegalities and violations going on with the subsidies: taking money and not paying people. . . . And they shut it down." For Johnny, in this case at least, justice was served.

Although the procedures for such legal mobilization were relatively well defined for the workfare and incarcerated workers I interviewed,[31] they were less standardized and more opaque for both graduate students and athletes, even though universities—and athletic programs and academic departments within them—often have some guidelines for filing complaints.[32] Yet most of these student workers did not know how they might lodge such a complaint and, even more, whether doing so would be useful. As Suzanne said, "I don't even know where you *would* complain. . . . The PIs are pretty well protected by the universities. I don't think there's a lot that can be done."

In fact, the ex–graduate students I interviewed often lamented the apparent absence of formal grievance procedures in their workplaces. Henry, for example, contrasted such procedures in private-sector labs with those in academic labs. In the former, he said, "there is a pretty clear line" for how to deal with workplace issues: "You should talk to your supervisor. There's going to be somebody in HR that you should talk to. If your supervisor is unresponsive, you can talk to your supervisor's supervisor." But "in academia, it's like,"

> *Who the hell is your supervisor's supervisor?* I guess you can go talk to the department chair, but the department chair is not the boss of your PI. It's not an accurate characterization. Even the dean, who is arguably more [the PI's boss], it's still a tenuous argument.

Emily made a similar point: "People who are real employees who are abused can appeal to their boss's boss or to HR for some sort of intervention. But," the 30-year-old white woman said, "your best solution in grad school . . . is to leave your [lab]—and not just your best solution, but in many cases your *only* solution." Thus, legal mobilization for graduate students was almost unheard of. For them, job exit seemed to be the "*only* solution."

In this regard, Gustavo was an exception among the graduate students I interviewed, though a few others had informally (and usually anonymously) contacted some kind of authority about problems with their advisors. For his part, Gustavo said that he filed a complaint with the university's ombudsman because he believed that his authorship of a paper had been unfairly revoked. While in graduate school, he explained, he had written an article based on a set of viruses he had developed. Before submitting it for publication, however, his advisor wanted to replicate the results, and so publication was delayed. Gustavo then left graduate school, and a new student joined his advisor's lab and ran the replications. That student was given first authorship by the advisor, and Gustavo was removed from the paper altogether. "But the truth is," Gustavo said, "I developed all the technology that went into that, which was six months' worth of work to develop a full suite of viruses. . . . I developed all the technology that made that shit happen." Ultimately, however, his complaint was unsuccessful. The other student remained first author because,

Gustavo explained, "the advisor has the final say."[33] Such authority is simply a given in the academy.

Meanwhile, none of the former college athletes I interviewed said that they had lodged formal complaints. Indeed, as others have observed, college athletes—in particular—have little practicable recourse against coaches' mistreatment and abuse.[34] They "just have to go with the flow," as former basketball player Mike Smith said, or leave the team altogether, as Bruce did.

Collective legal mobilization was, not surprisingly, even less common than individual rights claims. Of the 121 workers I interviewed, only one— former prisoner James D.—took part in a class action lawsuit, though two others were the beneficiaries of such suits: A.T. was awarded a settlement for his injuries during the 1971 Attica uprising, and athlete Sebastian Majella was awarded a settlement for the commercial use of his likeness in video games. James, for his part, was involved in a lawsuit against racial discrimination in prison; he even testified in court about the ways officers routinely discriminated against African American and Latino prisoners in job assignments, punishment, housing, and more. "The best assignments were going to Caucasian guys," he explained. "And if I got caught with a razor and you got caught with a razor," James told me, as African American "I would get an outside charge and you wouldn't. And housing, the best house blocks were mostly, you know, Caucasians. . . . It was very serious." Though the prisoners eventually won the case, James said that those who had testified were targeted for retribution as the case was moving through the legal system. "We were attacked by some staff who said that we were snitching on them," James recalled. The prisoners were physically beaten, he said, showing me his scars, and then they were put in solitary confinement on trumped-up charges. "They tried to say that we assaulted them," James recalled, "but when the District Attorney investigated, all of our stories were the same, because we told the truth, and theirs wasn't, so they ended up indicting some of the correction officers." Once again, the prisoners won their case, but by that time James had been in "the box" for two full years (of a five-year sentence). Ultimately, James and the other prisoners got justice, but at great personal cost.

In addition to such collective legal mobilization, some of the workers I interviewed engaged in other forms of collective action, including work stoppages and worker advocacy and organizing. For instance, A.T. said that he and his coworkers in the prison mess hall refused to serve break-fast one morning to protest the officers' treatment of a fellow prisoner. As A.T. explained,

> There was a guy, he had some juice, working in the mess hall. . . . We'd all gotten juice at the same time. Now they were on him for whatever reason. It wasn't really about the juice, it was about something else, but they ran up to this guy and told him that the juice was fermented, that he was making, you know, hooch, right? *No.* If *his* is fermented, mine is [too], you know? So . . . we were all going to stick together for this guy. . . . [The next day] we just refused to feed the population. . . . When the guys filed into the mess hall . . . we all stood against the wall and said, "If you want it, you got to get it your-self." Oh man! They went nuts. You know, they just took what they wanted. It was like almost a food fight.

As a consequence, A.T. said, the protesters were put in solitary confine-ment and then separated from each other by being transferred to different prisons across the state. "It just goes to show what they will do," he said. "There was like one hundred, I want to say about a hundred and twenty guys, they transferred every single one of us to other facilities."

O.G. was also involved in a prison work stoppage. The goal of the pro-test, the 62-year-old African American man explained, was to make parole possible for maximum-security prisoners. "We tried to push them for good time," he said, because even though early release for good behavior was law "on the books," it was not law "in action."[35] "In New York State, they say you got good time, but it was never—it *was* no good time," O.G. said. In order to change the system, he said, prisoners first "tried to peti-tion the commissioners and then they tried to go through the courts, but they wasn't trying to give it up. So, [the prisoners] said, we can force their hand by [going on strike]. But that didn't work either." As O.G. recalled,

> So different prisons went on strike. Everybody refused to go to programs, stayed in their cells. But then, they forced everybody back out. . . . They brought in what they call the CERT team.[36] These guys dressed in orange and they got these big long sticks, and they come in and they start tearing up everybody's cells, going to beat you down. That was to force individuals out of fear and intimidation to go back to work.

The strike was broken, and the system remained intact. But even though such protests did not unequivocally attain justice, both O.G. and A.T. felt morally affirmed by their part in them. "It was the idea that if they can do it to him, they're going to do it to you," A.T. said. "We had no unions, so we couldn't fight it," O.G. explained. "Sticking together," A.T. said, was the only way to do so.

Meanwhile, all five of the workfare workers I interviewed in New York City were active in community organizations that organized and advocated for the rights of poor people. As Johnny Dominoes recalled, it was his very first interaction with a community organizer that sparked his oppositional legal consciousness and led him to become involved in this advocacy work.

> [The organizer] said, "Do you like the way you're being treated?" I said, "No." [She asked,] "Do you think you have a voice?" I said, "No." "Do you think you could make things change for the system currently as they are?" I'm like, "I hope so." She said, "Well, attend one of our meetings. You have rights that you're not aware of, and you also can make the legislature change things." . . . I never thought I had those rights. I never thought I could have a voice, and so that's what brought me to the organization.

For Johnny, the fact that he had served in the military fueled his anger at this sense of rightslessness and voicelessness as a workfare worker and welfare recipient. "I felt humiliated and disgraced," he said.

> Because I protected my country for twelve years [in the Middle East] and I just don't understand why Americans—people—are being treated this way. I don't understand. I mean, we do so much for every other country, so why is it looked down upon when we need food or, like, a little handout or help. Like it's a disgrace. And, you know, you feel like a pariah. And I just don't understand that. I mean, I thought America would take good care of Americans first, like, what the democracy is for, what the Constitution stands for. . . . Yet when we [veterans] go through this system, it's an eye-opener. It's very humiliating.

"So, this is my new battle," Johnny avowed. "I can become a soldier for human rights—not just to fight with the bullets and take life, but now I can fight for human rights."

.   .   .   .   .

Through these strategies of resistance, the workers I interviewed sought to protect their bodies and minds from punishment, maintain and proclaim their sense of dignity in the face of subjugation and exploitation, and affirm and assert their legal rights and sense of justice. If measured by whether they generated outright change, however, such strategies were largely unsuccessful. Yet as previous scholarship has shown, it can be hard to gauge what "successful" resistance looks like. This is especially true in labor regimes as intensively coercive and subjugating as those behind bars, in which workers are expected to look down and not speak, as O.T.I. described. Therefore, even though A.T. believed that filing grievances "doesn't really change much"—and dismissed doing so as merely "[letting] them know what you're thinking"—I argue that, for prisoners, letting officers know what they are thinking is indeed a form of resistance. For in doing so, they are challenging the subjugation that suffuses the very structure of the prison. Thus *how* workers resist is fundamentally shaped by the particular "micro-physics of power" imposed on them, as well as by the institutional structures in which they are embedded. One cannot analyze resistance apart from its context.

Ultimately, I hope, by examining all of these workers together—as both workers and resisters—this analysis highlights not only their analytical points of intersection but also their political points of intersection. For in challenging their coercion and subjugation, all of these workers—*as different from each other as they are*—laid claim to the same category from which they are excluded: sovereign, rights-bearing workers. They argued that they are "grown" adults, not kids, servants, or slaves. They argued that they deserve "respect" and respectable jobs, not "disrespect" and "ignorant" work. They argued that they should get equal rights and equal treatment, and they are willing to "stand up" against injustice. In so doing, they discursively drew on the ideological strands of productive citizenship in America—sovereignty, morality, and rights—to argue against their exclusion from it, a form of ideological resistance which I examine next.

5 "I'm Getting Ethiopia Pay for My Work"

HEGEMONY AND COUNTER-HEGEMONY

I didn't feel like a worker, I felt like a football player. I mean, I love football, and that's the whole deal.

—Bill Murdock, former college football player

They should at least have us some jobs though. Like, that's not a job: going out there, going to pick up somebody's trash, used condoms, and stuff out on the floor. That's not no job.

—Shara White, workfare worker

I felt like [my job] was prestigious, professional . . . I felt like a person that was going to work. I never really looked at it as "us versus them" or "slavery" or, you know, the pay. I learned to accept it as a condition of my actions.

—Miguel Fine, former prisoner

We see ourselves as employees. And because we're employees, we should be able to have certain rights. We should be able to unionize. . . . [But] when we started to act that way, all of a sudden people talked to us about how we're "students," not "employees." But they want us to work like employees.

—Scott, former graduate student in molecular biology

In this chapter, I continue my examination of resistance, but I shift my focus from the realm of actions to that of ideas by exploring how the workers I interviewed conceptualized the sociolegal category of "work" and their exclusion from it. Their perspectives ranged widely. Some, like football player Bill Murdock above, broadly accepted—indeed, embraced—their status as something other than "workers" doing something other than "work." Thus, they did not oppose their exclusion from the sociolegal category of "work" and they did not make any claims to the rights that this category typically yields. More often, however, the workers I interviewed contested their exclusion from "work" in some way, and in so doing they challenged its hegemonic social construction. Some, such as workfare worker Shara White above, agreed that their labor was not "work" but argued that they deserved access to this category and the rights and privileges it offers. "They should at least have us some jobs," Shara said, because workfare is "not a job." Meanwhile, workers such as former prisoner Miguel Fine and former graduate student Scott argued that their labor was indeed "work," but they did not agree as to whether it should yield employment rights. On the one hand, even though Miguel felt almost like an "employee" or a "professional" in his job behind bars, he did not expect the wages, benefits, and other rights that such status usually entails. He accepted the low pay and constraints of prison labor "as a condition of [his] actions." On the other hand, Scott argued that graduate students were indeed workers and should also have full access to employment rights and protections. "We see ourselves as employees . . . [and] they want us to work like employees," he said. "We should be able to unionize."

Scott, Miguel, Shara, and Bill thus represent the range of ways that the workers I interviewed justified or challenged hegemonic constructions of "work" and their exclusion from it. Despite this range, nearly all of these workers drew on the same two ideological frames: work and citizenship. This is not surprising, perhaps, as these interrelated ideologies are the foundation of modern notions of work in America. Indeed, work and citizenship are mutually constitutive social constructions, jointly built on raced, classed, and gendered notions of morality and immorality, independence and dependence, productivity and idleness, rights and rightslessness.[1] Earlier I analyzed how cultural narratives stemming from these ideologies have been deployed to construct various categories of labor as something other than "work," including the labor regimes in this book.

Here I examine how workers themselves deployed these ideologies, invoking interrelated notions of labor productivity, responsibility, work ethic, independence, sovereignty, slavery, rights, and citizenship in both accepting and resisting hegemonic definitions of "work."

In doing so, these workers were engaging in practices of hegemony and counter-hegemony. Yet as is typical for such practices, even ideological resistance often reifies hegemonic ideals in some way.[2] For instance, calling prison work "slave labor" in an effort to challenge prisoners' lack of pay, autonomy, and rights as workers—as my informants often did[3]—nonetheless reinforces the sociolegal construction of incarcerated labor as distinct from rights-bearing "work." However, as scholars have argued, the same tools that reify hegemony can also be used to challenge it.[4] I find the same in this chapter: cultural ideologies of work and citizenship can be deployed toward both hegemonic and counter-hegemonic ends, sometimes simultaneously.

Parsing such ideological resistance is important because it is the foundation of social movements and, thus, social change. For as studies of social movements have shown, in order for acts of resistance (such as those I analyzed earlier) to become sustained social movements, activists—including workers themselves—must engage in a process of ideological framing: they must identify the problems that they believe can and should be solved; they must point to the causes of such problems; and they must specify the remedies they seek.[5] In short, *ideological* resistance is a necessary precursor to sustained social resistance and cultural change. As Antonio Gramsci and others have argued, moreover, subaltern groups—or "organic intellectuals"—are a prime source of such ideological resistance.[6] "By paying focused attention to the accounts of subaltern people," political scientist Paul Apostolidis writes, one "can discover unsuspected kernels of counterhegemony."[7] Here I undertake this task, examining the accounts of these subaltern workers to identify such "kernels" of counter-hegemony.

EMBRACING HEGEMONIC DEFINITIONS OF WORK:
"YOU'RE NOT DOING NOTHING"

As Bill Murdock's comments above suggest, not everyone I interviewed argued that their labor should be sociolegally reconstructed as rights-bearing "work" and themselves as rights-bearing "workers." The incarcerated and workfare workers who held this view usually conceptualized "work" as a distinct and privileged category of productive labor that yielded independence, rights, and respect—which, they believed, they did not entirely deserve because of their (real or perceived) criminality, idleness, or dependence. For instance, as Apache said at the start of this book, "I couldn't really conjure somebody getting a lot of money working in prison. It wouldn't really make sense to me. . . . I mean, you're in prison, people are paying taxes and you're not doing nothing." Apache believed that prisoners are not productive workers, despite their labor, because they are (socially constructed as) dependent: other "people are paying taxes," he said, and prisoners are "not doing nothing." As a result, in his view incarcerated workers deserved neither rights nor respect. "Yes, [it's] slave labor," Apache said. "And I'm not an advocate—especially me being a Black man—of anything that got anything to do with slave labor. But we can't put ourselves in prison," he argued. "If you don't want to be put in that position, *then don't go.*" In Apache's view, then, prison labor *should be* excluded from rights-bearing work. Requiring prisoners to perform "slave labor" made "sense" to him. Although as a Black man he recognized the discordance of sanctioning "slave labor," at heart he believed that it was prisoners' fault for putting themselves "in that position."

Rodney Williams generally agreed, though he did not characterize prison work as "slave labor." For the 41-year-old African American man, incarcerated labor was "just part of my punishment for the crime I committed."

> I have to be here, and they're going to want you to do something here. You can't just sit around all day and lay around. So, it was all part of the process really. I didn't think of myself as a slave or a worker. No, no. I just felt like it was part of doing the time that I have to do, you know. That's it.

Forty-seven-year-old Glenn also accepted compulsory prison labor as a reasonable part of his punishment. "We went ahead and really got ourselves in trouble," he said. "If you get in trouble, you got to do what you got to do."

For Rodney, Glenn, and Apache, being required to work—even "slave"—in prison was a natural consequence of their bad decisions, their criminality.

Each emphasized his personal responsibility for landing himself in prison and considered mandatory labor behind bars to be a just outcome of his actions. It was "punishment for the crime I committed," Rodney said. "We . . . got ourselves in trouble," Glenn said. And, in prison, "you got to do what you got to do." Idleness was not an option. "You can't just sit around all day," Rodney avowed. "If you don't want to be put in that position, *then don't go*," said Apache.

Workfare workers similarly drew on notions of responsibility, dependence, idleness, and productivity in justifying their compulsory labor and their exclusion from hegemonic definitions of work. "I don't disagree" that welfare recipients should have to work, 23-year-old Tasha Love said.

> I feel like, if you didn't have to work, then it'd be a lot more people that's being lazy, and not really understanding the facts of working. . . . I really don't mind it, because it's like, if you're not doing something, you're just doing nothing. You know what I mean? I'd rather do something than nothing.

This young Black woman did not mind being required to work, and she condemned laziness to underscore her point. In so doing, she—like many of the workfare workers I interviewed—drew stark symbolic boundaries between herself and the mythical and much-maligned population of "lazy" welfare recipients.[8] In her view, as in much of the rhetoric surrounding welfare (as well as incarceration), mandatory non-rights-bearing labor was the only culturally available alternative to unacceptable laziness and dependence. For as both Tasha Love and Apache argued, even though workfare and incarcerated workers were, and should be, excluded from rights-bearing work, they were not exempt from the cultural obligation to perform labor and avoid idleness and "dependence."[9]

A number of other workfare workers agreed. As 26-year-old Alice Perry said of workfare, "I guess it made me feel like you was working instead of just doing nothing and getting their money. So, I guess that was a good thing, because they put you to work." Had she not been doing workfare, this Black woman went on to argue, she felt that she would have been unfairly "using" the welfare system. "I'm not the type of person, you know, to just take from a person and just use them," Alice explained. In her view, her labor for the welfare system offset her sense of dependence.

Twenty-six-year-old Tasha Mack felt the same. "If they wasn't doing this [workfare program]," this African American woman said, "we would be at home not doing nothing."

> It just made me feel a little bit better to just go and do something. . . . It's not like I'm sitting in the house doing nothing. . . . I treat it as a job, because they pay my bills. And if I don't come here, that means me being sanctioned, and that leads to me having problems paying my rent, paying my bills. So I pretty much do what I got to do.

As her comments suggest, even though Tasha characterized workfare as a "job," she did so to frame it as an obligation rather than productive labor. She did not expect it to offer the rights and privileges of legally defined employment. It was enough that it helped "pay [her] bills" and prevented her from being sanctioned—and, perhaps even more important, that it kept her from being idle: she felt "a little bit better to just go and do something." In her view, even though workfare was neither productive labor nor rights-bearing work, at least she was not "sitting in the house doing nothing."

In a similar vein, April Johnson argued that workfare enabled welfare recipients to avoid idleness and dependence and thus fulfill the central obligations of responsible adulthood. "Yeah, I think people should [be required to work for public assistance]," the 36-year-old African American woman said.

> They shouldn't get it for free. They should work, people should work. You don't want people just to think they can just sit around all day and just receive welfare for nothing. And people should want to not *want* to sit around, and want to show their kids what life is really all about.

Adults have an obligation to work, April argued, and parents have an obligation to "show their kids what life is really all about," which in her view was work and responsibility, not laziness and dependence. "Nobody gets free money," Ambrosia Washington said, echoing April. "You got to work. It's like having a job, but at lower terms, standards." Like the others, the 29-year-old Black woman accepted and legitimized workfare's exclusion from rights-bearing employment, while also affirming the expectation that workfare workers perform labor to avoid (socially constructed) dependence and idleness. In just one sentence, Ambrosia perfectly captured these workfare workers' embrace of hegemonic definitions of work.

Some former college athletes and graduate students also embraced their exclusion from the sociolegal category of "work." Unlike workfare and incarcerated workers, however, they did not frame this category as more privileged than their own. In their view, perhaps not surprisingly, theirs was not "a job . . . at lower terms," as Ambrosia said of workfare. Rather, they viewed their status as athletes and PhD students as distinct from—and sometimes even preferred over—being a "worker." As 29-year-old M.K. said, she "didn't feel exploited at all" as a college athlete.

> I'm actually probably one of the few athletes that is against paying college athletes. I mean, it is what it is in my eyes. I didn't feel exploited in any way, because I was doing what I love . . . I was doing something that I was so passionate about, and that I loved so much. That was all that mattered to me.

For M.K., because she was doing something that she "loved so much," she did not feel like a worker and she certainly did not feel "exploited." As this African American former basketball player went on to explain, even though she believed that athletes could be given "more perks," she strongly believed that they should not "get paid." In her view, athletes are already overly "entitled," which would only be exacerbated by remuneration—that is, worker rights and privileges.

> I feel like paying these athletes is just going to further entitle them, because these athletes are getting paid in college [via cost-of-living stipends]. And then they turn around and they don't make pros, or they're in a sport that doesn't have a professional need. And then they're like, "Okay, well." [They don't know what to do]. They're not just going to be handed a job when they leave college, but they've been handed money for four years. I know one freshman, and she lives in Maryland, she saved twelve thousand dollars in her freshman year just from money that the university had given her for different things. I'm like, that's insane, twelve thousand dollars, that's crazy. . . . And all the other [athletes] just spent it on ridiculous things. So, it's like you're just giving them money to blow, essentially.

Echoing the workfare workers above, M.K. drew on notions of dependence and responsibility in her embrace of athletes' exclusion from hegemonic definitions of work. College athletes are not workers, she argued forcefully, and so they are not appropriately earning their stipends (which, it should be noted, M.K. and the other athletes I interviewed did not receive, as they graduated before the stipends were implemented in 2015). Because athletes are just being "handed money," M.K. argued, they are not gaining a proper sense of responsibility; they "blow" their money "on ridiculous things"[10] and they assume that they will "be handed a job" after college. "That's insane," she said, "that's crazy." Being an athlete "is what it is," M.K. argued, which in her view is not rights-bearing work.

Bill Murdock agreed. As the 34-year-old white man said, "I didn't feel like a worker, I felt like a football player."

> I mean, I love football, and that's the whole deal. Like, that's what I felt like I was doing. And, just like our coach said, "football is second" with his finger pointing number one, and "academics first" with his fingers pointing number two, right? That's for sure how I felt.

As with M.K., Bill's "love" for football precluded any sense of being a "worker." First and foremost, he felt like an athlete—"a football player"—in contrast to NCAA and university rhetoric that college athletes are always "students first, athletes second."[11] As Bill recalled, his coach clarified his team's true priorities with his fingers (even as he gave lip service to the party line): football was number one, and academics was number two. Bill wholeheartedly agreed.

Many of the former athletes I interviewed said that they had felt the same during much of their college careers, though they also often recounted a shift away from this full-fledged embrace of college sports as a labor of love distinct from "work." For instance, Kyle Bronstein said that when he was in college, he identified entirely as "an athlete." "It's almost like, I don't even like the term 'student-athlete.' . . . I mean, I would say 'athlete-student,'" the 26-year-old white man explained. "People asked what I majored in, [and I'd say] I majored in football my first two years. That's what I cared about." In retrospect, however, Kyle saw himself as a "worker" more than an "athlete" while he was in college, because, he explained, Division I football players are "the ground floor to the revenue stream." Thus, for Kyle, because athletes generate financial returns, they are indeed workers.

Likewise, though Lawrence ultimately came to feel like an exploited worker (or "slave") as a college athlete—largely because of the commodification of his body—at first he proudly embraced his identity as an athlete. "I have mixed emotions," the 31-year-old African American man explained.

> I'd say more so in the beginning, you know, I took pride in being an athlete on campus and stuff like that, because everybody's going to know who you are. . . . But later on, like when I started preparing for the NFL draft and everything, I felt like a slave.

Lindsay recounted a similar transformation. At the start of her college career, she recalled,

> I'm thinking like, "Holy shit, this is awesome" because, you know, my school is paid for. Like, "This is such a good opportunity." My family wouldn't have been able to afford for me to go here, and . . . I probably wouldn't have gotten into [this exclusive school] just on my own. So, I was like just super naïve, and just thankful.

But "the more [she] went through," the 25-year-old Black woman recalled, the more she "started to realize that it's not really adding up."

> So, I started to see things like, for example, we went to the Final Four. And I think we got a watch or something. Like, we didn't get anything extra from that. But our coaches made . . . like twenty, thirty thousand dollars off of our Final Four round in their bonuses. *Off of our backs*, and our labor. And so, I said, you know, this system is broken. . . . The people in power [are] benefiting off of student-athletes.

Although Lindsay eventually came to see college athletics as a highly exploitative system, for most of her college career she did not. She felt "thankful" for the "opportunity" to play basketball at an elite level and to study at an elite institution.

Most of the former graduate students I interviewed believed that their lab research was indeed "work," but a few did not. M.G., for example, said that she did not feel like a "worker" while she was doing her graduate research. Rather, she "felt like a scientist-in-training" or "like an intern." As the 35-year-old biracial woman explained,

> I wasn't like just a worker or a number. I felt like I was an important contributor to science. . . . I was a student in a sense, yeah, I was learning. . . .

But I felt like it was always towards my ultimate goal to be able to be an independent scientist working on important scientific questions.

M.G. did not see herself as a "worker" because, in her view, workers are dehumanized ("just . . . a number") in a way that she did not experience as a graduate student. Instead, she saw herself as relatively privileged—more than "just a worker"—while also being dependent in a way that workers are not. She felt like "an intern," a trainee on her way to becoming an "independent scientist." "Looking back," M.G. continued,

> I don't know how much I would change [about graduate school]. I think I got what I really wanted to get out of it. If there was a way to make more money out of it, I guess that would be cool. But I don't know. . . . It was actually a really positive experience.

For M.G., more money would have been "cool" but not necessary. She "got what [she] really wanted" from graduate school: education, training, and mentorship. Yet by her own account, her experience was unique. M.G. was already a parent before entering graduate school, and so her main criterion for selecting a lab and advisor was family-friendliness—not research agenda or reputation—and she was able to get what she wanted. Her graduate advisor, M.G. said, was "very much aware of family needs coming first." "He was a great guy, very supportive, family oriented," she went on, but he was an "exception." Thus, unlike most of the other former graduate students I interviewed, M.G. had a strong sense of her advisor's support for her family, training, and research, which led her to interpret her graduate school experience as distinct from—and better than—the dehumanizing world of "work."

Nik's experience was also unique among the former students I interviewed, which similarly shaped his views of graduate school and his sense of himself as a graduate student. As the 35-year-old man explained, he had worked in a high-paying "corporate environment" before graduate school. Though he had "enjoyed it in the beginning," Nik said of his corporate job, "it got very boring."

> I wasn't learning as much, and . . . it wasn't actually very satisfying for me. So, when I started thinking about grad school . . . I had, I think, a different perspective than most grad students. . . . Because I felt my brain was a bit

starving, and I had all these things: all these ideas and all these questions. And I wanted to have the time to read all these papers that I would download while I was working, but never had time to read. And I wanted hands-on training, you know, learning actually how to do experiments with animals, and neuroscience experiments, and learning about actual methods—and then actually doing them. And so, for me, my main goal was just to learn, to sort of satisfy this curiosity that I had about the brain, neuroscience. And in my lab I had full freedom to do that, and that was good.

As his comments suggest, Nik's prior work experience was not the only thing that distinguished him from the other graduate students I interviewed; his "full freedom" in the lab was also a key point of difference. For though the other graduate students reported varying degrees of autonomy in their lab work—ranging from some to very little—none of them reported anything like the "full freedom" that Nik described. As he explained, his was a "very unique lab environment," in which students "basically got to do whatever [they] wanted. So," Nik said, "I got to spend the first three years trying some crazy idea I had, that no one had ever tried before. . . . It failed. But I learned a lot along the way." For Nik, then, as for M.G., graduate school was centered on learning rather than labor. His expansive freedom to pursue his own "crazy idea"—combined with his belief that he could return to the corporate world whenever he wanted ("I knew at any time if I was unhappy, I could just leave and go back")—allowed him to embrace his role as student rather than worker.

CHALLENGING HEGEMONIC DEFINITIONS OF WORK:
"I DON'T SEE WHY WE SHOULD BE GETTING ANY
LESS THAN ANYBODY ELSE"

More often than fully embracing hegemonic definitions of work, the workers I interviewed challenged them in some way. In the sections that follow, I analyze their ideological resistance across three categories. First, some workers—all of them in workfare—agreed with their labor's exclusion from hegemonic definitions of work, but challenged their exclusion from rights-bearing employment. Rather than "wasting" their time with workfare, they wanted a "real" job, which workfare prevented them from getting. The second group of workers argued the opposite: their labor was indeed valuable and productive (not "slave" labor or punishment, as argued above), but even so, it should not yield the full rights and privileges typically associated with such work. The third group combined these two counter-hegemonic ideals by arguing that their labor was productive and valuable work and should therefore provide all of the rights and privileges of legally defined employment. Throughout, as we will see, these workers arranged and rearranged the same ideologies of work and citizenship in an effort to challenge (in one way or another) their exclusion from hegemonic constructions of work.

"This is not a job. . . . I'd rather go punch a clock"

When I asked Shara White whether welfare recipients should have to work for public assistance, the 30-year-old African American woman said, "I understand what the welfare is trying to say, like, it's not going to be just sitting on your butt and collecting our money. So, that's why it's called 'welfare to work.' . . . But, at the same time," she said, "they should at least have us some jobs though. Like, that's not a job: going out there, going to pick up somebody's trash, used condoms, and stuff out on the floor. That's not no job, you know what I'm saying?" In Shara's view, workfare was not "work," and welfare recipients should have access to real "jobs" rather than "going to pick up somebody's trash." To justify such claims, Shara condemned both laziness and dependence: you cannot "be just sitting on your butt and collecting [state] money," she avowed. By underscoring her own dedication to work and independence, as well as her own aversion to laziness, Shara laid claim to rights-bearing employment. She could—and should—be a productive worker-citizen.

Many of the workfare workers I interviewed echoed Shara's claims, similarly drawing on notions of work ethic, laziness, dependence, and responsibility to differentiate workfare from "real" jobs and argue for access to rights-bearing work. As Makita Ross said, "I mean, you should do something" in order to receive public assistance.

> You shouldn't just sit at home and, you know, not do nothing. So you won't be comfortable and be stuck on the system. You should be able to do something for anything somebody gives you.

But, the 32-year-old African American woman continued, that "something" should be centered on employment, not workfare. Public assistance programs, Makita argued, should be helping people "seek jobs, preparing you résumés, getting you ready for job interviews, making sure you have daycare after your job, and stuff like that." But as it was, Makita said, workfare is "just a waste of time." "Because they take fifty people to do a job that five people can do. It's not like the job they're asking us to do is a waste. It's just that you don't need that many people." Thus, unlike many of the other workfare workers I interviewed, Makita thought the labor of workfare was at least somewhat valuable—she believed that people should clean the parks—but on the whole she saw workfare as a "waste" of potentially productive labor. In her view, the goal of workfare was just "keeping you busy . . . making you do something." "That's just the way the system is set up," she said.

Chandrea Jackson agreed. "I mean, I'm cool with everything I got to do," the 32-year-old African American woman said. "I know it's a responsibility [to work] to collect your benefits. . . . I don't have no problem with doing this." But, she said, she wanted a real "job" instead of "picking up paper, cleaning up the bathrooms." "Find me a job," Chandrea avowed, "a full-time job." Chandrea believed in work (as well as in individual responsibility), and she believed that she deserved the rights and respect it garnered. Likewise, 23-year-old Felisha Jones said, "We're supposed to be here looking for jobs, not cutting grass, not picking up rocks. We're supposed to be here looking for a job, not mowing lawn." For Felisha, having to do unpaid labor that city employees should be doing for pay made workfare "slave work." As the African American woman went on to explain,

Shoo! It's just crazy, how we got to do this, and they're supposed to be having the city doing this. . . . Because, like, we were planting flowers over there at that circle, and I was like, "Why are the [city workers] not doing it?" I was like, "That's slave work." And cutting grass and doing that stuff behind [this building], that's slave work. . . . I think it's slave work because the city supposed to be doing this. Not us.

Tara Collins felt the same, emphasizing the unjustness of workfare workers' unpaid "dirty" jobs as well as the lack of respect for them. "People be sitting up there like, 'I'm about to go to work, I'm about to go to work,'" the

38-year-old Black woman said of other workfare workers. "This not your 'job.' They don't even respect you here. *They don't even know your name*," she declared. Workfare, as Tara argued, "is supposed . . . to help you learn how to succeed and how to keep a job. [But] it's really a deterrent. We're coming here every day, getting ate up, dirty, mowing grass, shoveling snow. . . . That's not 'work,' that's ignorant." In Tara's view, having to do the "ignorant" labor of workfare prevented her from gaining the rights and respect of real employment.

Kim Hunky strongly agreed, and like many of these workfare workers, she marshaled notions of work ethic, responsibility, productivity, dependence, and slavery to make her point. For example, when I asked whether she felt "like a worker" while doing workfare, Kim said, "No. I feel like a slave. I feel like a slave, because—for one—it's not a job." Workfare workers, the 25-year-old African American woman argued, are performing labor that others are "actually getting paychecks for . . . which is not fair."

> I think it's a waste of time, period. Like, it's not working for welfare, it's slaving for welfare. It's slaving. . . . Why would I have to come to this park and pick up some cigarette butts of somebody else's, when I could be out here doing more? . . . I'd rather go punch a clock. . . . My sister's been here for like a couple of years, and she'll rather pick up the garbage from the parks and everything, because she will call it her "job." This is not a job. You're working for some assistance, when you could be working for a paycheck every week.

In Kim's view, then, workfare is not the productive labor that she wants and deserves. "It's not a job," she repeatedly proclaimed, while also emphasizing her own ethic of work. She wanted to be "doing more," "working for a paycheck," and "punch[ing] a clock." "And you would expect for them to help you with something like that," Kim continued.

> If you tell me my long-term goal is to have a full-time job, why you can't help me get that? . . . Why don't you do that instead of making me come clean up a park, which is not going to benefit me? Because ain't nobody is going to come passing by, "Oh yeah, she picked up the most garbage, I'm going to hire her." You see what I'm saying? I don't see it benefiting anybody. It's not. Because every day you still go clean the same parks, pick up the same garbage you picked up yesterday, but ain't *nobody* going to hire you.

Thus, despite widespread rhetoric to the contrary,[12] Kim argued that workfare would not lead to employment. No one would hire her for having "picked up the most garbage." Even more, she believed that workfare prevented her from finding such employment and, therefore, precluded her from adhering to the welfare system's (and her own) construal of "independence" and "responsibility." "Once you go to an appointment" with a caseworker, Kim explained,

> The first thing they say is, "Well, we don't want to take care of you and your kids forever." *Well, this is what you are doing.* I can't get a job, because y'all want me to be here. By the time I leave here—guess what—it's time for me to go pick my kids up from daycare. So, I'm still in the same position, because every day it's the same thing. . . . Y'all giving us the right to do nothing, and accept these benefits, which is not fair.

For Kim, requiring workfare workers to perform unproductive labor— "nothing," labor that was not "benefiting anybody"—was already wasteful and unjust but all the more so because it prevented them from attaining rights-bearing employment and conforming to cultural expectations of responsible adulthood. For like all of the workfare workers I interviewed, Kim only had subsidized daycare for her children during workfare hours. Therefore, she could not search for employment—at least not during normal work hours or without her kids in tow—and remain in compliance. Yet like most Americans, and the workfare workers in this book,[13] Kim believed deeply in the importance of work, independence, and individual responsibility. And so to her great frustration she felt forced into a cycle of dependence from which she could not break free. "If you get cash assistance, you need to work for it," she avowed. "But make me get out here and work. Don't make me get out here and slave. I'm not a slave. Those days are over."

"I looked past how much they were paying me"

While the workfare workers above argued that their labor was not work but that they deserved rights-bearing employment, the workers in this section argued the reverse: that their labor was indeed valuable and productive "work," but that they did not deserve the full rights and privileges that such work typically provided. Like those above, these workers accepted some aspects of hegemonic definitions of work while rejecting others; but in their case, they accepted their exclusion from the status of "worker" while, contrary to hegemonic portrayals of their labor, asserting that theirs was nonetheless "real" work.

Many of the workers in this category were prisoners. "I thought about myself as a worker," 27-year-old D.Q. said of his many jobs behind bars, which included working in the mess hall and on the grounds-keeping crew.

> Because, I guess, for the simple fact that . . . I'm in prison. So I just felt the [low] pay came with me being in prison. But when I was going to work, I was going to work. It was just the difference of how much I was getting paid. But I accepted it, you know. At least it was something, at least I wasn't working for free.

Likewise, Miguel Fine said that he "felt like a person that was going to work" in his job as an inmate grievance representative.[14] "I felt very confident in who I was, and learned to accept that these are the rules here," the 27-year-old Hispanic man explained.

> Even though I didn't agree with it, I said, *this is jail,* like, this is not a hotel or whatever, Hollywood or whatever like that. So, I knew there were certain restrictions, you just have to accept them.

Both D.Q. and Miguel accepted—and legitimized—prison labor's exclusion from employment rights and privileges. In their view, the low pay and other "restrictions" of incarcerated labor were simply a function of the institution and did not prevent them from seeing themselves as "workers" performing important and productive labor.

Jack Johnson agreed, even though there were moments when he and his fellow prisoners would complain about their low pay and hard work behind bars. As the 60-year-old Black man recalled,

> There were times—private times—we talked about, "Man, they're just dogging us out for thirty-seven cent, blah, blah, blah." . . . You know, I talk [like that] because I'm human and I'm locked up . . . so let's talk about how they're just working us to death.

But in general, Jack continued, "I looked past how much they were paying me." Particularly in his job as a facilitator in anger management classes, Jack believed that he "was giving the knowledge to help somebody else. We take so much from our community," he went on. "Why not give something back?" For Jack, his labor was deeply important and, like Miguel and D.Q., he highlighted notions of responsibility, hard work, and productivity to emphasize his point.

Qwon also felt that his labor behind bars was valuable, even his less prestigious jobs, such as janitorial work. Yet like Apache, Qwon equated prison labor to slavery. "I never wouldn't say that it ain't the new slave trade," the 31-year-old African American man said. But "I never felt like no slave. . . . I was never exploited. I felt the value" even though, he allowed, prisoners work extremely hard. "You work. You're going to work. Them industries, oh, you're going to work. By all means, you're going to be hot, sweaty, everything." Even still, Qwon argued, the labor was valuable. "Say, if I didn't do my job," he explained,

> Then it wouldn't get done. If I don't do A, then B won't get done. If B don't get done, C won't get done. So I looked at myself as an employee, because I was a part of it. I was working. I ain't looked down on myself or nothing. Because, like I said, I was open-minded. I gave myself the benefit of the doubt. . . . And I was ambitious. I was determined to be right there. So, I looked at myself in the positive light, despite where I was at, what I was doing.

Even though he was incarcerated, then, earning minimal wages and (at times at least) performing what might be considered menial labor, Qwon felt like "an employee." He "felt the value" in his labor and therefore "looked at [him]self in the positive light." He "was working." He never felt like a "slave."

Yet later in the interview, Qwon also argued that prisoners should earn more for their labor—not as much as nonprisoners, he said, but more than they currently earn (which in New York State is usually 10–33 cents an hour).[15] In his view, the "bare minimum" wage for prisoners should be "at least twenty dollars every two weeks," or no less than 34 cents per hour.[16] "Because, I'm going to be real," Qwon told me, "it really don't cost that much to be in prison." Even still, he believed that prisoners' wages should

reflect the value of their labor to the institution. Therefore, in his estima-
tion, while basic jobs might garner just $20 every two weeks, "the bare
minimum for industry [jobs] should at least be two hundred dollars"
every two weeks (or about $3.33/hour) and $100 for food service workers
($1.66/hour). "If it wasn't for these inmates," he avowed, "the facility won't
be ran, period." In Qwon's view, prisoners' labor was essential to the institution,[17] and their wages should reflect such value, even as they should not
match free-world wages.

Variants of this argument were relatively common among the incarcerated workers I interviewed. Some 60 percent of my ex-prisoner informants
believed that prisoners should earn higher wages but not as high as the
federal minimum wage. They accepted their exclusion from employment
rights, in this case the Fair Labor Standards Act, while still contesting the
meagerness of their remuneration. In doing so, they usually made one of
three overlapping arguments. Some, such as Qwon, argued that prisoners'
wages should better reflect the value of their labor to the prison. Others
similarly highlighted the value of their labor, but emphasized more their
sense of exploitation. Paying prisoners higher wages, they argued, would
diminish the outsized—and therefore unduly exploitative—disparity
between their wages and the value of their labor to the institution. As
24-year-old Dom said, "They make so much money off of us that they can
give us a little more than sixteen cents an hour. . . . Like, I've seen dudes
getting four dollars every two weeks, and they're working hard! That's
crazy. That's crazy. That's slavery. It was slavery." Even still, the African
American man said, he "didn't pay too much attention to it like that."

> Because I didn't want to, you know, degrade myself. I didn't want to look at
> myself no lower than . . . what I already am. . . . So I just stuck with it. I
> didn't want to categorize myself as a lowlife. So I just didn't categorize
> myself at all, because it was too much.

For Dom, such low wages made prison labor "slavery." But, by exerting
considerable emotional labor it seems, he "didn't pay too much attention
to it like that." He did not want to "degrade [him]self" even more.

Meanwhile, other former prisoners cited the costs of incarceration—as
well as the costs of simply living behind bars—as the primary reason why
incarcerated workers should be paid more. In point of fact, prisoners are

responsible for a range of expenses, including fees and surcharges levied by the criminal justice system,[18] as well as the cost of purchasing provisions at the prison commissary (including toiletries, food, and over-the-counter medications).[19] Over and again, prisoners told me that surviving financially behind bars could be difficult, especially for those who did not receive "outside" money from family members. Accordingly, prisoners such as Tim Jones argued that incarcerated workers should be paid "enough to get by" in prison. As the 28-year-old African American man explained,

> I'm not going to count on talking about nobody's smoking habits, cigarettes and so forth. I'm just talking about food. If a guy—with no family support— only makes ten dollars every two weeks (because that's what you make, ten dollars every two weeks) . . . and the water system in the jail was coming out grayish, rusted-looking water. So, obviously, you know that's what they're using down there to cook the food. [Or] they may be serving something you do not eat, you're allergic to it or whatever case may be. So, if you want to be able to cook some food in the dorm for hisself, I'd say at least let them make eighteen or nineteen dollars [every two weeks]. It's not a lot, but . . . it's enough to get by. It's enough to where you could buy you some food to help you last through the week. And enough to buy cosmetics,[20] a few stamps, envelopes to write to your family and stay in contact with them.

James D. agreed. In his view, prison wages "should be commensurate with whatever living wage is for prison." But even as he applied free-world "living wage" language to prisoner remuneration, James did not believe that prisoners should earn free-world wages. Thus, largely conforming to hegemonic constructions of them and their labor, James and these other former prisoners accepted their exclusion from the rights and privileges of "work," even as they did not entirely "look past" their low pay (as did Jack, D.Q., and Miguel above). Instead, they drew on attenuated notions of work and citizenship to argue for living wages behind bars.

Workers in the other groups made parallel arguments. For instance, workfare workers such as Chandrea Jackson argued that they should get more than the meager cash benefits they received for their labor, but not as much as the federal minimum wage. Though, as quoted above, Chandrea ultimately argued that she wanted a "job" rather than workfare, she also said, "If we were getting over one thousand dollars [a month], then that's something to work for. But the little petty cash we get, it's not enough to go out there and work for." Having to work for so little money made her feel "like a lowlife." John T. agreed. "I think [workfare workers] should get a little more," the 53-year-old African American man said.

> If I got to go in there and do the same thing you do, I may not get as much as you [since you're not doing workfare], but I may get a little more money than what they give. . . . Maybe not even minimum wage, but something that you will feel appreciated.

"But the way they do it [now]," he explained,

> you go in there with a mind-set: "These people dogging me, man. I don't even want to be here." And this is where my mind was, especially when I sat up there and figured how much they were giving me an hour.

Although John did not believe that workfare workers should earn minimum wage—"as much as you"—he believed that the system's minimal benefits rendered workfare degrading. He felt they were "dogging" him. Likewise, 52-year-old Peter Blacker said, "I'm not asking for, you know, X amount, a great amount. Just make it worth my while, because they [only] give you enough to cover the bare, bare, bare minimum."

In a similar vein, a number of former athletes argued that while college athletes should not be paid wages per se, they should be able to earn money from their athleticism. "I have a very strong opinion about this," Jayce said. "I don't think that they should be paid by the university, [but] I think that it's ridiculous that you cannot endorse yourself." As scholarship athletes, the 29-year-old white man went on to explain,

> you're getting a lot from a university. I mean, I've graduated with no student loans, and every single thing paid for, my room and my board, everything. To me that was worth thirty thousand dollars a year, which I thought was fantastic. . . . But for someone to tell me that I can't take money from somebody else, that I can't endorse myself, or I can't do local commercials, or I can't go out and do this and that—that, to me, is hurting my future in football.

Former basketball player Mike Smith agreed. "I think they can give these kids more opportunity to make a little more money," the 37-year-old white man said.

If you're a star player, or whatever, if you can make money off the court, away from basketball, you know, why *not* do it? Why can't a star player go do an appearance in the mall or something? I don't see how that will hurt anything . . . I don't see the downside. . . . I don't know how that will hurt college sports.

Likewise, Tom Vine argued that college athletics should be "more of a free-market system," not by paying athletes but by allowing them to "earn money outside of the university." Thus, while Tom, Mike, and Jayce accepted many of athletes' exclusions from the sociolegal category of "worker," they challenged others. In particular, they believed that athletes' economic independence should not be so highly constrained. They argued that athletes should be able to profit from their athleticism as if they were free-market workers, even though they should not be paid free-market wages by their universities.

Yet other athletes did not challenge such limits on their economic independence. Echoing D.Q., Miguel Fine, and Jack Johnson above, these former athletes simply accepted the constraints of the institution for which they labored, even as they also believed that theirs was valuable labor. For instance, though 33-year-old Paulo said that he could "see both sides" of the debate about paying college athletes, the Mexican man ultimately argued against their remuneration. "For me, I don't know. I feel like, 'Hey, listen, you're playing college football. You get your school paid for. *Enjoy it.* And then if you get a chance to go to the next level, good for you.'" Molly agreed, even as she also characterized basketball as her "job" in college. As the 23-year-old African American woman explained,

> You're there to play the sport. So, the scholarship is what's getting you into the school. So, even though we're technically student-athletes first, it usually feels like you're an athlete-student, because your job is to play the sport. . . . So, yeah, we're "student-athletes"—technically—but our job and our priority is kind of like "athlete-student."

But, Molly continued, she "didn't feel like [she] was exploited." Though she recognized that other athletes might feel that way, especially football players, "because football generates the most money at schools," Molly did not. She felt that her university had done everything it could to help her succeed in her "job" as an athlete.

They provide, I mean, everything they provide for us is in support of that. So, we have resources academically, and resources for nutrition, and resources to physically do [our] best. So, like everything that they do is to make your athlete experience as comfortable and as easy as possible.

For Molly and these other athletes, then, their work as athletes was both important and valuable, but it should not be included in sociolegal definitions of "work." Like Qwon in prison, Molly did not feel "exploited." "You're there to play the sport," she said. "You're getting a lot from a university," Jayce said, "which I thought was fantastic." "You're playing college football," Paulo said, emphasizing its distinction from real work. "*This is jail,*" former prisoner Miguel said in a similar vein. "This is not a hotel." "I'm in prison," D.Q. said. "I just felt the pay came with me being in prison." These workers accepted the "restrictions" of the institutions for which they labored and found the "value" in their work. "*Enjoy it,*" Paulo said.

"We're not getting what we're supposed to get, we're still Americans"

While the workers in the previous two sections espoused various combinations of hegemonic and counter-hegemonic definitions of work, here I analyze those who articulated more full-fledged ideological resistance against their labor's exclusion from rights-bearing work. Yet much like the workers above, those in this section tended to draw on the same ideologies—notions of rights and slavery, labor value and productivity, independence and responsibility—to make their case, although they were more likely than those above to emphasize rights and citizenship.

In prison, 27-year-old Garcia argued, incarcerated workers should get "*at least* the minimum wage. I mean, I don't see why we should be getting any less than anybody else," the Black and Hispanic man avowed. "Because we do *all the same* work and have *all the same* responsibilities." Their current wages, Garcia avowed, are "slave wages" (though he then amended that claim, saying that it is an "oxymoron to say it's 'slave wages'" and therefore "it's more like sharecropper wage"). In so doing, Garcia—like the many workers in this study who deployed "slavery" as a discursive tool— was simultaneously invoking notions of labor productivity, rights, citizenship, dependence, and independence.

D.D.G. agreed, but instead of emphasizing prisoners' "work" and "responsibilities," he underscored—again and again—their rights as American citizens. "We're not getting what we're supposed to get," the 28-year-old Black man argued. "We're still Americans. We're still in America. We still all grew up with the same American flag."

> I got the American flag on my shirt right now, miss. So I'm American. I'm here in this country, I'm a citizen. So, I still got certain rights . . . I got human rights. So, if that's the case, then I'm denied my human rights [in prison]. Just because I'm incarcerated, it doesn't mean I'm denied.

Being "denied" such rights while working behind bars, D.D.G. went on to argue, made him feel like a "slave." "I thought of myself as a slave because of the pay," he said.

> Nobody else in the state of New York is getting paid that. . . . That's what made me feel like a slave, because I'm the only person in America that's getting paid X amount—maybe fifty cents for doing all this. The same thing that people is getting six dollars or seven, eight dollars an hour for, I'm getting three dollars every week. Let's be serious. That's where the concept of a slave is at. Yes, that's some slave stuff. . . . Nobody else around the country is making that. *We're in America* . . . I'm buying American things, I'm buying American food products, I'm spending American money, but now I get some foreign pay like I was in Ethiopia. I'm getting *Ethiopia* pay for my work. That doesn't make sense. That just contradicts the whole scenario.

D.D.G. thus repeatedly invoked (racialized) notions of citizenship rights to argue for higher wages—and in fact full employments rights and protections—for prisoners. He believed that they should not get "Ethiopia pay" for "American" work. Though citizenship was his primary justification, he also highlighted prisoners' work ethic to bolster his point. "I don't believe that inmates and convicts mind working," he explained, "it's just what they're working for." For D.D.G., prisoners' ready adherence to the Protestant work ethic in addition to their American citizenship (and American consumerism) should give them full rights of substantive citizenship. Being required to work without such rights, D.D.G. believed, produced a profoundly problematic disjuncture; it "just contradicts the whole scenario," he said. Sal Winter, another former prisoner, made the same point in remarkably similar terms. "The whole scenario is just twisted," the 24-year-old white man said. "You're working for nothing. You're work-ing *hard* for nothing. That violates your constitutional rights, because you're working for pennies."

O.T.I. also repeatedly invoked notions of rights and citizenship to con-test incarcerated workers' exclusion from the sociolegal category of work. "Just because you're in prison shouldn't subject you to a lower pay," the 27-year-old African American man argued.

> You should get minimum wage or whatever the job offers [outside of prison]. . . . It should be the same minimum wage as it is on the streets, because even though you're in jail, you're still a citizen. . . . So they should get the same rights as citizens.

Outside of prison, he went on to explain,

> I can quit my job, or a random person on the street can't say, "Hey, you're going to put up all this trash today and I'm going to give you two dollars and fifty cents." I'm going to say, "No, that's too much. I think I'm worth more than that." But in prison, really, you don't have that option. So when you take that option away, you kind of become a slave in a sense. . . . You really don't have any rights. . . . Even in Attica, you got Corcraft that is a multimillion dollar company,[21] but all their products are made by inmates who don't have the right standard laws or right grade of pay. It's just like kids in India mak-ing Nikes and volleyballs—you know what I'm saying?—and then not receiv-ing the right wages. I'm not saying we were the underage kids, but it's the same aspect. Sometimes *they're* forced to work just like we are; *they* don't get the right grade of pay, just like we do. Sometimes, in their situation, they don't have the choice, just like we do. And if they buck or stand up or say no, they get penalties, just like we do.

Much like D.D.G., then, O.T.I. compared prison labor to other racialized forms of unfree labor: historical slavery in the American South as well as modern-day child labor in the global South. In some ways, his analogy is even more pointed. Not only are prisoners earning third-world wages, he argued; they are laboring for the profit of American companies without access to American citizenship rights. "It's just like kids in India making Nikes and volleyballs," he said. "They should get the same rights as citizens."

Workfare workers also drew on notions of slavery, work, and rights to contest their labor's exclusion from the sociolegal category of "work." For instance, 56-year-old Jackie Robinson argued that workfare workers should earn "*at least* minimum wage."

> Because, at this point, thirty-five hours a week for a hundred and fifty-five dollars a month is—what is that?—two dollars, one seventy-five [an hour] maybe?[22] I think the minimum wage would *at least* leave us with our dignity. Come on, man. Don't do that. To me it's slave labor, I'm sorry.

After I probed Jackie on that point—"It felt like slave labor?" I asked—she responded, "It looks like it, smells like it, tastes like it. . . . It is what it is. If it quack like a duck, it's a duck."

John T. also invoked slavery to argue for full employment rights for workfare workers. "I was angry," the 53-year-old African American man said of his time in workfare. "Because I got to do this work, ain't getting paid for it. All of you are dogging us, and won't even hire us." "When I sat there and figured it out," John said of his hourly wage rate, "I got even madder, because they treat us like slaves. Like back in the old days. Or like you're in jail, where they want to pay you ten cents an hour. That ain't right. That ain't right." Workfare, John argued, "should be a regular worker's job, not a slave worker," and welfare recipients should get "employment . . . instead of dogging them and keeping them stuck where they're at."

A number of other workfare workers agreed, including Lisa Williams and Pauline Wilson. "I'm basically between a slave and a welfare recipient," 26-year-old Lisa said. "We're busting our butts, like, how much we be working and stuff. This could be a real job for eight fifty and twelve dollars." Likewise, Pauline said that when she realized her welfare benefits amounted to just "two or three dollars a day" in exchange for her labor,[23] she was "like, *Are you kidding me?*" "I called it slavery," the 57-year-old African American woman declared. "It's slavery. That's what it is." As Pauline went on to explain, "It ain't like you don't try."

> Like, it's not like people don't try to do better or get better. It's just the economy, it's not there. It's just not there. So, when we come to social service for help and you get slapped in the face with this job thing—this bull crap. It's slavery. It's back in slavery days.

As Pauline argued—along with most social scientists—people who seek public assistance do so not because they do not want to work but because social and economic structures impede them from securing family-sustaining employment.[24] In my interview with Lisa Williams, in fact, she described trying to "do better or get better," as Pauline put it. "It's so hard to find a job out here," the young African American woman said, echoing Pauline.

> You got to have the qualifications, the education. I have a high school diploma, by the way. [But] it's not enough. It's like, I wanted to be a police officer; they said I have to go back to college to get credit. [And] I'm going back, but it's like this welfare stuff keeps holding me back. I went to my caseworker the other day, because I told her I wanted to go back to school. . . . She said, "No." She told me, "No, you have to go to your work site if you want your benefits."

Much like Tara Collins and Kim Hunky above, Lisa felt that workfare was "holding [her] back," preventing her from being an independent, productive worker-citizen. Pauline agreed, though she was more pointed in her critique: workfare was "bull crap"; it was being "slapped in the face" rather than being helped. Yet in contrast to Tara and Kim, both Lisa and Pauline believed that workfare could and should be a "real job," as Lisa said, "for eight fifty and twelve dollars" an hour.

Although most of the former athletes I interviewed did not argue that college athletes should be paid—that is, that they should be full-fledged, rights-bearing "workers"—a few of them did, including Zachary Lane. In fact, echoing many of the incarcerated and workfare workers above, the 29-year-old African American man invoked slavery in doing so. "We got treated like slaves," he said. "Like I said, we were getting pimped," referring to his analogy between pimps and Division I athletics. His primary point of evidence was that he did not have enough to eat while he was in college, and because he was a Division I athlete, he felt he had no way to earn money to buy food. "I was hungry," Zachary said. "Granted, this was our job," he said of football, but because of NCAA rules, "we couldn't go out [and] get jobs, and we can't profit off of our own signatures, and things like that."

> That's the struggle of being a student-athlete: you have this job, it's a full-time job. Granted you're getting your education paid for . . . but we still got a job. You were still working us the whole week. We should get paid for those days we work.

For Zachary, athletes' scholarships were not adequate remuneration, despite pervasive rhetoric to the contrary.[25] Being a college football player is "a full-time job," he argued, and it should be remunerated accordingly. He should not have gone "hungry." He and the other athletes, he said, "were getting pimped."[26]

Lawrence agreed, emphasizing the profit of college sports as well as athletes' financial need. "I understand we're getting scholarships for the amount of time that we put in," the 31-year-old African American man said, but "the schools are actually making money off of us."

> I feel like we should get something. You know, different guys come from different families, so different guys, like, have to have a job. [But] they can't work a job, because they take up so much of our time. And I feel like if we were compensated, if players were compensated, they'd be able to help out [their families]. You know, I've seen different players had to drop out because they had to go back and help their family.

When I asked how much compensation would be reasonable, Lawrence replied, "They definitely need to pay us hourly. Because, if they paid us hourly, then, as I just told you [referring to the long hours his team practiced], we'd be making career money." Then Lawrence chuckled, thinking about how many hours he and teammates had worked and how much money they would have made.

Both Lindsay and JohnJohn made similar points, though they focused exclusively on the profits that various entities—but not athletes—earned from their athletic labor. Like Zachary, moreover, Lindsay invoked slavery in doing so. Although, as described above, she felt "thankful" to play basketball for much of her college career, the 25-year-old Black woman said that by the end, she "started to see that something is a little faulty here."

> I really kind of got my eyes opened to be like, it's a modern-day slavery thing, of like, they should be paying athletes. They should be being compensated more. It's easy to point to the male revenue sports, but [in my college career], it was like, we went to the Final Four, and so, our school made money off of that. And our coaches—literally, people who weren't playing— made money off of my hard work.

For Lindsay, it was the realization that her coaches were profiting handsomely from her athletic success—while she was not (and not even allowed to)—that led her to reconceptualize athletes as "workers." In her view, the system was "faulty": she and her teammates only got watches for going to the Final Four, while her coaches got tens of thousands of dollars.

"If you're on the team, when you're playing, you definitely should get [paid]," JohnJohn said, and not just because of how long and hard athletes work. "I think they should also get it because of merchandise, all these jerseys and images that are being sold, and so much money is being made." Repeatedly pointing to the commodification of athletes' success and bodies, this Black Jamaican man continued, "There's just so much money being made off of the images and likeness of these players."

> They definitely should be compensated. Because, I mean, it's really even bigger business than NFL, and the reason why is because a big part of the cut is not taken out to compensate players. So, it's bigger business than the NFL, because you don't have a million-dollar salary to pay these players. They just keep our money, basically. And TV deals are just as lucrative. Merchandising deals are just as lucrative, selling college player jerseys and he's not getting a dollar of it. But "the scholarship" is what everyone says is equal pay. It's not. It's pretty ridiculous actually.

Given how much others profited from their labor, JohnJohn argued, athletes' scholarships were not fair compensation, and those profits represented an unfair usurpation of what rightly belonged to the athletes. "They just keep our money," he said. Others are making "so much money," but athletes are "not getting a dollar of it."

Meanwhile, the graduate students who argued for worker rights did not emphasize students' financial needs or others' profits but, rather, the need to offset imbalanced power relations and to protect students. Still, like all of the workers in this section, they too underscored just how much they worked—their productivity, their labor as "real" work—as the underlying justification for such rights. For instance, as Elizabeth said of graduate school, "It sure did not feel like I was a student, especially after you get your coursework out of the way. Nothing about it felt like a traditional academic-like student environment. It felt more like 'work.'" Gustavo was even more pointed in his characterization of graduate school as work—indeed, as labor exploitation. "Graduate school is relentless and long," he said. "I mean, it's basically being a modern indentured servant, because you work very, very long hours for very low money under the premise that you will gain in the future. You know, one day, basically your master just signs off, and you're released." For the 35-year-old Chicano man, it was not just long work hours that rendered graduate school "indentured servitude." It was the long hours laboring under someone who had expansive power over you—"your master."

Emily also pointed to such power dynamics as the reason why graduate students should "unionize" and gain full employment rights. As the 30-year-old white woman said, faculty advisors "have a frightening amount of power" over graduate students. Indeed, she emphasized this point again and again in our interview, variously saying that advisors "have unchecked dominion," "total discretion," and "total power" over graduate students' lives. Such power, she said, as quoted before, "is what really turns [graduate student labor] into some kind of like—like, it's hard to believe that people can have that much control over your life in a country where otherwise, you know, you're protected by all kinds of labor laws." Unlike Gustavo, Emily stopped just short of describing graduate student work as some form of unfree labor, perhaps because it seemed culturally inappropriate or perhaps because of the very real distance between graduate work and, say, indentured servitude. Instead, she shifted gears midsentence to focus on rights and citizenship. Echoing D.D.G. and O.T.I. above, Emily highlighted what she saw as the unjust disjuncture of American workers laboring without access to standard U.S. employment rights and protections. "I think the whole way that it's done is really exploitative," she said.

Scott also saw graduate student labor as exploitative. In fact, the 32-year-old white man believed that denying graduate students employment rights was a deliberate strategy to extract the most surplus value from their labor. "We see ourselves as employees," he said.

> And because we're employees, we should be able to have certain rights. We should be able to unionize. . . . [But] when we started to act that way, all of a sudden people talked to us about how we're "students," not "employees." But they want us to work like employees.

As Scott continued, he drew parallels between graduate student labor and college athletics (without any prompting from me). "I think 'exploitation' would be a great way to describe" them both, he said.

I see definite parallels between student-athletes and graduate labor. I think a lot of the same things apply. And I would say that, if anything . . . student-athletes actually have it worse than graduate students. But, yeah, I mean, I would definitely say that student-athletes—just like graduate students—are "employees," but they're treated like students [in order] to be denied the employee protection that you have in other professions.

But getting such employee protections, particularly at private universities such as his own, Scott explained, was difficult.

In public universities, graduate students and postdocs are able to sort of band together and get some sort of labor protections for themselves in place. . . . I feel like a lot of these private institutions kind of abuse the fact that like, "Oh, well, we have a big name. You know, we don't have to necessarily play by the rule that these lesser-name institutions play by." And to some degree, that's correct, because in a big-name institution, if you want to work in a way that emphasizes work-life balance, then that's fine, because they can get rid of you and have a hundred other applicants ready to take your place.

For this reason, Scott believed that employment protections were crucial for graduate students at private and public institutions alike. His goal was "to help find some ways for graduate students and postdocs to regain . . . a greater degree of control in their lives"; because although most faculty advisors do not "abuse their power," he said, "for the ones that do decide to abuse their power, there's very little that will stop it." For him, worker rights—particularly unionization—was the answer.

.   .   .   .   .

Among the workers I interviewed at least, hegemonic and counter-hegemonic ideologies were comprised of nearly identical "kernels." The same ideologies of work and citizenship—interrelated notions of labor productivity, responsibility, work ethic, independence, sovereignty, and rights—were deployed toward these very different ends. For some incarcerated and workfare workers, beliefs about the importance of individual responsibility, work ethic, and productivity (combined with an abhorrence of laziness) served as justification for the compulsion of their labor, while beliefs about their "dependence" served as justification for their exclusion from employment rights. "If you didn't have to work," Tasha Love said, "then it'd be a lot more people that's being lazy." "Nobody gets free money," Ambrosia Washington said. Yet for other such workers, the very same beliefs served as justification for their opposition to hegemonic definitions of work and their exclusion from it. As Kim Hunky argued, workfare prevented welfare recipients from gaining skills and long-term employment, thereby prolonging their (socially constructed) dependence and idleness, "giving us the right to do nothing, and accept these benefits," she said, "which is not fair." Meanwhile, other workfare and incarcerated workers used these same ideologies to argue for their full inclusion in the sociolegal category of rights-bearing work. As John T. argued, workfare "should be a regular worker's job, not a slave worker." In prison, "You're working *hard* for nothing," Sal Winter said. "That violates your constitutional rights." "I don't see why we should be getting any less than anybody else," Garcia said. "Because we do *all the same* work and have *all the same* responsibilities."

Athletes and graduate students also drew on these ideologies toward both hegemonic and counter-hegemonic ends. While many of these student workers pointed to their hard work and long hours on the court and in the lab as evidence that theirs was, indeed, "work," others did not. As Bill Murdock said, "I love football, and that's the whole deal." "I didn't feel exploited in any way," M.K. said. "I was doing what I love." Meanwhile, Nik felt fortunate to be able to "satisfy [his] curiosity," spending "three years [in the lab] trying some crazy idea . . . that no one had ever tried before." And M.G. "got what [she] really wanted" from graduate school. "I wasn't like just a worker," she said. "I felt like I was an important contributor to science." Yet others pointed to the same hard work, long hours, and valuable contributions as evidence that they should be rights-bearing workers. College athletics is a "modern-day slavery thing," Lindsay argued, because only the "people who weren't playing . . . made money" from it. Likewise, Gustavo argued that graduate student labor is highly exploitative, even though he also believed that it could be valuable. (Recall his description of his contribution to an academic paper: "I developed all the technology that made that shit happen.")

This analysis suggests that waging a Gramscian "war of position" may be less about identifying new kernels of counter-hegemony than understanding how long-standing hegemonic ideals can be rearranged toward counter-hegemonic ends—even if they do not upend such ideals altogether. None of the workers in this study, for example, questioned the centrality of work, the importance of productive labor, and the disdain for idleness in American culture. Nonetheless, many of them posed substantial challenges to the sociolegal construct of work by arguing, in various ways, against their exclusion from it. For such workers, this is indeed a powerful claim because it attacks the very premise of these categories of "nonwork": that they are somehow fundamentally different from "real" work. For it is this distinction, at least in part, which allows them to be characterized by the particularly powerful form of labor coercion I have examined in this book.

Conclusion

Labor coercion is alive and well in American labor relations. Through status coercion, an unmeasured number of bosses have expansive punitive power over workers' lives, families, and futures. Of course, *all* bosses have significant power over their workers: their ability to hire and fire, schedule and reschedule, promote and demote workers is substantial indeed. But in the coercive workplaces I examine in this book, the scales are tipped even more in their favor, because their power extends beyond those forms of economic coercion to include control over workers' social *status* and all of the rights and privileges such status entails.

In graduate school in the sciences, for example, faculty advisors can dismiss their student workers from the status of graduate student (and future PhD), or they can keep students from leaving that status (and becoming a PhD)—in both cases, preventing students from completing their education, being accredited, and (hopefully) obtaining high-status work in that field. Such power is amplified by advisors' control over student publications and letters of recommendation, both of which also have significant effects on students' careers. In short, faculty advisors have near-total power to exclude their subordinates from the elite status of "Scientist, PhD."

Similarly, in Division I college athletics, coaches can remove their football and basketball players from the status of elite athlete by withdrawing their scholarships, which may also revoke their status as university student (and future college graduate). And even if coaches do not officially remove athletes from their team, they can indirectly revoke players' athlete status by not allowing them to compete. Doing so can affect athletes' lives and careers in significant and long-lasting ways, including impeding their ability to play professionally—that is, obtain high-status (and sometimes high-paying) work in that field. Such power is amplified by coaches' influence over NFL and NBA recruiters, the informal recommendation system upon which these professional sports rely. In short, college coaches have the power to exclude their subordinates from the status of "Star Athlete," an elite status which can bring fame and, for some, future fortune.

For both of these groups of student workers, then, supervisors have expansive power over their education and careers. But for most, such power does not inflict lifelong physical and mental harm. In part this is because for both of these groups there are alternative courses of action, however inferior. When science students are dismissed from their graduate programs, for example, they are typically awarded a master's degree (instead of a PhD) and can seek science-related employment in industry or education. Though for most aspiring PhDs this option is vastly inferior, it is nonetheless an avenue through which these former students can find some form of success. Likewise, when athletes are formally or informally removed from their teams (by being kicked out or benched), they may be able to transfer to another team (though they may also lose a year of playing time), or they can relinquish their sports career altogether (though some may then also lose their ability to attend college). As with graduate students, even though such options are vastly inferior, they are nonetheless courses of action through which former athletes can find some form of success. I would describe employers' powers of status coercion in these two labor regimes as serious but not extreme.

For workfare and incarcerated workers, however, employers' powers of status coercion are extreme indeed. For these workers (and often their families as well), such powers are likely to inflict lifelong physical and mental harm, and there are no viable alternatives. In the welfare system, for example, supervisors have the power to remove workfare workers from the status of deserving citizen—that is, welfare recipient—by revoking their access to critical components of the social safety net. The consequences for them and their children—housing instability, food insecurity, physical and mental health problems, and more—are profound and permanent. They are also unavoidable. Because welfare recipients are, by definition, already in poverty, they have no inferior-but-viable course of action when they are sanctioned. They simply lose the status of welfare recipient and its much-needed rights and privileges (however meager). The same is true of incarcerated workers. Their bosses can remove them from the status of "good" prisoner and, therefore, revoke their access to the many essential facets of everyday life that become "privileges" in prison, including family visits, phone use, store purchases, educational classes, exercise and recreation, socializing and human interaction, freedom within prison (albeit constrained), and freedom from prison. For prisoners, as for welfare recipients, there is no inferior-but-viable course of action when they are put in solitary confinement or on keeplock. They simply lose the status of "good" prisoner and its much-needed rights and privileges. And the consequences for them and their families are severe: severed family ties, long-term physical and mental health problems, and for some, even death.[1]

Because of these power dynamics behind bars, Apache evocatively argued that incarcerated workers are made into "cowards" by the institution. "Out here on Main Street," he explained, "you can't put me to work on slave labor. There are too many laws against it, you know what I'm saying?" But behind bars, he said, prisoners can indeed be "put to work on slave labor." To emphasize his point—this distinction between free labor and prison labor, rights and rightslessness—he then drew on notions of hegemonic masculinity. On "Main Street," Apache went on, "real" men can assert their rights. "A man stands up and a coward lays down." But "when you are in prison," he said, "you're a coward" no matter what.

> I don't care how tough you are, but when your family comes to visit you, they strip you down after that visit to make sure you're not bringing nothing into the system. . . . You *have* to be [a coward]. I mean, you can't be a tough guy. *How tough can you be?* You're fighting against a system that you can't win against.

In Apache's view, prisoners are "stripped down," both literally and figuratively, by the institution. They are made weak in the face of a "system" they "can't win against."

Though most of the workers I interviewed did not characterize their labor relations as a "fight" against the "system" in this way, nearly all of them recognized their relative powerlessness within their respective systems. Again and again, they described feeling like "lowlifes," "peons," "workhorses," and "slaves"—or like they simply "didn't exist." Their bosses' ability to wield expansive punitive power over them left them feeling deeply powerless. In prison "you can't really talk back to a superior officer," O.T.I. said, "because then you put your life in jeopardy." Workfare supervisors, Jennifer Rose said, "are like God: they control everything in the palm of their hands." "You just learn to, like, take it and move on," Haley said of coaches' abusive treatment. If you do not, Shevontae said, "everything can be tarnished." "You're just so vulnerable," Laine said of graduate students.

Indeed, even when their labor had achieved hard-won goals—a PhD and a faculty job, athletic success and a professional sports career, welfare compliance and family support, or "good behavior" behind bars and early release from prison—these workers could not overlook the punitive power dynamics at the heart of these labor relations. For some, simply talking about such dynamics elicited strong emotions. In fact, former graduate student Rebecca was so concerned about the potential for negative repercussions from our interview that I decided not to include her comments in this book. Similarly, though to a lesser degree, former basketball player Kate said that she felt anxious when talking about her coaches and the power they wielded, even though she was no longer in the sports world. As she said in an effort to explain why, "It's kind of like, if I don't speak on it . . . then it doesn't harm me in any way."

Others were excited to talk about such power dynamics in the hope of shedding light on their hardships and the broader social problems they revealed. For instance, Lisa Williams said that talking to me about workfare was "a good protest" and then added, "I wish I could be on strike for this stuff." But when I asked if that might be possible, she replied, "No. . . . We're used to getting up at seven o'clock in the morning, coming here and busting our butts until two-thirty. We done got used to it." Former prisoner K.H. also saw our interview as an opportunity for protest. Though he had "swallowed a lot of things that [he] really wanted to speak out on," K.H. said that he had also surreptitiously documented prisoners' mistreatment "for a time like right now," referring to our interview. "This is prime time for me," he declared. "It's important that this message gets out and someone does something about it. I'm hoping that this can get in the right hands." When I told him that I was not sure that mine were the "right hands," he replied, "I understand. But if you need some help, I can help you . . . whatever way that you can deem possibly to get this information out."

Other ex-prisoners made a similar argument, though even more pointedly. As described earlier, both Ron D. and Bruce W. told me that prisoners' mistreatment—*not* their labor—should be the focus of this book. "I think you should do more about how we get treated in prison instead of work," Ron said to me, "because how the people get treated in there is just absolutely crazy." Likewise, when I asked Bruce, "What else do you think I should know about work in prison?" he replied,

> I think you should talk about human equality. I believe you should shine a light on human equality between people, because they feel our social status gives them authority and power to abuse what they had been given, and they were given a position to oversee people do something [prisoners' labor]. Instead of seeing them doing it, they treat them—inhumane treatment. They treat them like dogs. They treat them like as if they peasants, like their footstools. They don't have no respect. Maybe you should shine a light more on the humanizing, the human equality.

Even though Bruce and Ron had left prison, they could not leave behind what they saw as the injustice at the heart of their labor and lives behind bars. And they both strongly believed that these unjust power dynamics should be at the center of this book.

Despite the centrality of such power dynamics to these workers' lives, they are not typical concerns of most studies of work, labor, and employment. At the risk of my being overly (and perhaps unfairly) broad, such studies, especially in the U.S. context, tend to focus on formal, legally defined employment, and as a result they tend to find specific versions of these dynamics—the forms of economic power that employers in such labor relations wield and the consequences of such power for workers, including precarity, wage stagnation, and economic inequality.

This broad characterization does not account for the *many* studies that examine other types of work and workers, different forms of employer power, and noneconomic consequences for workers. Indeed, there are numerous studies of off-the-books, underground, and illicit work (e.g., paid domestic labor, scavenging, sex work, and drug dealing),[2] labor that is legally characterized as "noneconomic" (e.g., workfare, prison labor, and internships),[3] gendered "invisible" work (e.g., care work, housework, emotion work, and aesthetic labor),[4] and nontraditional types of workers in traditional jobs (e.g., undocumented immigrants, immigrant guest workers, and workers under criminal justice supervision).[5] Such studies have also uncovered various forms of employer power and their negative consequences for workers, often by analyzing the ways in which gender, race, class, ethnicity, and citizenship shape workplace power dynamics. For instance, studies of guest workers and undocumented immigrant workers have shown how employers' operative power of deportation is linked to a host of illegal practices, including wage theft, dangerous working conditions, retribution for worker complaints and labor organizing, and other forms of worker abuse.[6] In a similar vein, studies of workers who labor under the ambit of the criminal justice system—parolees, probationers, and those with court-ordered debts—have shown how employers' operative power of incarceration is linked to degraded labor standards, wage theft, and other illegal workplace practices.[7] The consequence of such power dynamics for these workers is not labor precarity, though that may also be of concern. It is abiding fear and stress, workplace injury and even death, physical abuse and harassment, deep poverty and social isolation—even when threats of deportation and incarceration are not carried out.

In this book I have sought to synthesize and extend the insights of these studies which have looked beyond the traditional confines of work and labor sociology. By comparing radically different groups of nontraditional work and workers, I have sought to uncover the power structures that shape many such groups. Thus, although some might object to the unusual—even illogical—comparisons that I draw in this book, it is only through such comparisons that I have been able to look past the idiosyncrasies of these labor relations to find the common ground between them. Therefore, even though I do not intend to suggest that, for example, PhD students and prison workers are the same in any way, I do argue that they face the same type of coercion at work (just as corporate managers and day laborers both face employment precarity). In short, I believe that "odious comparisons,"[8] such as those in this book, can yield new insight into the landscape of work in America.

Yet this book's analysis does not simply add new points of interest to this landscape. It changes our understanding of it in its entirety. Consider, for example, how these findings complicate the oft-drawn binary between "good" and "bad" jobs.[9] The preeminent work in this field is *Good Jobs, Bad Jobs: The Rise of Polarized and Precarious Employment Systems in the United States, 1970s–2000s*, in which sociologist Arne Kalleberg analyzes numerous dimensions of job quality for workers—wages and benefits, autonomy and control, career ladders and security—and then sorts jobs into two broad categories, "good" and "bad" (the latter with less of all of the above). The gap between these two types of work, Kalleberg finds, has grown substantially, though all workers have confronted increasing levels of employment precarity.

But while this good/bad job binary is both politically and analytically useful, it does not easily accommodate the categories of work I examine in this book. For example, although security and stability are widely considered hallmarks of "good" jobs, they are also hallmarks of these coercive labor relations. Prison jobs, workfare assignments, college sports, and PhD lab research are not characterized by workplace restructuring, seasonal unemployment, unpredictable scheduling, mass layoffs, and high turnover. Likewise, while fringe benefits—particularly employer-provided health insurance plans—are standard features of "good" jobs, they are also common (in some form at least) in the labor relations I analyze here: incarcerated workers receive healthcare in prison; workfare workers are often covered by Medicaid; and many graduate and undergraduate students have access to campus healthcare. On the other hand, while wages—particularly those complying with state and federal minimums—are basic components of even "bad" jobs in the mainstream economy, aside from prisoners' meager remuneration none of the workers in this book earned legal "wages" for their labor, let alone the minimum wage.[10] In addition, even workers in many "bad" jobs have legal rights and protections—on the books if not always in practice—including the right to safe working conditions, freedom from discrimination and harassment, and union organization and collective bargaining. Yet because they were not legally deemed "employees," the workers in this book largely did not have access to such protections, even on the books.[11] Finally, while the good/bad job binary accounts for various types of employer power (e.g., control over scheduling, promoting, and firing workers, as well as control over work activities), it does not account for the expansive type of employer power documented in this book.

These are not hair-splitting distinctions. They have real-world significance for those who want to respond to these problems, because in fact solutions for "bad" jobs will not solve the bad aspects of coercive labor regimes. For instance, to remedy the problem of precarity, Kalleberg endorses the Danish model of "flexicurity," which seeks to enhance employee security while preserving employer flexibility. Thus, Kalleberg advocates for a variety of welfare and labor policies, including a stronger social safety net, government creation of good jobs, immigration reform, employment rights for part-time workers, and sick leave and vacation time for all (legally defined) workers. Though these are important and much-needed reforms, any benefit they provide to the workers in this book would be indirect at best. In particular, only if a stronger social safety net were to decrease the use of sanctions and minimize work requirements for welfare would it remedy the bad aspects of workfare. Otherwise, a greater number of (traditionally defined) "good" jobs and increased benefits for (traditionally defined) "employees" will not mitigate the negative effects of status coercion for the workers in this book.

Ultimately, incorporating these power dynamics and labor relations into the broader landscape of work in America changes our understanding of this landscape in multiple and sometimes surprising ways. For instance, when compared to these coercive labor regimes, even "bad" jobs can be reframed as sites of relative privilege *as well as* disadvantage. At the same time, the very meaning of "privilege" is called into question, as we have seen how this term has been used to undermine college athletes' and graduate students' claims for worker rights. Echoing 19th-century characterizations of white middle-class "housewives," they are said to be too "privileged" to be workers.

Meanwhile, this book has revealed precarity as only one source—albeit an important one—of worker vulnerability and employer power. In fact, as we have seen, workers' susceptibility to precarity (and economic coercion in general) is intensified by employers' powers of status coercion. For workers in these coercive labor regimes are often primed to accept precarious work on entering the mainstream economy. Graduate students are groomed for low-paid and unstable (but often long-term) positions as postdocs and adjuncts; workfare workers are primed for (and even pushed into) low-wage and unstable jobs, often in the service sector; and prisoners are primed for low-wage, unstable, and frequently dangerous jobs in day labor, roofing, construction, and the like. As C. Parks said, "If you can get through work in prison, when you come home you can do anything." Moreover, for some coercive labor relations not examined here, the compounding effects of status coercion and economic coercion may be even more acute. This is likely the case for workers who are required to maintain employment—regardless of its "bad" qualities—as a condition of their freedom from incarceration, as well as for noncitizen workers who can be deported if they challenge the "bad" aspects of their jobs.

Even in less extreme cases, such as the otherwise traditional workers who are bound by noncompete agreements, workers' vulnerability to economic coercion is intensified by their employers' powers of status coercion. When workers cannot leave their job for another in their field of expertise, they have fewer viable courses of action when their employers put them on the night shift, cut their wages and benefits, or harass them. Noncompete agreements are only one mechanism of status coercion I have identified for "regular" workers. What other such mechanisms are there, and who is affected? Only further research will tell, but by identifying status coercion as a distinct form of employer power, this book lays a foundation for doing so.

This book does not only expand our understanding of employers' "arsenal" against workers. It can also help workers build their own arsenal. By classifying the nontraditional groups of workers in this book *as workers,* this book affirms their identity as such. Whatever else they are doing and whatever else they are gaining, they are performing *labor* for someone else's benefit, and therefore they should be able to claim rights as workers. Indeed, many of the workers I interviewed had already embraced this identity, even if they also felt isolated and powerless within their particular labor regimes.

This book may also offer some remedies for that sense of isolation and powerlessness, further building workers' arsenal. By identifying status coercion as the central mechanism of their bosses' punitive power, this book gives them a target for change. Just as worker-activists have fought to restrict (at least to some degree) employers' powers of economic coercion through welfare and employment protections, workers can fight to restrict employers' powers of status coercion. Indeed, there are already organizations of former prisoners and their allies working to limit the reasons and duration for which prisoners can be put in solitary confinement. These organizations might also seek to strengthen prisoners' ability to file grievances by implementing third-party complaint procedures in prisons, jails, and detention centers. Similar procedures would benefit all of the workers in this book—and many others—by giving them greater recourse when workplace problems arise. But such policies are only the tip of the iceberg. When worker-activists have a target, they can develop and deploy innovative strategies to remedy the problems, just as they have done with economic coercion (as with "Fight for $15" and "alt-labor" organizing).

By revealing how status coercion affects a wide range of workers, this book broadens their community of allies. Graduate students and student-athletes who labor for the same university, for example, might join forces to develop policies that curtail the particular variants of status coercion they experience as student workers. Likewise, incarcerated and workfare workers, some of whom could be members of the same family, might recognize in each other allies against the coercion they both face at work. And workers in tech jobs as well as in tree service jobs might protest together the growing use of noncompete clauses, which inhibit their economic freedom and exacerbate their employers' power of economic coercion.

In order to do these things, however, we must recognize that Americans face coercion as well as precarity at work.

APPENDIX A The Story of This Book

When I started this project, I did not set out to study labor coercion. Rather, I wanted to learn about the experiences and perspectives of workers who were not protected by labor and employment laws. Thus, my original research design included three group of workers who were unevenly excluded from labor and employment laws in New York State: incarcerated workers were at one end of the spectrum, as they are almost entirely excluded from such protections; workfare workers were in the middle, as they are protected by only some labor laws, such as discrimination and (in a convoluted way) minimum wage statutes; at the other end of the spectrum were domestic workers—nannies, caretakers, and house-cleaners—who had recently gained many employment protections in New York State, except for the right to organize and bargain collectively.

Yet my early interviews with incarcerated and workfare workers[1] revealed the centrality of coercion (which I later identified as "status coercion") to their work lives, and my analytical focus began to shift toward such power dynamics. I continued with my original framework, however, and interviewed 20 domestic workers in Western New York.[2] To my surprise, such coercion was absent from their work lives. This is not to say that their labor was devoid of hierarchy, economic coercion, or even mistreatment. Like all workers, they could be vulnerable to such power dynamics in the workplace. But it was clear that their understanding and experience of their bosses' power differed markedly from that of incarcerated and workfare workers. In those labor relations, status coercion was so central, so pervasive, so palpable that it had come to the fore of my research without my intending to study it.

However, the fact that these domestic workers did not fit into this paradigm was unexpected, as a range of studies has shown this to be a highly vulnerable workforce, unusually subject to punitive employer power and abuse.[3] Yet the workers in such studies, I realized, were nearly always immigrants or migrants—variously documented, undocumented, or on temporary visas—because nonnative workers dominate domestic labor in many large cities in the United States and across the globe. This did not seem to be true of Western New York, as all but one of the domestic workers I interviewed were native-born in the United States. So I began to explore whether the power dynamics described in those other studies were due more to the workers' precarious immigration status than the structure of domestic work itself. Ultimately, I came to believe this to be true because, as I discuss in the introduction, employers have expansive coercive power over undocumented immigrant and temporary migrant workers' status as *workers* in the United States—power which can pervade even documented workers' labor, as they may also fear the revocation of their legal worker status. Thus, I came to understand that the same coercion that pervades workfare and prison labor also likely pervades the labor of many nonnative workers—housecleaners, nannies, and otherwise—but not that of the native-born domestic workers I had interviewed.

In short, even though my interviews with domestic workers are not included in this book, they were essential to its analytical development. By pushing me to make sense of *how* and *why* they differed from the others, these interviews helped me delineate the concept of "status coercion." And so I learned that what might initially seem to be an analytical detour can in fact be analytical progress.

I then looked for other categories of coerced labor to include in my analysis. In doing so, I sought variation in the severity of such coercion in order to understand how this power dynamic operates across very different workplaces and for very different workers. I identified Division I college athletes (particularly in the revenue-generating sports) and graduate students in the sciences as workers who would likely fit in this analytical framework, and I interviewed 38 former worker-students across these two groups.[4] As my findings show, such workers do indeed fit in this analysis, even though there are *significant* differences between them and the others.

Comparing such diverse groups not only reveals the ways that dissimilar workers experience similar power dynamics. It also shows how this type of coercion is not relegated to extreme cases. This expansive and punitive employer power, which some might consider justifiable for, say, prisoners, is not unique to them. It is also experienced by elite athletes and soon-to-be PhDs. Thus, this form of labor governance cannot be easily dismissed as a condition of "the other."

Still, some might object to the comparison of these groups. They are indeed radically different. At times, their past, present, and future trajectories could not seem more different. But while I do not argue that they are the same, I do argue that they experience the same type of coercion, even as they do so in profoundly different ways.

In comparing the experiences of these diverse groups, I have sought to analyze the various ways they make sense of the world, while also culturally contextualizing their perspectives. Such analytical work is, of course, central to qualitative sociology as a methodology. For as sociologist Allison Pugh has argued, interpretive interviewers are not just "stenographers."[5] They do not merely report what people say. They analyze what people say and how they say it. Rather than taking my informants' perspectives at face value, I have had to look beyond—and sometimes even controvert—them in order to make sense of their broader context and multiple meanings. As Harel Shapira writes, sociologists must "distinguish our informants' truth from sociological truth—a truth that asks us to make visible the social forces that others are often blind to."[6] Doing so, Shapira contends, requires an "important and *necessary* epistemological gap between [oneself] and the people [one] writes about. It is not an empathy gap," he explains, but a gap between "what it is that the researcher understands and what it is that the people we write about understand."[7] This is the task of qualitative sociology, and the task I have undertaken in this book.

But this task is not always uncomplicated, especially when one is a privileged white upper-middle-class researcher—as am I—studying largely marginalized populations. The ethics of doing so have been roundly and rightly debated.[8] Though such debates often focus on ethnographic rather than interviewing methods, I have kept such ethical concerns at the forefront of my research and writing. In particular, heeding sociologist Mario Small's advice, I have sought to pursue "empathy" rather than "sympathy," and "understanding" rather than "pity," for the workers in this study.[9]

In an effort to maintain transparency throughout my research, I did not attempt to mask or bridge the often-significant social distance between myself and my informants (though it is debatable whether that is ever truly possible). Without a doubt, I was an outsider to their social world, which informed how they spoke to me of their experiences and worldviews in ways that cannot be measured. Yet because I knew little of their world—and because they did not expect me to—they were willing to explain seemingly quotidian matters in great detail, and I was not worried about losing insider status for having to ask basic questions (such as the meaning of "O.G."). To be sure, they sometimes teased me for my lack of knowledge, rightly reifying their status as experts of their own lives, owners of their own stories. For their sharing those stories, I am deeply grateful. I hope I have done them justice.

APPENDIX B People qua Data

This appendix provides more detail about the workers at the heart of this study: their demographic characteristics and their labor as well as how they compare to their broader populations. For each category of work, there are two tables. The first is intended to serve as a quick reference guide for the informants in that group, listing them in alphabetical order by the first name of their self-chosen pseudonym. This table lists their self-identified race/ethnicity, sex, age, and—if they were not born in the United States—a general descriptor of their nationality. Because I did not explicitly ask about nationality, however, all of my informants are presumed to be native-born unless they indicated otherwise. A few described their ethnoracial identity in such a way that readers might mistake them to be foreign-born. In those cases, I have added my own notation in brackets for clarification; for the two informants (both athletes) about whom I was uncertain, I have inserted question marks alongside my notation. This table also includes these informants' jobs—that is, a selection of their (sometimes many) jobs in prison, some of the types of labor they performed for workfare, their NCAA Division I college sport (football or basketball), or the scientific discipline in which they pursued their PhDs.

The second table for each category of work summarizes the demographic characteristics of the informants in that group and their broader populations around the time of my fieldwork. For the informants in this study, race and ethnicity are not discrete categories. Thus, for example, if an informant identified himself as Black and Hispanic, he is listed as both "African American" and "Hispanic." (However, if an informant identified herself as "biracial" or "Black and White," she is listed only in the "multiracial" category.) Most informants in this study were no longer in their reported labor position at the time of our interview. This includes all of the incarcerated, athlete, and graduate student informants and some of the workfare workers. Though the incarcerated workers had only recently left prison, for the other groups there was some variation in the time lapse. For the former athletes and graduate students, in particular, this means that their ages do not correspond to those of their broader populations, although such age data were not readily available.

Though these demographic data are important, it is not possible to draw meaningful comparisons between the demographic groups in this book. To be sure, race, gender, and other demographics have profoundly shaped these workers' labor and lives. Indeed, there are well-documented differences between white, Black, and Brown prisoners in their work, wages, and skill acquisition behind bars,[1] just as there are well-documented differences between men and women—and between racial groups—in graduate work within the academic sciences.[2] But this study cannot interrogate such differences; even with a relatively large number of interviews, it is unequivocally "small-n research." As such, it is designed to develop theory—in this case, identifying a mechanism by which power is deployed (and resisted) in the workplace—rather than documenting variation across groups in how such power is experienced. I hope subsequent research will undertake this task, as documenting such variation is essential to understanding workers' experience of employers' punitive and coercive power.

Table 3 Incarcerated workers: Quick reference guide

Pseudonym	Demographic characteristics	Prison jobs (selected)
A.T.	Black, male, 64	Food service; porter; laundry; metal shop
Apache	Black American, male, 34	Food service; porter
Black P.R.	Black, male, 22	Porter
Brenda Smith	Black African American, female, 53	Food service; porter
Bruce W.	African [African American], male, 23	Porter
C. Parks	African American, male, 27	Food service; porter
D.D.G.	Black, male, 28	Outside work crew; porter
D.Q.	African American, male, 27	Porter; lawns and grounds
Derrick	African American, male, 33	Food service; lawns and grounds
Dom	African American, male, 24	Food service
Dominique	Black, female, 31	Porter; beauty salon
F.E.	African American, male, 21	Teacher's aide; porter
F. Gordon	African American, male, 25	Lawns and grounds; painting
Garcia	Black and Hispanic, male, 27	Porter; facility maintenance
Glenn	Black, male, 47	Porter; laundry
J.D.	African American, male, 22	Porter
J.P. Smith	African American, male, 55	Teacher's aide
Jack Johnson	Black, male, 60	Anger management facilitator
Jahad	African American and American Indian, male, 49	Welding; facility maintenance
James D.	African American, male, 52	Asbestos abatement; anger management facilitator; porter
Jane D.	African American, female, 25	Facility maintenance
Jarome Wilks	Black African American, male, 20	Outside work crew
John D.	African American, male, 20	Lawns and grounds
John S.	White, male, 24	Porter; laundry
K.H.	African American, male, 47	Food service; porter
Kendrick	African American, male, 41	Porter; biohazard cleanup
Larry G.	Black American, male, 50	Tool clerk; porter
Linda H.	Black and White, female, 24	Porter; facilitator for addiction group
Mary	White, female, 52	Welder; porter

Table 3   (Continued)

Pseudonym	Demographic characteristics	Prison jobs (selected)
Miguel Fine	Hispanic, male, 27	Inmate grievance representative; flooring
Mike Harris	African American, male, 20	Porter; lawns and grounds
Mike Russ	Hispanic and Black, male, 19	Utilities; porter
O.G.	African American, male, 62	Food service; license plate shop
O.T.I.	African American, male, 27	Porter; school clerk
Paul D.	Italian [white], male, 22	Outside work crew; food service
Qwon	African American, male, 31	Food service; barber shop; porter
Rodney Williams	African American, male, 41	Porter; lawns and grounds
Ron D.	African American, male, 24	Tool clerk; porter; food service
Sal Winter	White, male, 24	Food service
Santos	Black, male, 28	Porter; caustics
Tim Jones	African American, male, 28	Porter; recreation aide

Table 4   Incarcerated workers: Descriptive statistics

Demographic characteristics	Ex-incarcerated respondents	New York State prison population[a]
Sex		
Male	88% (n = 36)	96%
Female	12% (n = 5)	4%
Age		
Average	33 yrs.	37.7 yrs.
Median	27 yrs.	—
Race/ethnicity		
African American	85.3% (n = 35)	49.6%
Hispanic	7.3% (n = 3)	24.1%
White	9.7% (n = 4)	23.6%
Multiracial	2.4% (n = 1)	—
Asian	0% (n = 0)	—
Native American	2.4% (n = 1)	—
Non-U.S. native	0% (n = 0)	10%
Total	n = 41	53,928

[a] Department of Corrections and Community Supervision, *Under Custody Report: Profile of Inmate Population under Custody on January 1, 2013* (Albany: DOCCS, 2013).

Table 5 Workfare workers: Quick reference guide

Pseudonym	Demographic characteristics	Workfare jobs (selected)
Alice Perry	Black, female, 26	Trash pickup; food pantry; thrift store
Ambrosia	Black, female, 29	Trash pickup; food pantry
Antonella	White, female, 60	Clerical; dishwashing
April Johnson	African American, female, 36	Trash pickup; thrift store
April Smith	African American, female, 30	Janitorial; thrift store
B. Brown	Black, female, 52	Food pantry
Chandrea Jackson	African American, female, 32	Trash pickup
Ciara	Black, female, 30	Trash pickup; thrift store; food pantry
Cindy	American Polish Puerto Rican Jew [white], female, 47	Clerical
Clevelanda Pace	Black, female, 33	Clerical; janitorial
DiMaggio	White, male, 51	Clerical; janitorial
Felisha Jones	African American, female, 23	Painting; lawns and grounds
Gail	African American, female, 56	Thrift store
George	Afro-American, male, 55	Clerical
Ilana	Afro-American, female, 57	Trash pickup
Jackie Lewis	Black, female, 57	Janitorial; food preparation
Jackie Robinson	Black, female, 56	Janitorial; clerical
James Griggs	Afro-American, male, 50	Janitorial
James Pondos	African American, male, 52	Painting; trash pickup; building maintenance
Jennifer Rose	Black and Hispanic, female, 27	Thrift store
John T.	African American, male, 53	Hospital laundry and patient transport
Johnny Dominoes	Hispanic, male, 54	Clerical; truck delivery
Kathy Johnson	White, female, 45	Thrift store
Kierra Ross	African American, female, 51	Trash pickup; janitorial; thrift store
Kim Collins	Black African American, female, 46	Trash pickup
Kim Hunky	African American, female, 25	Trash pickup; janitorial; thrift store
Lisa Williams	African American, female, 26	Trash pickup; janitorial; thrift store
Makita Ross	African American, female, 32	Trash pickup; food pantry; clerical
Michael Perry	Black, male, 35	Building maintenance; janitorial
Pauline Wilson	African American, female, 57	Janitorial; trash pickup
Peter Blacker	Black, male, 52	Building maintenance; trash pickup; lawns and grounds

Table 5 (Continued)

Pseudonym	Demographic characteristics	Workfare jobs (selected)
Phil Jackson	African American / American German, male, 48	Building maintenance; trash pickup; lawns and grounds
S.R.	African American, female, 34	Thrift store
Sasha Reed	African American, female, 26	Trash pickup; thrift store
Shara White	African American, female, 30	Trash pickup
Steven Rodriguez	Hispanic, male, 35	Trash pickup; lawns and grounds
Tara Collins	Black, female, 38	Trash pickup; lawns and grounds
Tasha Love	Black, female, 23	Trash pick-up; janitorial
Tasha Mack	African American, female, 26	Trash pickup; lawns and grounds; food pantry
Tashia Green	African American, female, 31	Trash pickup; janitorial
Tracy Martin	Native American, female, 37	Clerical
Will Jones	African American, male, 30	Trash pickup; building maintenance

Table 6   Workfare workers: Descriptive statistics

Demographic characteristics	Workfare respondents	New York State adult TANF population[a]
Sex		
Male	26% (*n* = 11)	12.3%
Female	74% (*n* = 31)	87.7%
Age		
Average	40 yrs.	48.1% = 20–29 yrs.
Median	36 yrs.	27.3% = 30–39 yrs.
Race/ethnicity		
African American	80.9% (*n* = 34)	39.8%
Hispanic	7.1% (*n* = 3)	33.5%
White	9.5% (*n* = 4)	21.1%
Multiracial	2.3% (*n* = 1)	1.4%
Asian	0% (*n* = 0)	3.4%
Native American	2.3% (*n* = 1)	0.7%
Non-U.S. native	0% (*n* = 0)	10.7%
Total	*n* = 42	69,253 (adult)

[a] Administration for Children & Families, *Characteristics and Financial Circumstances of TANF Recipients, 2013* (Washington, DC: ACF, 2015).

Table 7   College athletes: Quick reference guide

Pseudonym	Demographic characteristics	Job (sport)
Bill Murdock	White, male, 34	Football
Bruce	White/Caucasian, male, 33	Football
Haley	White, female, 23	Basketball
Jayce	White, male, 29	Football
JohnJohn	Black Jamaican [African American?], male, 34	Football
Kate	Black, female, 24	Basketball
Kyle Bronstein	White, male, 26	Football
Lawrence	African American, male, 31	Football
Lindsay	Black, female, 25	Basketball
M.K.	African American, female, 29	Basketball
M. Max	Black, male, 37	Football
Mike Smith	White, male, 37	Basketball
Molly	African American, female, 23	Basketball
Paulo	Mexican [Mexican American?], male, 33	Football
Sebastian Majella	White, male, 33	Football
Shevontae	Black, female, 26	Basketball
Tom Vine	White, male, 36	Basketball
Zachary Lane	African American, male, 29	Football

Table 8   College athletes: Descriptive statistics

Demographic characteristics	Ex-athlete respondents	Division I NCAA football[a]	Division I NCAA basketball[a]
Sex			
Male	67% (n = 12)	100%	52.3%
Female	33% (n = 6)	0%	47.7%
Age			
Average	29.9 yrs.	—	—
Median	29 yrs.	—	—
Race/ethnicity			
African American	50% (n = 9)	47.4%	53.6%
Hispanic	6% (n = 1)	2.7%	2.1%
White	44% (n = 8)	39.6%	28.2%
Multiracial	0% (n = 0)	4.4%	5.4%
Asian	0% (n = 0)	0.4%	0.3%
Native American	0% (n = 0)	0.4%	0.4%
Non-U.S. native	0% (n = 0?)	0.4%	6.6%
Total	n = 18	28,380	10,462

[a] "Student-Athlete Data," *NCAA,* http://web1.ncaa.org/rgdSearch/exec/saSearch (November 22, 2018).

Table 9   *Graduate students: Quick reference guide*

Pseudonym	Demographic characteristics	Job (academic discipline)
Charlie	White, female, 38	Cancer biology
D.N.	Asian, male, 33, Southeast Asian	Electrical engineering
Elizabeth	White, female, 31	Inorganic chemistry
Emily	White, female, 30	Chemistry
Gustavo	Chicano, male, 35	Neuroscience
Henry	White, male, 42	Chemistry
Iris	Latina, female, 34	Chemistry
Kimberly Mays	African American, female, 37	Cancer biology
Laine	White, female, 30	Inorganic chemistry
Lisbeth Jordan	White, female, 30	Chemistry
M.G.	Biracial Asian American, female, 35	Pharmacology
Michelle Fisher	White, female, 29	Chemistry
Nik	[Race/ethnicity not given], male, 35	Neuroscience
Rebecca	White, female, 40	Biomedical sciences
Ron	White, male, 36, European	Chemistry
Scott	White, male, 32	Molecular biology
Sunny	Hispanic American, female, 41	Pharmacology
Suzanne	White, female, 42, European	Molecular biology
Tiffany	White, female, 38	Biomedical sciences
Zane	White, male, 28	Chemistry

Table 10   Graduate students: Descriptive statistics

Demographic characteristics	Ex-graduate student respondents	Graduate students in science and engineering[a]
Sex		
Male	35% (*n* = 7)	58%
Female	65% (*n* = 13)	42%
Age		
Average	34.8 yrs.	—
Median	35 yrs.	—
Race/ethnicity		
African American	5% (*n* = 1)	4.9%
Hispanic	15% (*n* = 3)	6.1%
White	65% (*n* = 13)	39.1%
Multiracial	5% (*n* = 1)	1.6%
Asian	10% (*n* = 2)	5.6%
Native American	0% (*n* = 0)	0.3%
Non-U.S. native	15% (*n* = 3)	38.1%
Total	*n* = 20	618,008

[a] National Science Foundation, "Survey of Graduate Students and Postdoctorates in Science and Engineering, Fall 2015," *NCSESData.NSF.gov*, https://ncsesdata.nsf.gov/datatables/gradpostdoc/2015/ (November 22, 2018). Note that these race/ethnicity data refer to U.S. citizens and permanent residents only, unlike my summary statistics, which include the three nonnative students.

Notes

1. "Apache" and all of the names in this book are pseudonyms chosen by the informants themselves. Their ethnoracial identities are also self-designated.

2. New York State prison wages range from $0.10 to $0.33 per hour for most jobs, while industry jobs in Corcraft factories pay, on average, $0.62 per hour. For state and federal prison wage rates, see Prison Policy Initiative, "State and Federal Prison Wage Policies and Sourcing Information," www.prisonpolicy.org/reports /wage_policies.html (November 17, 2018). For more on Corcraft prison industries, see "About Corcraft," *Corcraft Products*, www.corcraft.org/webapp/wcs/stores /servlet/WhoWeAreView (November 17, 2018).

3. The use of italics in quotations indicates informants' own emphases.

4. Evelyn Nakano Glenn, *Unequal Freedom: How Race and Gender Shaped American Citizenship and Labor* (Cambridge: Harvard University Press, 2002); Linda Kerber, *No Constitutional Right to Be Ladies: Women and the Obligations of Citizenship* (New York: Hill and Wang, 1998); T. H. Marshall, *Class, Citizenship and Social Development* (New York: Doubleday, 1964 [1949]); Judith Shklar, *American Citizenship: The Quest for Inclusion* (Cambridge: Harvard University Press, 1991); Max Weber, *The Protestant Work Ethic and the Spirit of Capitalism* (New York: Scribner's, 1958); Kathi Weeks, *The Problem with Work: Feminism, Marxism, Antiwork Politics, and Postwork Imaginaries* (Durham: Duke University Press, 2011).

5. Emphasis added. "Primary Documents in American History," www.loc .gov/rr/program/bib/ourdocs/13thamendment.html (October 27, 2017).

6. E.g., Hale v. Arizona, 967 F.2d 1356, 1990. For in-depth analysis of prisoners' legal status as workers, see Noah Zatz, "Working at the Boundaries of Markets," *Vanderbilt Law Review* 61, no. 3 (2008): 857–958; Noah Zatz, "Prison Labor and the Paradox of Paid Nonmarket Work," in *Research in the Sociology of Work*, vol. 18, ed. Nina Bandelj (Bingley: Emerald, 2009), 369–98.

7. Shklar, *American Citizenship;* Margaret Somers, *Genealogies of Citizenship: Markets, Statelessness, and the Right to Have Rights* (Cambridge: Cambridge University Press, 2008).

8. In fact, in New York City workfare is called the "work experience program" (or "WEP") and references to such programs as "work experience" are widespread; e.g., Mathematica Policy Research, Inc., *Strategies for Increasing TANF Work Participation Rates: Providing Unpaid Work Experience Opportunities for TANF Recipients* (Washington, DC: US Department of Health and Human Services, 2008).

9. Although welfare benefits are not legally construed as "wages" (but see Matter of Walter Carver v. State, 26 N.Y. 3d 272, 2015), the sum of an individual's cash benefits and food stamps divided by the number of hours worked is required to comply with the federal minimum wage (Stone v. McGowan, 308 F. Supp. 2d 79, 2004). For more on the meagerness of welfare benefits, see Kaaryn Gustafson, *Cheating Welfare: Public Assistance and the Criminalization of Poverty* (New York: New York University Press, 2011); Sharon Hays, *Flat Broke with Children: Women in the Age of Welfare Reform* (New York: Oxford University Press, 2004). As this book is being written, moreover, some states have extended (or sought to extend) work requirements to additional social welfare programs, including Medicaid and SNAP, though such efforts are facing legal challenges.

10. Gustafson, *Cheating Welfare;* Julilly Kohler-Hausmann, "'The Crime of Survival': Fraud Prosecutions, Community Surveillance and the Original 'Welfare Queen,'" *Journal of Social History* 41, no. 2 (2007): 329–54; Julilly Kohler-Hausmann, *Getting Tough: Welfare and Imprisonment in 1970s America* (Princeton: Princeton University Press, 2017); Kenneth Neubeck and Noel Cazenave, *Welfare Racism: Playing the Race Card against America's Poor* (New York: Routledge, 2001); Joe Soss, Richard Fording, and Sanford Schram, *Disciplining the Poor: Neoliberal Paternalism and the Persistent Power of Race* (Chicago: University of Chicago Press, 2011); Loïc Wacquant, *Punishing the Poor: The Neoliberal Government of Social Insecurity* (Durham: Duke University Press, 2009).

11. E.g., "The Welfare State's Cost to American Taxpayers," *Discover the Networks,* www.discoverthenetworks.org/viewSubCategory.asp (October 28, 2017); "I HateWelfareBums!"*IsItNormal?*http://isitnormal.com/story/i-hate-welfare-bums-32539/ (October 28, 2017); "The Statistics Do Not Lie! Welfare Is the Best Paying Entry Level Job in 35 States!" *D.C. Clothesline,* www.dcclothesline.com/2014/08/05 /statistics-lie-welfare-best-paying-entry-level-job-35-states/ (October 28, 2017).

12. See chapter 5 in this book, as well as Jane Collins and Victoria Mayer, *Both Hands Tied: Welfare Reform and the Race to the Bottom of the Low-Wage Labor Market* (Chicago: University of Chicago Press, 2010); Gustafson, *Cheating Welfare;* Hays, *Flat Broke with Children.*

13. Kaaryn Gustafson, "The Criminalization of Poverty," *Journal of Criminal Law and Criminology* 99, no. 3 (2009): 643–716; Gustafson, *Cheating Welfare;* Kohler-Hausmann, "'Crime of Survival'"; Kohler-Hausmann, *Getting Tough;* Neubeck and Cazenave, *Welfare Racism;* Frances Fox Piven and Richard Cloward, *Regulating the Poor: The Functions of Public Welfare* (New York: Pantheon, 1971); Wacquant, *Punishing the Poor.*

14. Gustafson, *Cheating Welfare;* Neubeck and Cazenave, *Welfare Racism;* Piven and Cloward, *Regulating the Poor;* Soss, Fording, and Schram, *Disciplining the Poor;* Wacquant, *Punishing the Poor;* Bruce Western and Becky Pettit, "Incarceration & Social Inequality," *Dædalus* (Summer 2010): 8–19.

15. Katherine Beckett and Bruce Western, "Governing Social Marginality: Welfare, Incarceration, and the Transformation of State Policy," *Punishment & Society* 3, no. 1 (2001): 44.

16. Wacquant, *Punishing the Poor*, 11; see also David Garland, *Punishment and Modern Society: A Study in Social Theory* (Chicago: University of Chicago Press, 1990); Gustafson, "Criminalization of Poverty"; Gustafson, *Cheating Welfare;* Julilly Kohler-Hausmann, "Guns and Butter: The Welfare State, the Carceral State, and the Politics of Exclusion in the Postwar United States," *Journal of American History* 102, no. 1 (2015): 87–99; Bruce Western and Katherine Beckett, "How Unregulated Is the U.S. Labor Market? The Penal System as a Labor Market Institution," *American Journal of Sociology* 104, no. 4 (1999): 1030–60. But see Mona Lynch, "Theorizing Punishment: Reflections on Wacquant's *Punishing the Poor*," *Critical Sociology* 37, no. 2 (2011): 237–44.

17. Kohler-Hausmann, *Getting Tough;* Beckett and Western, "Governing Social Marginality."

18. Erin Hatton, "When Work Is Punishment: Penal Subjectivities in Punitive Labor Regimes," *Punishment & Society* 20, no. 2 (2018): 174–91.

19. Wacquant, *Punishing the Poor*, 42.

20. Michel Foucault, *Discipline & Punish: The Birth of the Prison* (New York: Random House, 1977), 297.

21. John Krinsky, *Free Labor: Workfare and the Contested Language of Neoliberalism* (Chicago: University of Chicago Press, 2007); Zatz, "Prison Labor."

22. There is significant lack of transparency in terms of who profits from college sports and how much; Taylor Branch, "The Shame of College Sports," *The Atlantic*, October 2011, www.theatlantic.com/magazine/archive/2011/10/the-shame-of-college-sports/308643/. Yet partial data are available regarding coaches' pay, universities' revenue, and NCAA revenue; see "College Athletics Revenues and Expenses—2008," *ESPN*, www.espn.com/ncaa/revenue/_/type/expenses, and

www.espn.com/ncaa/revenue (October 28, 2017); "Revenue & Expenses," *NCAA,* www.ncaa.org/sites/default/files/2015%20Division%20I%20RE%20report.pdf (October 28, 2017); "Where Does the Money Go?" *NCAA,* www.ncaa.org/health-and-safety/sport-science-institute/ncaa-budget-where-money-goes (October 28, 2017); "Revenue," *NCAA,* www.ncaa.org/about/resources/finances/revenue (October 28, 2017). These data suggest that although coaches and the NCAA often profit handsomely from college sports, the numbers are only ambiguously positive for universities. Aside from the top football and basketball programs, which yield sizeable returns for their universities, most sports are reportedly net losses for their universities. However, these calculations do not account for various indirect returns from teams' athletic success, including increased legislative spending, alumni support, and student recruitment.

23. E.g., O'Bannon v. NCAA, Nos. 14–16601, 14–17068 (9th Cir. September 30, 2015).

24. Sheila Slaughter, Teresa Campbell, Margaret Holleman, and Edward Morgan, "The 'Traffic' in Graduate Students: Graduate Students as Tokens of Exchange between Academe and Industry," *Science, Technology, & Human Values* 27, no. 2 (2002): 285; see also Richard Freeman, Eric Weinstein, Elizabeth Marincola, Janet Rosenbaum, and Frank Solomon, "Careers and Rewards in Bio Sciences: The Disconnect between Scientific Progress and Career Progression," *American Society of Cell Biology,* 2001, https://depts.washington.edu/envision/resources /CareersBiosciences.pdf; Viviane Callier and Nathan Vanderford, "Mission Possible: Putting Trainees at the Center of Academia's Mission," *Nature Biotechnology* 32, no. 6 (June 2014): 593–94; Richard Freeman, Frank Solomon, Janet Rosenbaum, Elizabeth Marincola, and Eric Weinstein, "Competition and Careers in Biosciences," *Science,* December 14, 2001, www.sciencemag.org/careers/2001/12 /competition-and-careers-biosciences.

25. Freeman et al., "Careers and Rewards"; Callier and Vanderford, "Mission Possible"; Freeman et al., "Competition and Careers"; Slaughter et al., "'Traffic' in Graduate Students."

26. For graduate students, see *Brown University,* 342 NLRB 483 (2004); *The New School,* NLRB Case 02-RC-143009 (2015); but see *New York University,* 332 NLRB 1205 (2000). For college athletes, see Amicus Brief by National Association of Collegiate Directors of Athletics and Division 1A Athletic Directors' Association, *Northwestern University,* NLRB Case 13-RC-121359 (2015); but see *Northwestern University,* NLRB Case 13-RC-121359 (2015).

27. However, such stipends for Division I athletes were implemented in 2015, after all of my athlete informants had completed their undergraduate careers. For more, see Ray Glier, "Pets, Car Repairs and Mom: How College Football Players Use Their Stipends," *New York Times,* January 5, 2017, www.nytimes.com /2017/01/05/sports/ncaafootball/pets-car-repairs-and-mom-how-football-players-use-their-stipends.html.

28. E.g., "Graduate School Handbook: Information for All Graduate Students," *Brown University Graduate School,* www.brown.edu/academics/gradschool /graduate-school-handbook-information-all-graduate-students#employment (October 28, 2017); "Guidelines for Part-Time Employment of Full-Time Graduate Students in Arts & Sciences," *Washington University in St. Louis: The Graduate School,* http://graduateschool.wustl.edu/files/graduateschool/imce/part-time_employment_policy.pdf (October 28, 2017); "Graduate Policies & Procedures," *MIT: Office of Graduate Education,* https://odge.mit.edu/gpp /assistance/employment/conflict-of-interest-commitment/ (October 28, 2017).

29. *NCAA Division I Manual, 2015–16-January* (Indianapolis: National Collegiate Athletic Association, 2015); see also "Amateurism," *NCAA,* www.ncaa .org/amateurism (October 27, 2017).

30. Alan Binder, "N.C.A.A. Athletes Could Be Paid Under New California Law," *New York Times,* September 20, 2019, https://www.nytimes.com/2019/09 /30/sports/college-athletes-paid-california.html.

31. "Amateurism," *NCAA.*

32. Football and basketball athletes are not allowed to go directly to the NFL and NBA from high school. Football "players must have been out of high school for at least three years"; "The Rules of the Draft," *NFL,* http://operations.nfl .com/the-players/the-nfl-draft/the-rules-of-the-draft/ (October 27, 2017). Basketball players "must be 19 years old during draft calendar year, and at least one season has passed since graduation of high school"; "NBA Draft Rules," *Draft Site,* www.draftsite.com/nba/rules/ (October 27, 2017).

33. Unless otherwise noted, in this book "graduate students" and "college athletes" refer to the particular subgroups in this study: science graduate students and Division I football and basketball players.

34. In 2015–16, among NCAA Division I athletes, 60 percent of football players, and 72 percent of men and 68 percent of women basketball players, were racial minorities; "Student-Athlete Data," *NCAA,* http://web1.ncaa.org /rgdSearch/exec/saSearch (October 28, 2017).

35. Some of these parallels have been noted by sports scholars and commenters; e.g., Billy Hawkins, *The New Plantation: Black Athletes, College Sports, and Predominantly White NCAA Institutions* (New York: St. Martin's Press, 2010); Cord Jefferson, "The Dementia Bonus: Football as Black Servitude," *The Awl,* August 11, 2010, www.theawl.com/2010/08/the-dementia-bonus-football-as-black-servitude/; William Rhoden, *Forty Million Dollar Slaves: The Rise, Fall, and Redemption of the Black Athlete* (New York: Three Rivers Press, 2006).

36. Different state prison systems—and their prisoners—have different official and unofficial names for solitary confinement; e.g., "FAQ," *Solitary Watch,* http://solitarywatch.com/facts/faq/ (January 14, 2018).

37. "FAQ," *Solitary Watch;* New York Civil Liberties Union, *Boxed In: The True Cost of Extreme Isolation in New York's Prisons* (New York: NYCLU, 2012);

New York State Bar Association, *Solitary Confinement in New York State* (Albany: NYSBA, 2013); Anna Flagg, Alex Tatusian, and Christie Thompson, "Who's in Solitary Confinement?" *The Marshall Project*, November 20, 2016, www.themarshallproject.org/2016/11/30/a-new-report-gives-the-most-detailed-breakdown-yet-of-how-isolation-is-used-in-u-s-prisons.

38. Bruce Arrigo and Jennifer Leslie Bullock, "The Psychological Effects of Solitary Confinement on Prisoners in Supermax Units," *International Journal of Offender Therapy and Comparative Criminology* 52 (2008): 622–40; Mary Murphy Corcoran, "Effects of Solitary Confinement on the Well Being of Prison Inmates," *Applied Psychology OPUS* (2015), https://steinhardt.nyu.edu/appsych/opus/issues/2015/spring/corcoran; Craig Haney, "Restricting the Use of Solitary Confinement," *Annual Review of Criminology* 1 (2018): 285–310; Terry Allen Kupers, *Solitary* (Oakland: University of California Press, 2017); Nathaniel Penn, "Buried Alive: Stories from Inside Solitary Confinement," *GQ*, March 2, 2017, www.gq.com/story/buried-alive-solitary-confinement; New York State Bar Association, *Solitary Confinement in New York State;* Andrew Urevig, "The Confined Mind," *Lateral Magazine,* December 18, 2018, www.lateralmag.com/articles/issue-30/the-confined-mind.

39. George Dvorsky, "Why Solitary Confinement Is the Worst Kind of Psychological Torture," *Gizmodo,* http://io9.gizmodo.com/why-solitary-confinement-is-the-worst-kind-of-psycholog-1598543595 (January 14, 2018).

40. Welfare sanctions vary by state and category of assistance. Some states—though not New York—impose "full-family sanctions," which revoke not only the adult's benefits but also those of their dependent children. For more, see Dan Bloom and Don Winstead, *Sanctions and Welfare Reform,* Policy Brief no. 12 (Washington, DC: Brookings Institute, 2002); General Accounting Office, *Welfare Reform: State Sanction Policies and Number of Families Affected* (Washington, DC: US General Accounting Office, 2000); LaDonna Pavetti, Michelle Derr, and Heather Hesketh, *Review of Sanction Policies and Research Studies* (Princeton: Mathematica Policy Research, 2003); Legal Momentum, *The Sanction Epidemic in the Temporary Assistance for Needy Families Program* (New York: Women's Legal Defense and Education Fund, 2010).

41. Andrew Cherlin et al., *Sanctions and Case Closings for Noncompliance: Who Is Affected and Why* (Baltimore: Welfare, Children, & Families Study, Johns Hopkins University, 2001); Ariel Kalil, Kristin Seefeldt, and Hui-chen Wang, "Sanctions and Material Hardship Under TANF," *Social Service Review* 76, no. 4 (2002): 642–62; Taryn Lindhorst and Ronald Mancoske, "The Social and Economic Impact of Sanctions and Time Limits on Recipients of Temporary Assistance to Needy Families," *Journal of Sociology and Social Welfare* 33, no. 1 (2006): 93–114; Nancy Reichman, Julien Teitler, and Marah Curtis, "TANF Sanctioning and Hardship," *Social Service Review* 79, no. 2 (2005): 215–36.

42. "The Personal Responsibility and Work Opportunity Reconciliation Act of 1996," *US Department of Health & Human Services,* https://aspe.hhs.gov/report /personal-responsibility-and-work-opportunity-reconciliation-act-1996 (December 20, 2017); "TANF Federal Five-Year Time Limit," *Office of Family Assistance,* November 29, 2016, www.acf.hhs.gov/ofa/resource/tanf-federal-five-year-time-limit; Office of Temporary and Disability Assistance, "Temporary Assistance: Overview," *New York State OTDA,* http://otda.ny.gov/programs/temporary-assistance / (January 14, 2018). It is also true, though, that states have some flexibility in implementing such time limits. New York, for example, is one of the less stringent states on this issue, routinely transferring cases approaching TANF time limits to state and local sources of funding; Mary Farrell, Sarah Rich, Lesley Turner, David Seith, and Dan Bloom, *Welfare Time Limits: An Update on State Policies, Implementation, and Effects on Families* (Washington, DC: Lewin Group and MDRC, 2008); Cherlin et al., *Sanctions and Case Closings;* Pavetti et al., *Review of Sanction Policies.*

43. Karl Marx, *Capital: A Critique of Political Economy,* vol. 1 (New York: Penguin, 1992 [1906]).

44. Michael Burawoy, *The Politics of Production* (London: Verso, 1985), 123.

45. Marx, *Capital.*

46. E.g., Alexander Anievas, ed., *Marxism and World Politics: Contesting Global Capitalism* (New York: Routledge, 2010); Elisabeth Jean Wood, *Forging Democracy from Below: Insurgent Transitions in South Africa and El Salvador* (New York: Cambridge University Press, 2000).

47. Hira Singh, *Recasting Caste: From the Sacred to the Profane* (New Delhi: Sage Publications India, 2014); Joe Foweraker, *The Struggle for Land: A Political Economy of the Pioneer Frontier in Brazil from 1930 to the Present Day* (New York: Cambridge University Press, 1981).

48. Robert Steinfeld, *Coercion, Contract, and Free Labor in the Nineteenth Century* (Cambridge: Cambridge University Press, 2001).

49. Tom Brass, *Towards a Comparative Political Economy of Unfree Labour* (London: Frank Cass, 1999); Robert Evans, "Some Notes on Coerced Labor," *Journal of Economic History* 30 (1970): 861–66; Sébastien Rioux, "The Fiction of Economic Coercion: Political Marxism and the Separation of Theory and History," *Historical Materialism* 21 (2013): 92–128.

50. Edward Baptist, *The Half Has Never Been Told: Slavery and the Making of American Capitalism* (New York: Basic Books, 2014); Alex Lichtenstein, *Twice the Work of Free Labor: The Political Economy of Convict Labor in the New South* (New York: Verso, 1996).

51. Douglas Blackmon, *Slavery by Another Name: The Re-enslavement of Black Americans from the Civil War to World War II* (New York: Doubleday, 2008); Glenn, *Unequal Freedom;* Lichtenstein, *Twice the Work of Free Labor;* Rebecca McLennan, *The Crisis of Imprisonment: Protest, Politics, and the Making of the American Penal State, 1776-1941* (Cambridge: Cambridge University Press, 2008); Mae Ngai,

Impossible Subjects: Illegal Aliens and the Making of Modern America (Princeton: Princeton University Press, 2004); David Oshinsky, *Worse than Slavery: Parchman Farm and the Ordeal of Jim Crow Justice* (New York: Free Press, 1997).

52. Steinfeld, *Coercion, Contract, and Free Labor.*

53. Ralph Linton, *The Study of Man: An Introduction* (New York: D. Appleton-Century, 1936); see also Robert Merton, *Social Theory and Social Structure* (New York: Free Press, 1957).

54. This was particularly true for the graduate students I interviewed and to a lesser degree college athletes, whose class backgrounds, labor market experience, and career goals could buffer them—at least to some degree—from their bosses' coercive power. For instance, one former graduate student I interviewed, Nik, had previously worked in a high-paying tech job. His belief that he could return to that job at any time allayed his sense of vulnerability to his advisor's power over his research, degree, and career.

55. Southern Poverty Law Center, *Close to Slavery* (Montgomery: Southern Poverty Law Center, 2009), 15.

56. "Immigration Reform and Control Act of 1986 (IRCA)," *US Citizen and Immigration Services,* www.uscis.gov/tools/glossary/immigration-reform-and-control-act-1986-irca (October 28, 2017).

57. Annette Bernhardt et al., *Broken Laws, Unprotected Workers: Violations of Employment and Labor Laws in America's Cities* (New York: National Employment Law Project, 2009); Human Rights Watch, *Unfair Advantage: Workers' Freedom of Association in the United States under International Human Rights Standards* (New York: Human Rights Watch, 2000); National Employment Law Project, *Iced Out: How Immigration Enforcement Has Interfered with Workers' Rights* (New York: NELP, 2009); Southern Poverty Law Center, *Close to Slavery.* In fact, employers' coercive power over undocumented workers has only been strengthened in recent years by court rulings which assert that workers' illegality renders them consensual to their own exploitation; Kathleen Kim, "Beyond Coercion," *UCLA Law Review* 62 (2015): 1558–84.

58. E.g., Peter van der Meer, "Gender Unemployment and Subjective Well-Being: Why Being Unemployed Is Worse for Men than for Women," *Social Indicators Research* 115, no. 1 (2014): 23–44.

59. Office of Economic Policy, *Non-compete Contracts: Economic Effects and Policy Implications* (Washington, DC: US Department of Treasury, 2016); see also Conor Dougherty, "How Noncompete Clauses Keep Workers Locked In," *New York Times,* May 13, 2017, www.nytimes.com/2017/05/13/business/noncompete-clauses.html.

60. Dougherty, "How Noncompete Clauses."

61. In both of these institutions, in fact, there are specific terms used to describe the removal of workers from that status: "dishonorable discharge" (along with various types of "other than honorable discharge") for members of the military, and "defrocking" (or laicization) for clerics in some religious traditions.

62. For the now-disgraced film producer Harvey Weinstein, moreover, his legal, institutionally accepted power over actors' careers (i.e., status coercion) seemed to facilitate his illicit abuse of them as well.

63. Noah Zatz et al., *Get to Work or Go to Jail: Workplace Rights under Threat* (Los Angeles: UCLA Institute for Research on Labor and Employment, 2016); Noah Zatz, "Carceral Labor beyond Prison," in *Prison/Work: Labor in the Carceral State*, ed. Erin Hatton (Oakland: University of California Press, forthcoming).

64. Zatz, "Carceral Labor."

65. As quoted in Zatz et al., *Get to Work*, 12.

66. Gretchen Purser, "'You Put Up with Anything': The Vulnerability and Exploitability of Formerly-Incarcerated Workers," in *Prison/Work: Labor in the Carceral State*, ed. Erin Hatton (Oakland: University of California Press, forthcoming); Zatz et al., *Get to Work*.

67. Marx, *Capital*, 769.

68. Michel Wieviorka, "Case Studies: History or Sociology," in *What Is a Case: Exploring the Foundations of Social Inquiry*, ed. Charles Ragin and Howard Becker (Cambridge: Cambridge University Press, 1992), 159–72.

69. Wieviorka, "Case Studies," 170.

70. Wieviorka, "Case Studies," 170.

71. George Steinmetz, "Odious Comparisons: Incommensurability, the Case Study, and 'Small N's' in Sociology," *Sociological Theory* 22, no. 3 (2004): 371–400.

72. E.g., Baptist, *Half Has Never Been Told;* Blackmon, *Slavery by Another Name;* Brass, *Towards a Comparative Political Economy;* Lichtenstein, *Twice the Work;* Steinfeld, *Coercion, Contract, and Free Labor.*

73. E.g., Baptist, *Half Has Never Been Told.*

74. E.g., John Bowe, *Nobodies: Modern American Slave Labor and the Dark Side of the New Global Economy* (New York: Random House, 2008); Kathleen Kim, "The Coercion of Trafficked Workers," *Iowa Law Review* 96 (2011): 409–74; Louise Shelley, *Human Trafficking: A Global Perspective* (Cambridge: Cambridge University Press, 2010); Kendra Strauss, "Coerced, Forced and Unfree Labour: Geographies of Exploitation in Contemporary Labour Markets," *Geography Compass* 6 (2012): 137–48.

75. E.g., Gertrude Ezorsky, *Freedom in the Workplace?* (Ithaca: Cornell University Press, 2007); Todd Gordon, "Capitalism, Neoliberalism, and Unfree Labour," *Critical Sociology* (2018), doi: 10.1177/0896920518763936.

76. Erin Hatton, *The Temp Economy: From Kelly Girls to Permatemps in Postwar America* (Philadelphia: Temple University Press, 2011); Arne Kalleberg, *Good Jobs, Bad Jobs: The Rise of Polarized and Precarious Employment Systems in the United States, 1970s to 2000s* (New York: Russell Sage Foundation, 2011).

77. Guy Standing, *The Precariat: The New Dangerous Class* (New York: Bloomsbury, 2014).

78. Jamie Peck, "Zombie Neoliberalism and the Ambidextrous State," *Theoretical Criminology* 14, no. 1 (2010): 104–10; Wacquant, *Punishing the Poor.*

236   NOTES TO PAGES 20-22

79. Kalleberg, *Good Jobs, Bad Jobs;* Peck, "Zombie Neoliberalism"; Standing, *Precariat.*

80. Peck, "Zombie Neoliberalism."

81. Elizabeth Hinton, *From the War on Poverty to the War on Crime* (Cambridge: Harvard University Press, 2016); Khalil Gibran Muhammad, *The Condemnation of Blackness* (Cambridge: Harvard University Press, 2010).

82. Michelle Alexander, *The New Jim Crow: Mass Incarceration in the Age of Colorblindness* (New York: New Press, 2012); Wacquant, *Punishing the Poor;* Bruce Western, *Punishment and Inequality in America* (New York: Russell Sage Foundation, 2006).

83. Kohler-Hausmann, *Getting Tough;* Neubeck and Cazenave, *Welfare Racism;* Soss, Fording, and Schram, *Disciplining the Poor.*

84. Kohler-Hausmann, *Getting Tough;* Neubeck and Cazenave, *Welfare Racism;* Soss, Fording, and Schram, *Disciplining the Poor.*

85. Zatz, "Carceral Labor"; Zatz et al., *Get to Work.*

86. E.g., Joan Acker, "Hierarchies, Jobs, Bodies: A Theory of Gendered Organizations," *Gender & Society* 4, no. 2 (1990): 139–58; Dana Britton, *At Work in the Iron Cage: The Prison as Gendered Organization* (New York: New York University Press, 2003); Louwanda Evans and Wendy Moore, "Impossible Burdens: White Institutions, Emotional Labor, and Micro-Resistance," *Social Problems* 62, no. 3 (2015): 439–54; Adia Harvey Wingfield, "Racializing the Glass Escalator: Reconsidering Men's Experiences with Women's Work," *Gender & Society* 23, no. 1 (2009): 5–26; George Lipsitz, *How Racism Takes Place* (Philadelphia: Temple University Press, 2011); Wendy Moore, *Reproducing Racism: White Space, Elite Law Schools, and Racial Inequality* (Lanham: Rowman & Littlefield, 2008); Mary Nell Trautner, "Doing Gender, Doing Class: The Performance of Sexuality in Exotic Dance Clubs," *Gender & Society* 19, no. 6 (2005): 771–88.

87. For prisoners' demographic data, see E. Ann Carson, *Prisoners in 2016* (Washington, DC: US Department of Justice, 2018), www.bjs.gov/content/pub /pdf/p16.pdf. For race-gender-class constructions of prisons and the criminal justice system, see Anna Curtis, "'You Have to Cut It Off at the Knee': Dangerous Masculinity and Security inside a Men's Prison," *Men and Masculinities* 17, no. 2 (2014): 120–46; Rose Brewer and Nancy Heitzeg, "The Racialization of Crime and Punishment: Criminal Justice, Color-Blind Racism, and the Political Economy of the Prison Industrial Complex," *American Behavioral Scientist* 51, no. 5 (2008): 625–44; Loïc Wacquant, "Deadly Symbiosis: When Ghetto and Prison Meet and Mesh," *Punishment & Society* 3, no. 1 (2001): 95–133.

88. For welfare recipients' demographic data, see Office of Family Assistance, *Characteristics and Financial Circumstances of TANF Recipients, Fiscal Year 2015* (Washington, DC: Office of Family Assistance, 2018), www.acf.hhs.gov /sites/default/files/ofa/characteristics_and_financial_circumstances_of_tanf_ recipients.pdf. For race-gender-class constructions of the welfare system, see

Gustafson, *Cheating Welfare;* Kohler-Hausmann, *Getting Tough;* Neubeck and Cazenave, *Welfare Racism;* Soss, Fording, and Schram, *Disciplining the Poor.*

89. For athletes' demographic data, see "Student-Athlete Data," *NCAA.* For race-gender-class constructions of college athletics, particularly football and basketball, see Hawkins, *New Plantation;* Rhoden, *Forty Million Dollar Slaves.*

90. For science graduate students' demographic data, see "Survey of Graduate Students and Postdoctorates in Science and Engineering, Fall 2016," *NSF,* https://ncsesdata.nsf.gov/gradpostdoc/2016/ (March 26, 2018). For race-gender-class constructions of academic sciences, see Louise Archer, Jennifer Dewitt, and Jonathan Osborne, "Is Science for Us? Black Students' and Parents' Views of Science and Science Careers," *Science Education* 99, no. 2 (2015): 199–237; Wendy Faulkner, "Dualisms, Hierarchies and Gender in Engineering," *Social Studies of Science* 30 (2000): 759–92; Allison Gonsalves, Anna Danielsson, and Helena Pettersson, "Masculinities and Experimental Practices in Physics: The View from Three Case Studies," *Physical Review: Physics Education Research* 12 (2016): 020120-1-15.

91. Andrea Armstrong, "Race, Prison Discipline, and the Law," *UC Irvine Law Review* 5, no. 4 (2015): 759–82; Michael Schwirtz, Michael Winerip, and Robert Gebeloff, "The Scourge of Racial Bias in New York State Prisons," *New York Times,* December 3, 2016, www.nytimes.com/2016/12/03/nyregion/new-york-state-prisons-inmates-racial-bias.html; Jeremiah Wade-Olson, *Punishing the Vulnerable: Discrimination in American Prisons* (Santa Barbara: Praeger, 2018).

92. Shaun Harper, *Black Male Student-Athletes and Racial Inequities in NCAA Division I College Sports* (Philadelphia: University of Pennsylvania, Center for the Study of Race & Equity in Education, 2016); Hawkins, *New Plantation;* Corinne Moss-Racusin, John Dovidio, Victoria Brescoll, Mark Graham, and Jo Handelsman, "Science Faculty's Subtle Gender Biases Favor Male Students," *PNAS: Proceedings of the National Academy of Sciences of the United States of America* (2012), doi: 10.1073/pnas.1211286109; Julie Posselt, *Inside Graduate Admissions: Merit, Diversity and Faculty Gatekeeping* (Cambridge: Harvard University Press, 2016); Joan Williams and Jessica Lee, "It's Illegal, Yet It Happens All the Time," *Chronicle of Higher Education,* September 28, 2015, www.chronicle.com/article/Its-Illegal-Yet-It-Happens/233445; U.S. Commission on Civil Rights, *A New Paradigm for Welfare Reform: The Need for Civil Rights Enforcement* (Washington, DC: U.S. Commission on Civil Rights, 2002).

93. Cynthia Cockburn, "The Gendering of Jobs: Workplace Relations and the Reproduction of Sex Segregation," in *Gender Segregation at Work,* ed. Sylvia Walby (Philadelphia: Open University Press, 1988), 38.

94. In fact, I interviewed over 140 workers for this book. However, as I describe in appendix A, 20 were domestic workers who are excluded from this book's findings, even though my interviews with them were crucial to developing its argument and analysis.

95. Brown v. Plata, 563 U.S. 493, 2011.

96. "How Much Do Incarcerated People Earn in Each State?" *Prison Policy Initiative*, www.prisonpolicy.org/blog/2017/04/10/wages/ (March 27, 2019).

97. Freeman et al., "Competition and Careers in Biosciences"; see also "Policies and Notices," *National Institutes of Health: Research Training and Career Development*, https://researchtraining.nih.gov/resources/policy-notices (October 28, 2017); "Data, Outcomes, and Evaluations: Reports on the Biomedical Research Workforce," *National Institutes of Health: Research Training and Career Development*, https://researchtraining.nih.gov/resources/data-outcomes-and-evaluations (November 5, 2017).

98. In fact, I originally planned to interview prisoners behind bars, but the New York State Department of Corrections and Community Supervision (DOCCS) would not grant me access to the state's prisons "because"—an official stated in our e-mail correspondence—the study "does not promise to have value for the Department."

99. In order to preserve the full meaning and character of their words, worker quotations in this book are edited as little as possible for readability, brevity, and anonymity.

100. This insight is drawn, at least in part, from Matthew Desmond's discussion of Leslie Marmon Silko's novel *Ceremony* at the 2017 annual meeting of the American Sociological Association in Montréal. Silko's book explores the centrality of storytelling to Laguna Pueblo culture, and as Desmond noted, she begins the book with the following dictum: "I will tell you something about stories / . . . They aren't just for entertainment. / Don't be fooled / They are all we have, you see"; Leslie Marmon Silko, *Ceremony* (New York: Viking Press, 1977), 2.

101. This insight is drawn from Allison Pugh's perceptive feedback on an earlier draft of this manuscript.

102. Foucault, *Discipline & Punish*, 137.

103. Nancy Fraser and Linda Gordon, "A Genealogy of Dependency: Tracing a Keyword of the U.S. Welfare State," *Signs* 19, no. 2 (1994): 309–36; Glenn, *Unequal Freedom;* Kerber, *No Constitutional Right;* David Roediger, *The Wages of Whiteness: Race and the Making of the American Working Class* (New York: Verso, 1991); Shklar, *American Citizenship;* Weeks, *Problem with Work.*

104. Ta-Nehisi Coates, *Between the World and Me* (New York: Spiegel & Grau, 2015), 10.

CHAPTER 1. CULTURAL NARRATIVES OF COERCED LABOR

1. Graeme Wood, "From Our Prison to Your Dinner Table," *Pacific Standard*, March 3, 2015, https://psmag.com/from-our-prison-to-your-dinner-table-10d94a05edca#.nan8qo3le.

2. Seth Davis, "Will Players Ever Stage a Strike at the Final Four? Rumors Persist Each Year, But I'll Believe It When I See It," *Sports Illustrated,* March 28, 2016, www.si.com/college-basketball/2016/03/28/rumors-players-walking-out-final-four-persist-without-any-real-evidence.

3. Noah Zatz, "Working at the Boundaries of Markets," *Vanderbilt Law Review* 61, no. 3 (2008): 857–958; Noah Zatz, "Prison Labor and the Paradox of Paid Nonmarket Work," in *Research in the Sociology of Work,* vol. 18, ed. Nina Bandelj (Bingley: Emerald, 2009), 369–98; see also Hale v. Arizona, 967 F.2d 1356, 1990.

4. Nancy Fraser and Linda Gordon, "A Genealogy of Dependency: Tracing a Keyword of the U.S. Welfare State," *Signs* 19, no. 2 (1994): 309–36; Evelyn Nakano Glenn, *Unequal Freedom: How Race and Gender Shaped American Citizenship and Labor* (Cambridge: Harvard University Press, 2002); David Roediger, *The Wages of Whiteness: Race and the Making of the American Working Class* (New York: Verso, 1991); Kathi Weeks, *The Problem with Work: Feminism, Marxism, Antiwork Politics, and Postwork Imaginaries* (Durham: Duke University Press, 2011).

5. Fraser and Gordon, "Genealogy of Dependency," 316.

6. Fraser and Gordon, "Genealogy of Dependency," 316.

7. Fraser and Gordon, "Genealogy of Dependency"; Michael Katz, *In the Shadow of the Poorhouse: A Social History of Welfare in America,* 2nd ed. (New York: Basic Books, 1996); Anna Stubblefield, "'Beyond the Pale': Tainted Whiteness, Cognitive Disability, and Eugenic Sterilization," *Hypatia* 22, no. 2 (2007): 162–81.

8. Stubblefield, "'Beyond the Pale'"; see also Fraser and Gordon, "Genealogy of Dependency"; Glenn, *Unequal Freedom;* Chad Alan Goldberg, *Citizens and Paupers: Relief, Rights, and Race, from the Freedmen's Bureau to Workfare* (Chicago: University of Chicago Press, 2007); Roediger, *Wages of Whiteness;* Weeks, *Problem with Work.*

9. Katz, *In the Shadow of the Poorhouse.*

10. As the following passage reveals, however, such solitary confinement did not usually exceed three days, which is significantly less than solitary sentences in contemporary American prisons, which typically start at 30 days and can last indefinitely; Bill Rockwood, Evan Wexler, and Sarah Childress, "How Much Time U.S. Prisoners Spend in Solitary," *PBS Frontline,* April 22, 2014, www.pbs.org/wgbh/pages/frontline/criminal-justice/locked-up-in-america/how-much-time-u-s-prisoners-spend-in-solitary/.

11. "Poorhouse Rules & Regulations," Orange County, NY, 1831, *The Poorhouse Story,* www.poorhousestory.com/RULES_NY_ORANGE_Text.htm (December 20, 2017).

12. For rhetoric about slaves, see Eric Foner, *Reconstruction: America's Unfinished Revolution, 1863–1877* (New York: Perennial Classics, 2011); Eric Foner and Olivia Mahoney, *America's Reconstruction: People and Politics after the Civil War* (New York: HarperCollins, 1995); Charles Davis and Henry Louis Gates Jr., eds., *The Slave's Narrative* (New York: Oxford University Press, 1985); Eugene Genovese, *Roll, Jordan, Roll: The World the Slaves Made* (New York:

Random House, 1976). For rhetoric about colonial natives, see Robert Berkhofer Jr., *The White Man's Indian: Images of the American Indian from Columbus to the Present* (New York: Vintage, 2011); Edward Said, *Culture and Imperialism* (New York: Vintage, 1994); David Spurr, *The Rhetoric of Empire: Colonial Discourse in Journalism, Travel Writing, and Imperial Administration* (Durham: Duke University Press, 1993); Anthony Wallace, *The Long, Bitter Trail: Andrew Jackson and the Indians* (New York: Farrar, Straus and Giroux, 1993).

13. Genovese, *Roll, Jordan, Roll*, 302.

14. William Harper, *The Pro-Slavery Argument* (Philadelphia: Lippincott, Grambo, & Co., 1853), 60, https://archive.org/stream/proslaveryargume00harp #page/n5/mode/2up.

15. Harper, *Pro-Slavery Argument*, 95.

16. Harper, *Pro-Slavery Argument*, 49.

17. Harper, *Pro-Slavery Argument*, 26.

18. Foner and Mahoney, *America's Reconstruction;* see also Kenneth Neubeck and Noel Cazenave, *Welfare Racism: Playing the Race Card against America's Poor* (New York: Routledge, 2001); Weeks, *Problem with Work*.

19. Foner and Mahoney, *America's Reconstruction*, 58.

20. Douglas Blackmon, *Slavery by Another Name: The Re-enslavement of Black Americans from the Civil War to World War II* (New York: Doubleday, 2008); Sarah Haley, *No Mercy Here: Gender, Punishment, and the Making of Jim Crow Modernity* (Chapel Hill: University of North Carolina Press, 2016); Alex Lichtenstein, *Twice the Work of Free Labor: The Political Economy of Convict Labor in the New South* (New York: Verso, 1996); Daniel Novak, *The Wheel of Servitude: Black Forced Labor after Slavery* (Lexington: University Press of Kentucky, 1978); David Oshinsky, *Worse than Slavery: Parchman Farm and the Ordeal of Jim Crow Justice* (New York: Free Press, 1997).

21. Blackmon, *Slavery by Another Name*, 1; see also Lichtenstein, *Twice the Work;* Oshinsky, *Worse than Slavery*.

22. Lichtenstein, *Twice the Work*, 17–18.

23. Although prior to industrialization white women had been men's economic equals, they had not been their political equals. Hilary Land, "Family Wage," *Feminist Review* 6 (1980): 57; see also Jeanne Boydston, *Home and Work: Housework, Wages, and the Ideology of Labor in the Early Republic* (New York: Oxford University Press, 1994); Alice Kessler-Harris, *Out to Work: A History of Wage-Earning Women in the United States* (New York: Oxford University Press, 1982).

24. Kessler-Harris, *Out to Work;* Louise Michele Newman, *White Women's Rights: The Racial Origins of Feminism in the United States* (New York: Oxford University Press, 1999).

25. Kessler-Harris, *Out to Work*, 187.

26. Indeed, it was widely believed that slaves could not be physically overworked; Genovese, *Roll, Jordan, Roll*.

27. Some white women activists used claims of vulnerability to gain labor protections and a modicum of political power; Kessler-Harris, *Out to Work;* Newman, *White Women's Rights.*

28. Though African Americans were disproportionately incarcerated, the criminal justice system was overwhelmingly white in popular imagination as well as in reality in the mid-20th century. For longitudinal data on the U.S. criminal justice population, see Jeremy Travis, Bruce Western, and Steve Redburn, eds., *The Growth of Incarceration in the United States* (Washington, DC: National Academic Press, 2014). For more on the rehabilitative ideal, see David Garland, *The Culture of Control: Crime and Social Order in Contemporary Society* (Chicago: University of Chicago Press, 2001).

29. E.g., Steve Chapman, "Black Demands and White Fears," *Chicago Tribune,* July 13, 2016, www.chicagotribune.com/snews/opinion/chapman/ct-dallas-race-war-blacks-white-anxiety-perspec-20160713-column.html; Alice George, "The 1968 Kerner Commission Got It Right, but Nobody Listened," *Smithsonian Magazine,* March 1, 2018, www.smithsonianmag.com/smithsonian-institution/1968-kerner-commission-got-it-right-nobody-listened-180968318/; Mark Hare, "Riots Still Haunt Rochester," *Rochester City Newspaper,* July 16, 2014, www.rochestercitynewspaper.com/rochester/riots-still-haunt-rochester/Content; see also Jane Rhodes, *Framing the Black Panthers: The Spectacular Rise of a Black Power Icon* (New York: New Press, 2007); Sabrina Sérac, "Between Fact & Fiction: The Use of Fear in the Construct and Dissemination of the Black Panther Party Image," *Revue de Recherche en Civilisation Américaine* (August 10, 2018), http://journals .openedition.org/rrca/273.

30. For more on crime rates and fears of crime, see Garland, *Culture of Control;* Julilly Kohler-Hausmann, *Getting Tough: Welfare and Imprisonment in 1970s America* (Princeton: Princeton University Press, 2017).

31. Michelle Alexander, *The New Jim Crow: Mass Incarceration in the Age of Colorblindness* (New York: New Press, 2012); Kohler-Hausmann, *Getting Tough;* Doris Marie Provine, *Unequal under Law: Race and the War on Drugs* (Chicago: University of Chicago Press, 2007).

32. Bruce Western, *Punishment and Inequality in America* (New York: Russell Sage Foundation, 2006).

33. Loïc Wacquant, *Punishing the Poor: The Neoliberal Government of Social Insecurity* (Durham: Duke University Press, 2009).

34. Mimi Abramovitz, *Regulating the Lives of Women: Social Welfare Policy from Colonial Times to the Present* (Boston: South End Press, 1988); Michael Katz, *The Undeserving Poor: From the War on Poverty to the War on Welfare* (New York: Oxford University Press, 1989).

35. This was due to states' discriminatory welfare policies as well as caseworkers' discriminatory practices; Premilla Nadasen, *The Welfare Rights Movement in the United States* (New York: Routledge, 2005); Neubeck and Cazenave,

Welfare Racism; Joe Soss, Richard Fording, and Sanford Schram, *Disciplining the Poor: Neoliberal Paternalism and the Persistent Power of Race* (Chicago: University of Chicago Press, 2011).

36. Nadasen, *Welfare Rights;* Neubeck and Cazenave, *Welfare Racism.*

37. Robert Moffitt, "The Deserving Poor, the Family, and the U.S. Welfare System," *Demography* 52, no. 3 (2015): 729–49.

38. Julilly Kohler-Hausmann, "'The Crime of Survival': Fraud Prosecutions, Community Surveillance and the Original 'Welfare Queen,'" *Journal of Social History* 41, no. 2 (2007): 329–54.

39. For more on the welfare rights movements, see Felicia Kornbluh, *The Battle for Welfare Rights: Politics and Poverty in Modern America* (Philadelphia: University of Pennsylvania Press, 2007); Nadasen, *Welfare Rights.*

40. Kohler-Hausmann, "'Crime of Survival'"; Neubeck and Cazenave, *Welfare Racism;* Rickie Solinger, *Beggars and Choosers: How the Politics of Choice Shapes Adoption, Abortion, and Welfare in the United States* (New York: Hill and Wang, 2002).

41. Jane Collins and Victoria Mayer, *Both Hands Tied: Welfare Reform and the Race to the Bottom in the Low-Wage Labor Market* (Chicago: University of Chicago Press, 2010); Sharon Hays, *Flat Broke with Children: Women in the Age of Welfare Reform* (New York: Oxford University Press, 2004); Soss, Fording, and Schram, *Disciplining the Poor.*

42. Neubeck and Cazenave, *Welfare Racism;* see also Martin Gilens, *Why Americans Hate Welfare: Race, Media, and the Politics of Antipoverty Policy* (Chicago: University of Chicago Press, 1999).

43. For data on state educational spending, see State Higher Education Executive Officers, *SHEF: FY 2017: State Higher Education Finance* (Boulder: SHEEO, 2018); Michael Mitchell, Michael Leachman, and Kathleen Masterson, "A Lost Decade in Higher Education Funding," *Center on Budget and Policy Priorities,* August 23, 2017, www.cbpp.org/research/state-budget-and-tax/a-lost-decade-in-higher-education-funding.

44. Sheila Slaughter and Gary Rhoades, *Academic Capitalism and the New Economy: Markets, State, and Higher Education* (Baltimore: Johns Hopkins University Press, 2004).

45. Ryan King-White, ed., *Sport and the Neoliberal University: Profit, Politics, and Pedagogy* (Brunswick: Rutgers University Press, 2018). For longitudinal data on sports' costs and revenue, see National Collegiate Athletic Association, *Revenues and Expenses: 2004–15* (Indianapolis: NCAA, 2016), www.ncaapublications.com/productdownloads/D1REVEXP2015.pdf.

46. E.g., Marc Tracy, "NCAA Extends Basketball Deal with CBS Sports and Turner through 2032," *New York Times,* April 12, 2016, www.nytimes.com/2016/04/13/sports/ncaabasketball/ncaa-extends-basketball-deal-with-cbs-sports-and-turner-through-2032.html.

47. Walter Byers, *Unsportsmanlike Conduct: Exploiting College Athletes* (Ann Arbor: University of Michigan Press, 1995).

48. E.g., Emma Baccellieri, "Nigel Hayes Is the Latest High-Profile Athlete to Call the NCAA on Its Bullshit," *Deadspin,* October 15, 2016, https://deadspin .com/nigel-hayes-is-the-latest-high-profile-athlete-to-call-1787834394; Justin Block, "Cardale Jones Just Tore Into the NCAA for Exploiting Its Athletes," *Huffington Post,* April 11, 2016, www.huffingtonpost.com/entry/cardale-jones-rips-ncaa-for-exploiting-college-athletes_us_570be174e4b01422324991bb; John Culhane, "Hey, Hey, NCAA. Unionize College Sports Today!" *Slate.com,* January 29, 2014, www.slate.com/articles/sports/sports_nut/2014/01/northwestern_football_union_will_college_athletes_union_gambit_succeed_could.html; Alex Putterman, "College Athlete Activist Ramogi Huma Discusses Northwestern Union, More," *Sports Illustrated,* August 4, 2015, www.si.com/college-football/2015/08/04/ramogi-huma-northwestern-union-ncaa-reform-ncpa.

49. E.g., Billy Hawkins, *The New Plantation: Black Athletes, College Sports, and Predominantly White NCAA Institutions* (New York: Palgrave Macmillan, 2010); William Rhoden, *Forty Million Dollar Slaves: The Rise, Fall, and Redemption of the Black Athlete* (New York: Three Rivers Press, 2006).

50. Paula Stephan, *How Economics Shapes Science* (Cambridge: Harvard University Press, 2012).

51. Sheila Slaughter, Teresa Campbell, Margaret Holleman, and Edward Morgan, "The 'Traffic' in Graduate Students: Graduate Students as Tokens of Exchange between Academe and Industry," *Science, Technology, & Human Values* 27, no. 2 (2002): 285; Richard Freeman, Eric Weinstein, Elizabeth Marincola, Janet Rosenbaum, and Frank Solomon, "Careers and Rewards in Bio Sciences: The Disconnect between Scientific Progress and Career Progression," *American Society of Cell Biology,* 2001, https://depts.washington.edu/envision/resources/Careers Biosciences.pdf; Viviane Callier and Nathan Vanderford, "Mission Possible: Putting Trainees at the Center of Academia's Mission," *Nature Biotechnology* 32, no. 6 (June 2014): 593–94.

52. Richard Larson, Navid Ghaffarzadegan, and Yi Xue, "Too Many PhD Graduates or Too Few Academic Job Openings: The Basic Reproductive Number R_0 in Academia," *Systems Research and Behavioral Science* 31, no. 6 (2014): 745–50; see also Leah Cannon, "How Many PhD Graduates Become Professors?" *Life Science Network,* September 15, 2016, https://lifesciencenetwork11.connectedcommunity .org/blogs/leah-cannon/2016/09/15/how-many-phd-graduates-become-professors. For longitudinal data on graduate student enrollment (and postdocs) in the sciences, see "Survey of Graduate Students and Postdoctorates in Science and Engineering, Fall 2016," *NSF,* February 2018, https://ncsesdata.nsf.gov/gradpostdoc /2016/.

53. E.g., Michelle Chen, "Could Yale Graduate Students Be the Next to Unionize?" *Nation,* May 6, 2015, www.thenation.com/article/could-yale-graduate-

students-be-next-unionize/; Josh Eidelson, "Can Graduate Students Unionize? The Government Can't Decide," *Bloomberg Businessweek*, May 12, 2016, www .bloomberg.com/news/articles/2016-05-12/can-graduate-students-unionize-the-government-can-t-decide; Steven Greenhouse, "Columbia Graduate Students Push for a Labor Union," *New York Times*, March 3, 2015, www.nytimes .com/2015/03/04/nyregion/columbia-graduate-students-push-for-a-labor-union .html.

54. Henry Giroux, *Neoliberalism's War on Higher Education* (Chicago: Haymarket Books, 2014). For more on academic capitalism, see Slaughter and Rhoades, *Academic Capitalism;* Bob Jessop, "Varieties of Academic Capitalism and Entrepreneurial Universities," *Higher Education* 73, no. 6 (2017): 853–70.

55. E.g., "WV Correctional Industries," *West Virginia Division of Corrections,* www.wvdoc.com/wvdoc/WVCorrectionalIndustries/tabid/42/Default.aspx (December 20, 2017); "2017 Florida Statutes," *Official Internet Site of the Florida Legislature,* www.leg.state.fl.us/Statutes/index.cfm (December 20, 2017); "Quick Facts about the Florida Department of Corrections," *Florida Department of Corrections,* April 2017, www.dc.state.fl.us/oth/Quickfacts.html; "Inmate Labor Projects," *New York State Corrections and Community Supervision Directive,* Dir. #3055, Dtd. 7/30/2014, file:///C:/Users/USER/Documents/Working% 20But%20Not%20Employed/1-Prison%20Workers/NYS%20DOCCS%20directive%20for%20inmate%20labor%20projects.pdf (December 20, 2017); "Inmate Work Crew Information," DOC Operations Division: Prison, *Oregon.gov,* www .oregon.gov/doc/OPS/PRISON/pages/crci_workcrew.aspx (December 20, 2017); Bob Wignall, "Prison Labor Facilitates Inmate Rehabilitation," in *Prisons,* ed. James Haley, *Opposing Viewpoints in Context* (Farmington Hills: Greenhaven Press, 2005).

56. J.J. Hensley, "Cash-Strapped Arizona Municipalities Urged to Turn to Inmate Labor," *Arizona Republic,* June 20, 2010, http://archive.azcentral.com /news/articles/20100620department-corrections-inmate-labor.html.

57. "Washington Inmate Labor Programs," SJR 8212 (2007), *Ballotpedia*, https:// ballotpedia.org/Washington_Inmate_Labor_Programs,_SJR_8212_(2007).

58. E.g., "About," *CalPIA*, www.calpia.ca.gov/about/ (December 20, 2017); "Our Mission," *Washington State Correctional Industries,* www.washingtonci.com / (December 20, 2017); "Washington Inmate Labor Programs"; "Arizona Correctional Industries," *Arizona Department of Corrections,* https://corrections.az.gov /arizona-correctional-industries(December17,2017);"904.703ServicesofInmates— Institutions and Public Service," *Iowa.gov,* www.legis.iowa.gov/DOCS/IACODE /2003SUPPLEMENT/904/703.html (December 20, 2017); *Department of Corrections, Colorado Correctional Industries* (Denver: Colorado Office of the State Auditor, 2015), www.leg.state.co.us/OSA/coauditor1.nsf/All/908C1FE0217F7E0487257 DCE00701378/$FILE/1350P%20Colorado%20Correctional%20Industries,%20 Department%20of%20Corrections,%20January%202015.pdf; "Inmate Labor

Program," *Pasco's Sheriff Office,* https://pascosheriff.com/inmate-labor-program/ (December 20, 2017); Wignall, "Prison Labor Facilitates."

59. "Adult Corrections: Inmate Work Program," *South Dakota Department of Corrections,* https://doc.sd.gov/adult/work/ (December 20, 2017).

60. Beth Schwartzapfel, "Modern-Day Slavery in America's Prison Workforce," *American Prospect,* May 28, 2014, http://prospect.org/article/great-american-chain-gang.

61. Edward Said, *Orientalism* (New York: Random House, 1978).

62. E.g., "Adult Corrections," *South Dakota Department of Corrections;* "Benton County Sheriff's Office Using Inmate Labor: Move Expected to Save Budget Dollars," *OzarksFirst.com,* October 11, 2016, www.ozarksfirst.com/news/benton-county-sheriffs-office-using-inmate-labor/593799223; "Inmate Labor Program," *Monmouth County Sheriff's Office,* www.mcsonj.org/divisions/corrections/inmate-labor-program/ (December 20, 2017); "Inmate Work Crew Information," *Oregon.gov;* "2017 Florida Statutes"; "Our Mission," *Washington State Correctional Industries;* Robbie Brown and Kim Severson, "Enlisting Prison Labor to Close Budget Gaps," *New York Times,* February 24, 2011, www.nytimes.com/2011/02/25/us/25inmates.html; Russell Nichols, "Working Prisoners Save Taxpayers' Money," *Governing: The States and Localities,* May 2011, www.governing.com/topics/public-justice-safety/working-prisoners-saves-taxpayers-money.html; Wignall, "Prison Labor Facilitates"; Wood, "From Our Prison"; "Inmate Labor," *Arizona Department of Corrections,* https://corrections.az.gov/inmate-labor (December 20, 2017).

63. Robert Atkinson, "Prison Labor Reduces Incarceration Costs," in *Prisons,* ed. James Haley, *Opposing Viewpoints in Context* (Farmington Hills: Greenhaven Press, 2005).

64. "Inmate Labor," *Pasco's Sheriff Office.*

65. "Inmate Labor," *Pasco's Sheriff Office.*

66. "Inmate Labor," *Jackson County, Georgia,* www.jacksoncountygov.com/184/Inmate-Labor (December 20, 2017).

67. E.g., "Adult Corrections," *South Dakota Department of Corrections;* Michael Crowe, "Funding Approved for Blount County Animal Center after Inmate Reduction Left It Short-Handed," *WBIR 10News,* August 8, 2016, www.wbir.com/news/local/blount-county-animal-center-left-shorthanded-by-lost-inmate-labor/290760742; Jimmie Gates, "Counties Opt for Free State Inmate Labor," *Clarion Ledger,* August 8, 2016, www.clarionledger.com/story/news/local/2016/08/08/counties-opt-free-state-inmate-labor/88397914/; "Inmate Labor Work Crew," *Nassau County Sheriff's Office,* http://nassauso.com/inmate-labor-work-crew/ (December 20, 2017); "Inmate Labor," *Jackson County, Georgia.*

68. Brown v. Plata, 563 U.S. 493 (2011).

69. Defendants' Opposition to Plaintiffs' Motion to Enforce, Case No. C01-1351-THE, United States District Court, Eastern District of California and the Northern District of California (2014), 4.

70. See also Annika Neklason, "California Is Running Out of Inmates to Fight Its Fires," *The Atlantic,* December 7, 2017, www.theatlantic.com/politics/archive /2017/12/how-much-longer-will-inmates-fight-californias-wildfires/547628/; Jaime Lowe, "The Incarcerated Women Who Fight California's Wildfires," *New York Times,* August 31, 2017, www.nytimes.com/2017/08/31/magazine/the-incarcerated-women-who-fight-californias-wildfires.html.

71. E.g., Wignall, "Prison Labor Facilitates"; Wood, "From Our Prison"; Atkinson, "Prison Labor Reduces"; "About," *CalPIA;* "2017 Florida Statutes"; "FPI Inmate Programs," *UNICOR,* www.unicor.gov/About_FPI_Programs.aspx (December 20, 2017); Michael Berens and Mike Baker, "Broken Prison Labor Program Fails to Keep Promises, Costs Millions," *Seattle Times,* December 13, 2014, http://projects.seattletimes.com/2014/prison-labor/1/; *Department of Corrections, Colorado Correctional Industries.*

72. Wood, "From Our Prison."

73. Atkinson, "Prison Labor Reduces."

74. Atkinson, "Prison Labor Reduces."

75. Sarah Shemkus, "Beyond Cheap Labor: Can Prison Work Programs Benefit Inmates?" *The Guardian,* December 9, 2015, www.theguardian.com/sustainable-business/2015/dec/09/prison-work-program-ohsa-whole-foods-inmate-labor-incarceration; "Adult Corrections," *South Dakota Department of Corrections;* Wignall, "Prison Labor Facilitates"; *Department of Corrections, Colorado Correctional Industries;* "WV Correctional Industries," *West Virginia Division of Corrections;* "2017 Florida Statutes"; "P-I Endorsement: Smarter Prisoners," *Seattle PI,* October 9, 2007, www.seattlepi.com/local/opinion/article/P-I-Endorsement-Smarter-prisoners-1252014.php.

76. Berens and Baker, "Broken Prison Labor."

77. Brown and Severson, "Enlisting Prison Labor."

78. "FPI Inmate Programs," *UNICOR.*

79. Breanna Edwards, "Mass. Sheriff Offers Free Inmate Labor to Build Trump's US-Mexico Border Wall," *The Root,* January 5, 2017, www.theroot.com /mass-sheriff-offers-free-inmate-labor-to-build-trump-s-1791134186.

80. E.g., Herbert Gans, *The War against the Poor: The Underclass and Antipoverty Policy* (New York: Basic Books, 1995); Kaaryn Gustafson, *Cheating Welfare: Public Assistance and the Criminalization of Poverty* (New York: New York University Press, 2012); Hays, *Flat Broke;* Katz, *Undeserving Poor;* Michael Katz, ed., *The Underclass Debate: Views from History* (Princeton: Princeton University Press, 1993); John Krinsky, *Free Labor: Workfare and the Contested Language of Neoliberalism* (Chicago: University of Chicago Press, 2008); Neubeck and Cazenave, *Welfare Racism.*

81. E.g., David Whitman, "Despite Tough Talk, States Avoid Workfare," *U.S. News & World Report* 124, no. 1 (January 12, 1998); see also Jenifer Zeigler, "Statement of Jenifer Zeigler, Submitted to the Subcommittee on Human

Resources of the House Committee on Ways and Means," February 10, 2005, www.cato.org/publications/congressional-testimony/statement-jenifer-zeigler-submitted-subcommittee-human-resources-house-committee-ways-means#16.

82. E.g., E. Tammy Kim, "New York City Changes Course on Welfare-to-Work," *Aljazeera America*, October 16, 2014, http://america.aljazeera.com/articles /2014/10/16/an-activist-reformertakesonwelfareinnewyorkcity.html; Heather Mac Donald, "The de Blasio Stamp: Moving to Boost Dependency," *New York Post*, May 15, 2014, http://nypost.com/2014/05/15/the-de-blasio-stamp-moving-to-boost-dependency/; Whitman, "Despite Tough Talk"; "Another Sign of de Blasio's War on Welfare Reform," *New York Post*, February 21, 2016, http://nypost .com/2016/02/21/another-sign-of-de-blasios-war-on-welfare-reform/.

83. Mac Donald, "De Blasio Stamp."

84. "NYC Mayor Looks to Undo Giuliani-Era Welfare Reforms," *Fox News*, November 18, 2014, www.foxnews.com/politics/2014/11/18/nyc-mayor-looks-to-undo-giuliani-era-welfare-reforms.html.

85. Rachel Sheffield and Robert Rector, "Five Myths about Welfare and Child Poverty," *Heritage Foundation*, December 20, 2016, www.heritage.org/welfare /report/five-myths-about-welfare-and-child-poverty. The Trump administration has also argued that Medicaid should be attached to work requirements; e.g., Michelle Chen, "The Medicaid Work Requirements Could Make It Impossible to Qualify for Medicaid in Most States," *The Nation*, January 18, 2018, www.thenation.com/article/the-medicaid-work-requirements-could-make-it-impossible-to-qualify-for-medicaid-in-most-states/; Betsy McCaughey, "Why Work Requirements Are Good for Medicaid," *New York Post*, January 16, 2018, https://nypost.com/2018/01/16/why-work-requirements-are-good-for-medicaid/.

86. Chen, "Medicaid Work Requirements"; Ken Jacobs, Ian Perry, and Jenifer MacGillvary, *The High Public Cost of Low Wages* (Berkeley: UC Berkeley Labor Center, 2015), http://laborcenter.berkeley.edu/pdf/2015/the-high-public-cost-of-low-wages.pdf; Jennifer Sandlin, "Text, Lies, and the Welfare State: The Portrayal of Welfare Recipients in Welfare-to-Work Educational Programs," *Conference Proceedings of the Adult Education Research Conference*, 2002, http:// newprairiepress.org/cgi/viewcontent.cgi; "SNAP Increasingly Serves the Working Poor," *United States Department of Agriculture*, March 14, 2017, www.ers .usda.gov/data-products/chart-gallery/gallery/chart-detail/.

87. Indeed, such rhetoric even dominates the discourse of those who are critical of work-first policies, including Steven Banks himself, the so-called welfare chief, whom Mayor de Blasio appointed to lead New York City's rollback of workfare; e.g., Samar Khurshid, "In Departure from Predecessors, de Blasio Administration Overhauls City Welfare System," *Gotham Gazette*, February 19, 2016,www.gothamgazette.com/index.php/government/6177-in-departure-from-predecessors-de-blasio-administration-overhauls-city-welfare-system.

88. This has been a long-standing tenet of American discourse on poverty and public assistance; Gans, *War against the Poor;* Goldberg, *Citizens and Paupers;* Gustafson, *Cheating Welfare;* Katz, *Undeserving Poor.*

89. For the text of the bill, see "The Personal Responsibility and Work Opportunity Reconciliation Act of 1996," *U.S. Department of Health & Human Services,* https://aspe.hhs.gov/report/personal-responsibility-and-work-opportunity-reconciliation-act-1996 (December 20, 2017). For Clinton's speech, see "Text of President Clinton's Announcement on Welfare Legislation," *New York Times,* August 1, 1996, www.nytimes.com/1996/08/01/us/text-of-president-clinton-s-announcement-on-welfare-legislation.html.

90. E.g., "Another Sign of de Blasio's War," *New York Post;* Edwin Feulner, "Pulling People from Poverty," *Heritage Foundation,* May 25, 2016, www.heritage.org/welfare/commentary/pulling-people-poverty; "Back in the Dole-Drums," *New York Post,* March 14, 2015, http://nypost.com/2015/03/14/back-in-the-dole-drums/; Khurshid, "In Departure from Predecessors"; Heather Mac Donald, "De Blasio's New Welfare Plan: Anything to Stop People from Getting a Job," *New York Post,* August 9, 2015, http://nypost.com/2015/08/09/de-blasios-new-welfare-plan-anything-to-stop-people-from-getting-a-job/; Heather Mac Donald, "Say Goodbye to Welfare Reform, New York," *New York Post,* March 7, 2014, http://nypost.com/2014/03/07/say-good-bye-to-welfare-reform-new-york/; Mac Donald, "De Blasio Stamp"; "NYC Mayor Looks to Undo," *Fox News;* "Rolling Back Welfare Reform in New York," *New York Post,* December 6, 2015, http://nypost.com/2015/12/06/rolling-back-welfare-reform-in-new-york/; Fred Siegel, "Team de Blasio Is Quietly Gutting Welfare Reform," *New York Post,* September 15, 2015, http://nypost.com/2015/09/15/team-de-blasio-is-quietly-gutting-welfare-reform/; Rachel Sheffield, "Welfare Reform Must Include Work Requirements," *Heritage Foundation,* March 22, 2016, www.heritage.org/welfare/commentary/welfare-reform-must-include-work-requirements; Sheffield and Rector, "Five Myths"; Zeigler, "Statement of Jenifer Zeigler."

91. "After 20 Years, Critics Are Still Lying about the Success of Welfare Reform," *New York Post,* August 22, 2016, http://nypost.com/2016/08/22/after-20-years-critics-are-still-lying-about-the-success-of-welfare-reform/.

92. Michael Goodwin, "De Blasio Has Somehow Made the Homeless Problem Worse," *New York Post,* August 20, 2016, http://nypost.com/2016/08/30/de-blasio-has-somehow-made-the-homeless-problem-worse/.

93. See also "After 20 Years," *New York Post;* "Back in the Dole-Drums," *New York Post;* Nicholas Kristof, "Why I Was Wrong about Welfare Reform," *New York Times,* June 18, 2016, www.nytimes.com/2016/06/19/opinion/sunday/why-i-was-wrong-about-welfare-reform.html.

94. Feulner, "Pulling People."

95. Gustafson, *Cheating Welfare;* Hays, *Flat Broke;* Krinsky, *Free Labor;* Robert Moffitt and Stephanie Garlow, "Did Welfare Reform Increase Employment and Reduce Poverty?" *Pathways* (Winter 2018): 17–21.

96. Siegel, "Team de Blasio Is Quietly Gutting"; "Rudy Giuliani on Welfare & Poverty," *On the Issues,* www.ontheissues.org/Celeb/Rudy_Giuliani_Welfare_+_Poverty.htm (December 20, 2017).

97. In fact, Reagan merged the identities of two actual cases of welfare fraud while also often embellishing their stories; Gustafson, *Cheating Welfare;* Kohler-Hausmann, "'Crime of Survival.'"

98. Gustafson, *Cheating Welfare;* Kohler-Hausmann, "'Crime of Survival.'"

99. "Bill de Blasio's Path to the Welfare Horrors of Yesteryear," *New York Post,* November 3, 2016, http://nypost.com/2016/11/03/bill-de-blasios-path-to-the-welfare-horrors-of-yesteryear/.

100. "Another Sign of de Blasio's War," *New York Post;* see also Kim, "New York City Changes"; "Rolling Back Welfare," *New York Post.*

101. Christopher Jencks, *Rethinking Social Policy: Race, Poverty, and the Underclass* (Cambridge: Harvard University Press, 1992); Thomas Sugrue, "The Impoverished Politics of Poverty," *Yale Journal of Law & the Humanities* 6, no. 1 (1994): 163–79.

102. U.S. Department of Labor, *The Negro Family: The Case for National Action* (Washington, DC: U.S. Government Printing Office, 1965), https://web.stanford.edu/~mrosenfe/Moynihan%27s%20The%20Negro%20Family.pdf.

103. E.g., Mac Donald, "De Blasio's New Welfare Plan"; Jonah Goldberg, "A Way out of the Welfare Rate [*sic*] Maze," *New York Post,* January 10, 2014, http://nypost.com/2014/01/10/a-way-out-of-the-welfare-rate-maze/; Mickey Kaus, "Workfare Wimp-Out," *New Republic,* March 13, 1995.

104. Mac Donald, "De Blasio's New Welfare Plan."

105. Goldberg, "Way Out."

106. Weeks, *Problem with Work,* 62–63.

107. Weeks, *Problem with Work,* 62.

108. E.g., *Northwestern University Athletics, 2013–2014* (Lafayette: School Datebooks, 2013); Jimmy Grant, "Playing College Football Is a Privilege," *Her Loyal Sons,* August 24, 2016, www.herloyalsons.com/blog/2016/08/24/playing-college-football-is-a-privilege/; Ron Higgins, "College Football and Academics Aren't Easy, but Neither Is Real Life," *Times-Picayune,* August 12, 2017, www.nola.com/lsu/index.ssf/2017/08/college_football_and_academics.html; Chip Patterson, "President to Team: 'Playing Football for FSU Is a Privilege, Not a Right,'" *CBS Sports,* July 13, 2015, www.cbssports.com/college-football/news/president-to-team-playing-football-for-fsu-is-a-privilege-not-a-right/; Clay Travis, "Alabama Football Players Avoid Charges for Inane Reason," *Outkick the Coverage,* www.outkickthecoverage.com/alabama-football-players-avoid-charges-for-insane-reason-062016/ (December 21, 2017).

109. E.g., Mark Zoller, "Student Athletes Don't Realize How Lucky They Are," *Cincinnati.com*, April 14, 2014, www.cincinnati.com/story/opinion/readers /2014/04/14/student-athletes-dont-realize-how-lucky-they-are/7701691/; Baccellieri, "Nigel Hayes Is the Latest"; "Should College Athletes Be Paid?" *Tylt*, https:// thetylt.com/sports/should-college-athletes-be-paid (December 20, 2017).

110. Davis, "Will Players Ever"; see also Harry Cheadle, "College Athletes Should Get Paid Whether They Want the Money or Not," *Vice Sports*, July 21, 2014, https:// sports.vice.com/en_us/article/college-athletes-should-get-paid-whether-they-want-the-money-or-not; Stewart Mandel, "How the NCAA Botched Its Case in the Landmark Ed O'Bannon Antitrust Trial," *Sports Illustrated*, June 27, 2014, www .si.com/college-football/2014/06/27/ncaa-case-flops-ed-obannon-trial.

111. *NCAA 2015–16 Guide for the College-Bound Student-Athlete* (Indianapolis: National Collegiate Athletic Association, 2015), 23.

112. *NCAA Division I Manual, 2015–16-January* (Indianapolis: National Collegiate Athletic Association, 2015), 4; *NCAA Agent Guide* (Indianapolis: National Collegiate Athletic Association, 2008), 3.

113. E.g., Alex Prewitt, "Large Majority Opposes Paying NCAA Athletes, Washington Post-ABC Poll Finds," *Washington Post*, March 23, 2014, www .washingtonpost.com/sports/colleges/large-majority-opposes-paying-ncaa-athletes-washington-post-abc-news-poll-finds/2014/03/22/c411a32e-b130-11c3-95e8-39bef8e9a48b_story.html; see also Blake Lovell, "Student-Athletes Play for the Love of the Game," Room for Debate, *New York Times*, March 13, 2012, www .nytimes.com/roomfordebate/2012/03/13/ncaa-and-the-interests-of-student-athletes/student-athletes-play-for-the-love-of-the-game; Ashley DuPuis, "For the Love of the Game: A Survey of What Makes Athletes Walk Away from the Games They Love," *The Dartmouth*, October 31, 2016, www.thedartmouth.com /article/2016/10/for-the-love-of-the-game.

114. E.g., Jon Steingart, "NCAA, PAC-12 Hit with Claim Football Players Are Employees," *Bloomberg BNA*, www.bna.com/ncaa-pac12-hit-n57982077628 / (December 20, 2017).

115. Prewitt, "Large Majority Opposes."

116. Steingart, "NCAA, PAC-12."

117. E.g., Prewitt, "Large Majority Opposes"; Gary Mihoces, "Status of Student Athletes Again up for Debate at Villanova Conference," *USA Today*, April 10, 2015, www.usatoday.com/story/sports/college/2015/04/10/ncaa-student-athletes-kesler-sports-and-law/25589773/; Patrick Harker, "Student Athletes Shouldn't Unionize," *New York Times*, April 1, 2014, www.nytimes.com /2014/04/02/opinion/student-athletes-shouldnt-unionize.html; *NCAA Division I Manual*; Northwestern Football, *2013 Team Handbook*; *Northwestern University Athletics, 2013–2014*; *NCAA 2015–16 Guide*; "Big Presidents, Chancellors on O'Bannon Trial," *BTN: Big Ten Network*, http://btn.com/2014/06/24/big-ten-presidents-chancellors-on-obannon-trial/ (December 21, 2017); Michael

McCann, "NCAA Makes Strong Counterargument to Close O'Bannon Trial," *Sports Illustrated*, June 28, 2014, www.si.com/college-football/2014/06/28 /obannon-ncaa-trial-student-athlete-antitrust; Andy Staples, "Big Ten Advocates New Benefits for Student-Athletes, but Is It Too Late?" *Sports Illustrated*, June 24, 2014, www.si.com/college-football/2014/06/24/big-ten-student-athlete-ncaa-reform; see also Taylor Branch, "Toward Basic Rights for College Athletes," *The Atlantic*, November 11, 2015, www.theatlantic.com/business /archive/2015/11/ncaa-taylor-branch/415389/; Taylor Branch, "The Shame of College Sports," *The Atlantic*, October 2011, www.theatlantic.com/magazine /archive/2011/10/the-shame-of-college-sports/308643/2/.

118. *NCAA 2015–16 Guide*, 30.

119. Mihoces, "Status of Student Athletes."

120. O'Bannon v. NCAA, Nos. 14–16601, 14–17068 (9th Cir. September 30, 2015).

121. Mandel, "How the NCAA Botched."

122. This football team handbook, along with the *Northwestern University Athletics 2013–2014* handbook, was made part of the public record in a National Labor Relations Board case in which Northwestern football players sought to unionize; *Northwestern University*, NLRB Case 13-RC-121359 (2015).

123. Northwestern Football, *2013 Team Handbook*, 23–24.

124. E.g., Jack McCallum, "The Diary of a Student-Athlete," *Sports Illustrated*, February 13, 1995, www.si.com/vault/1995/02/13/133272/the-diary-of-a-student-athlete-meet-jacque-vaughn———-and-say-goodbye-to-some-old-notions-about-pampered-athletes; Christine Brennan, "Pampered from Childhood, Athletes Get Lost in the Real World," *Los Angeles Times*, December 30, 1990, http://articles.latimes.com/1990–12–30/sports/sp-10047_1_real-world; DeWayne Wickham, "Pampered Black Athletes Lose Sight of Past Struggles," *USA Today*, August 21, 2006, http://usatoday30.usatoday.com/news /opinion/columnist/wickham/2006-08-21-black-athletes_x.htm; "Rich, Pampered Athletes in Philly Plan on Protesting National Anthem," *Pirate's Cove*, September 18, 2016, www.thepiratescove.us/2016/09/18/rich-pampered-athletes-in-philly-plan-on-protesting-national-anthem/; William Rhoden, "Athletes on Campus: A New Reality—Athletes Find Life of Privilege and Isolation," *New York Times*, January 8, 1990, www.nytimes.com/1990/01/08/sports /athletes-campus-new-reality-second-three-articles-black-student-athletes-find .html; Barry Temkin, "Pampered Players Pay in Long Run," *Chicago Tribune*, December 27, 1991, http://articles.chicagotribune.com/1991-12-27/sports /9104260286_1_egos-coaches-attitude; "Readers Sound Off on a Fired Cop, Protesting Athletes and Smeared Victims," *Daily News*, September 16, 2016, www.nydailynews.com/opinion/sept-16-fired-protesting-athletes-smeared-victims-article-1.2794129; "College Students Complain That Athletes Are Pampered," *Fark.com*, February 2, 2004, www.fark.com/comments/817632/College-

students-complain-that-athletes-are-pampered; "Pampered Athletes Suck!" *DBS Universe*, August 4, 2011, http://dbsuniverse.blogspot.com/2011/08 /pampered-athletes-suck.html; Bob Hunter, "A Sad Week If You're Sick of Pampered Athletes," *Columbus Dispatch*, June 20, 2009, www.dispatch.com/content /stories/sports/2009/06/20/hunter_6-20.ART_ART_06-20-09_C1_5RE82A8 .html; "Study Finds Black Student-Athletes Graduate at Lower Rates," *NCSA*, www.ncsasports.org/blog/2016/03/15/study-finds-black-studentathletes-graduate-rates/ (December 21, 2017); Bill Plaschke, "Athletes' Union Movement at Northwestern Could Have Huge Implications," *Los Angeles Times*, January 28, 2014, http://articles.latimes.com/2014/jan/28/sports/la-sp-college-union-plaschke-20140129; Ray Hartmann, "Mizzou Quiet about Honor Student Athletes Received for Racial Protest," *St. Louis Magazine*, August 18, 2016, www .stlmag.com/news/think-again/mizzou-football-players-racial-protest/.

125. Darin Gantt, "Arian Foster Admits Getting Money in College," *NBC Sports*, September 20, 2013, http://profootballtalk.nbcsports.com/2013/09/20 /arian-foster-admits-getting-money-in-college/.

126. Gantt, "Arian Foster Admits."

127. See also Higgins, "College Football and Academics."

128. E.g., *NCAA 2015–16 Guide*, 5; *NCAA Division I Manual*, 4.

129. *Northwestern University Athletics, 2013–2014*, 5.

130. Northwestern Football, *2013 Team Handbook*, 20; emphasis in original.

131. Northwestern Football, *2013 Team Handbook*, 23–25.

132. Northwestern Football, *2013 Team Handbook*, 25.

133. E.g., Northwestern Football, *2013 Team Handbook*, 21, 22, 23, 26; *Northwestern University Athletics, 2013–2014*, 7.

134. *Northwestern University Athletics, 2013–2014*, 7.

135. As revealed in wrongful death suits, moreover, it seems that NCAA and team officials have not always protected athletes' physical well-being in action or legal rhetoric. In one such case, lawyers for the NCAA stated, "The NCAA denies that it has a legal duty to protect student-athletes"; Branch, "Toward Basic Rights"; see also David Dishneau, "NCAA to Pay $1.2 Million to Settle Lawsuit in Death of Frostburg Football Player," *Baltimore Sun*, August 8, 2016, www .baltimoresun.com/news/maryland/bs-md-ncaa-settlement-20160808-story.html.

136. Northwestern Football, *2013 Team Handbook*, 23.

137. Northwestern Football, *2013 Team Handbook*, 38.

138. E.g., *NCAA Division I Manual*, xiv, 4, 5.

139. *NCAA Division I Manual*, 4.

140. *NCAA Agent Guide;* see also Branch, "Shame of College Sports"; "Agents and Amateurism: Agent Information," *NCAA*, www.ncaa.org/enforcement /agents-and-amateurism (December 21, 2017); Maryann Hudson and Elliott Almond, "They Play by Their Own Rules: Colleges: Sports Agents Are Everywhere, and the NCAA Estimates 70% of Current Athletes Have Had Contact

with Them," *Los Angeles Times*, October 13, 1995, http://articles.latimes
.com/1995–10–13/sports/sp-56605_1_sports-agent; Darren Heitner, "Football
Agent Terry Watson Facing 14 Felony Counts for Violating North Carolina Athlete Agent Law," *Forbes*, October 9, 2013, www.forbes.com/sites/darrenheitner
/2013/10/09/football-agent-terry-watson-facing-14-felony-counts-for-violating-
north-carolina-athlete-agent-law/#509f9da11337; Terri Langford, "Sports
Agents Want Greater Access to Texas College Football Players," *Texas Tribune*,
June 22, 2014, www.texastribune.org/2014/06/22/texas-sports-agent-law-
offers-no-active-enforcemen/; "Report: State Agent Laws Unenforced," *ESPN*,
August 17, 2010, www.espn.com/college-sports/news/story.

141. Quoted in Branch, "Shame of College Sports."

142. *NCAA Division I Manual; NCAA Agent Guide.*

143. See also Northwestern University, Reply Brief to the Board on Review of
Regional Director's Decision and Direction of Election, *Northwestern University*, NLRB Case 13-RC-121359 (2015), 14; Mandel, "How the NCAA Botched";
Christian D'Andrea, "College Athletes Don't Get Paid Because They're Not
Adults, Real NCAA Executive Actually Says," *SBNation*, December 10, 2015,
www.sbnation.com/college-football/2015/12/10/9885188/college-athletes-pay-ncaa-
reasons-oliver-luck; *NCAA 2015–16 Guide.*

144. Sara Matthiesen, "Academic Work Is Labor, Not Romance," *Chronicle of
Higher Education*, August 26, 2016, www.chronicle.com/article/Academic-
Work-Is-Labor-Not/237592; Amy Hungerford, "Why the Yale Hunger Strike Is
Misguided," *Chronicle of Higher Education*, May 9, 2017, www.chronicle.com
/article/Why-the-Yale-Hunger-Strike-Is/240037; Sophie Moullin, "Elite Gradu-
ate Student Struggles Are Not Class Struggles," personal website, November 21,
2016, https://scholar.princeton.edu/smoullin/blog/elite-graduate-student-
struggles-are-not-class-struggles; Tyce Palmaffy, "Union and Man at Yale: Class
Struggle," *New Republic*, June 7, 1999, 18; Rick Perlstein, "Professors to Grad
Students: Focus on Studies, Not Wages," *The Nation*, December 4, 2013,
www.thenation.com/article/professors-grad-students-focus-studies-not-wages/;
Corey Robin, "When Professors Oppose Grad Student Unions," *Jacobin*, December 5, 2013, www.jacobinmag.com/2013/12/WHEN-PROFESSORS-OPPOSE-
STUDENTS-UNIONS/.

145. "Life as a Graduate Student," *Becoming a Historian*, www.chashca
committees-comitesa.ca/becoming%20a%20historian/chapterfour.shtml
(December 21, 2017); see also Jennifer Jordan, "The Privilege of Being a Yale
Graduate Student," *Yale Daily News*, March 24, 2003, http://yaledailynews.com
/blog/2003/03/24/the-privilege-of-being-a-yale-graduate-student/; "Other
Students Voice," *Graduate Student Unionization: A Critical Approach*, https://
criticalgsu.wordpress.com/other-students-voice/ (December 21, 2017); Jae Hyun
Lee, "Student Union Is No Magic Bullet," *Harvard Crimson*, October 28, 2015,
www.thecrimson.com/article/2015/10/28/lee-graduate-student-union/.

146. "Why Do Graduate Students Allow Themselves to be Exploited Like Cheap Labor?" *Quora.com,* https://www.quora.com/Why-do-graduate-students-allow-themselves-to-be-exploited-like-cheap-labor (December 21, 2017), emphasis in original.

147. E.g., John Coatsworth, "Provost's Letter on National Labor Relations Board Ruling," *Columbia News,* August 24, 2016, http://news.columbia.edu/content/Provost-Letter-National-Labor-Relations-Board-Ruling; Jordan, "Privilege of Being"; Matthiesen, "Academic Work Is Labor"; Preston Cooper, "The Faulty Logic of the NLRB College Student Unionization Ruling," *Forbes,* August 25, 2016, www.forbes.com/sites/prestoncooper2/2016/08/25/the-faulty-logic-of-the-nlrb-college-student-unionization-ruling/#536d086b7d6b; Joseph Ambash, "NLRB's Graduate-Assistant Ruling: Bad News for Administrators and Students," *Chronicle of Higher Education,* September 7, 2016, www.chronicle.com/article/NLRB-s-Graduate-Assistant/237714; Natasha Baker, "Unmanageable Quagmire or Elegant Distinction?" *Inside Higher Ed,* September 8, 2016, www.insidehighered.com/views/2016/09/08/concerns-about-impact-nlrbs-recent-ruling-grad-student-unionization-essay; Amicus Curiae Brief, National Right to Work Legal Defense and Education Foundation, Trustees of Columbia University v. Graduate Workers of Columbia, NLRB 02-RC-143012 (2016); NLRB v. Yeshiva University 444 U.S. 672 (1980). But see Dissent in *Brown University,* NLRB Case 1-RC-21368 (2004); Ambash, "NLRB's Graduate-Assistant Ruling."

148. E.g., Kaustuv Basu, "So Close," *Inside Higher Ed,* March 21, 2012, www.insidehighered.com/news/2012/03/21/unionization-battle-roils-university-michigan; Greenhouse, "Graduate Students Push"; Stacey Patton, "Union Battle Causes Rifts among Faculty and Graduate Students at U. of Michigan," *Chronicle of Higher Education,* March 1, 2012, www.chronicle.com/article/Union-Battle-Causes-Rifts/131019; Cooper, "Faulty Logic"; Ambash, "NLRB's Graduate-Assistant Ruling"; Baker, "Unmanageable Quagmire"; Peter Weber, "Important University Update on Doctoral Education," *Graduate School, Brown University,* September 12, 2012, www.brown.edu/academics/gradschool/important-university-update-doctoral-education; Tom Gantert, "State Agency Rules That Graduate Student Research Assistants Not Eligible for Unionization," *CapCon: Michigan Capitol Confidential,* June 20, 2014, www.michigancapitolconfidential.com/GSRAs-not-public-employees-cant-be-unionized; *NLRB v. Yeshiva University;* Amicus Curiae Brief, National Right to Work Legal Defense and Education Foundation, *Trustees of Columbia;* Brief of Amici Curiae, Brown University et al., Trustees of Columbia University v. Graduate Workers of Columbia, NLRB 02-RC-143012 (2016), 3; Amicus Brief, Higher Education Council of the Employment Law Alliance, Trustees of Columbia University v. Graduate Workers of Columbia, NLRB 02-RC-143012 (2016), 2.

149. Brief of Amici Curiae, Brown University et al., *Trustees of Columbia,* 10.

150. Amicus Brief, Higher Education Council, *Trustees of Columbia,* 2.

151. E.g., Amicus Curiae Brief, National Right to Work Legal Defense and Education Foundation, *Trustees of Columbia;* Amicus Brief, Higher Education Council, *Trustees of Columbia;* Brief of Amici Curiae, Brown University et al., *Trustees of Columbia University;* Coatsworth, "Provost's Letter"; Greenhouse, "Graduate Students Push"; Weber, "Important University Update."

152. Weber, "Important University Update."

153. Coatsworth, "Provost's Letter."

154. Amicus Curiae Brief, National Right to Work Legal Defense and Education Foundation, *Trustees of Columbia,* 5.

155. Palmaffy, "Union and Man," 18; see also Gabriel Winant, "Grad Students to the Barricades," *Dissent* (Fall 2012): 32–38.

156. Quoted in Mark Oppenheimer, "Graduate Students, the Laborers of Academia," *New Yorker,* August 31, 2016, www.newyorker.com/business /currency/graduate-students-the-laborers-of-academia.

157. "Grad Students Say Harvard Obstructed Vote over Joining Union," *Portland Press Herald,* December 30, 2016, www.pressherald.com/2016/12/30 /grad-students-say-harvard-obstructed-vote-over-joining-union/comments/.

158. "Other Students Voice," emphasis in original; see also Lee, "Student Union."

159. William Corsaro, *The Sociology of Childhood,* 2nd ed. (London: Sage, 2005).

CHAPTER 2. COERCION AND COMPLIANCE

1. Michel Foucault, *Discipline & Punish: The Birth of the Prison* (New York: Random House, 1977), 137.

2. In fact, most conventional employees are also employed "at will." However, graduate students, unlike most conventional employees, can be terminated "at will" not just from a particular job but also from their education, academic degree, and career trajectory.

3. Richard Freeman et al., "Careers and Rewards in Bio Sciences: The Disconnect between Scientific Progress and Career Progression," *American Society of Cell Biology,* August 2001, https://depts.washington.edu/envision/resources /CareersBiosciences.pdf.

4. Freeman et al., "Careers and Rewards"; Viviane Callier and Nathan Vanderford, "Mission Possible: Putting Trainees at the Center of Academia's Mission," *Nature Biotechnology* 32, no. 6 (June 2014): 593–94.

5. When graduate students do not perform labor for their advisors, such relationships are likely still characterized by status coercion, but they are not *labor relations.*

6. Most scholarships are single-year scholarships, though the NCAA started allowing universities to award multiyear scholarships in 2012; "Frequently

Asked Questions About the NCAA," *NCAA.org*, www.ncaa.org/about/frequently-asked-questions-about-ncaa (April 15, 2019); Jon Solomon, "Schools Can Give Out 4-Year Athletic Scholarships, But Many Don't," *CBS Sports*, September 16, 2014, www.cbssports.com/college-football/news/schools-can-give-out-4-year-athletic-scholarships-but-many-dont/.

7. According to the NCAA, 1.8 percent of college football players go on to play professionally (4.6% from Division I teams), and 1.1 percent of male basketball and 0.9 percent of female basketball players do so (3.6% and 3.2% from Division I teams, respectively); "Estimated Probability of Competing in Professional Athletics," *NCAA.org*, March 10, 2017, www.ncaa.org/about/resources/research/estimated-probability-competing-professional-athletics. For reminders, see, e.g., *NCAA 2015-16 Guide for the College-Bound Student-Athlete* (Indianapolis: National Collegiate Athletic Association, 2015).

8. National Collegiate Athletic Association, *Transfer 101: Basic Information You Need to Know about Transferring to an NCAA College, 2014-15* (Indianapolis: NCAA, 2014), 12; "Transfer Terms: Eligibility Timeline," *NCAA*, www.ncaa.org/student-athletes/current/transfer-terms (January 14, 2018).

9. Except for those bound by noncompete clauses, for example.

10. National Collegiate Athletic Association, *Transfer 101;* see also David Frank, "Transferring Colleges: It's Harder Than You Think," *AthNet*, www.athleticscholarships.net/2012/06/20/transferring-colleges-its-harder-than-you-think.htm (January 14, 2018).

11. Greg Bishop, "Want to Play at a Different College? O.K., but Not There or There," *New York Times*, June 7, 2013, www.nytimes.com/2013/06/08/sports/ncaafootball/college-coaches-use-transfer-rules-to-limit-athletes-options.html.

12. "Permission to Contact," *NCAA.org*, www.ncaa.org/student-athletes/current/permission-contact (January 14, 2018); National Collegiate Athletic Association, *Transfer 101;* see also John Infante, "NCAA Four Year Transfer Rules," *AthNet*, www.athleticscholarships.net/college-transfer-4-4.htm (January 14, 2018).

13. Frank, "Transferring Colleges."

14. National Collegiate Athletic Association, *Transfer 101.*

15. Bruce was not required to sit out for a year because he was not transferring from a Division I school. Being a "walk-on" means not having a scholarship.

16. Three of the eighteen athletes I interviewed reported feeling pressured and/or witnessing others being pressured to play through significant injuries.

17. Former basketball player Luke Bonner recalled feeling similarly—sweating, nervous—before publishing a critique of amateurism and NCAA athletics; CARE conference, Drexel University, Philadelphia, March 26, 2016.

18. For more on sanctions, see LaDonna Pavetti, Michelle Derr, and Heather Hesketh, *Review of Sanction Policies and Research Studies* (Princeton: Mathematica Policy Research, 2003).

19. Mary Farrell et al., *Welfare Time Limits: An Update on State Policies, Implementation, and Effects on Families* (Washington, DC: Lewin Group and MDRC, 2008), 3.

20. Jane Collins and Victoria Mayer, *Both Hands Tied: Welfare Reform and the Race to the Bottom of the Low-Wage Labor Market* (Chicago: University of Chicago Press, 2010); Pavetti et al., *Review of Sanction Policies.*

21. Premilla Nadasen, *The Welfare Rights Movement in the United States* (New York: Routledge, 2005); Kenneth Neubeck and Noel Cazenave, *Welfare Racism: Playing the Race Card against America's Poor* (New York: Routledge, 2001).

22. Though workfare supervisors cannot directly impose sanctions, they can report noncompliance to caseworkers, who then impose them. From workfare workers' perspective, however, this is only a technical detail, as their supervisors' ability to report them effectively gives them the power of sanctions. Moreover, the fact that welfare recipients can be sanctioned for missing work for this type of family emergency stands in contrast to the protections extended to (some) workers by the Family and Medical Leave Act.

23. In our interview, Pauline initially said "mmm-mmmm" instead of "ass," though she used the expletive in the original incident.

24. Legal Momentum, *The Sanction Epidemic in the Temporary Assistance for Needy Families Program* (New York: Women's Legal Defense and Education Fund, 2010); Pavetti et al., *Review of Sanction Policies.*

25. Francis Clines, "Welfare Reform Increases Homelessness," in *The Homeless,* ed. Louise Gerdes (Farmington Hills: Greenhaven Press, 2007); Legal Momentum, *Sanction Epidemic;* Nancy Reichman, Julien Teitler, and Marah Curtis, "TANF Sanctioning and Hardship," *Social Service Review* 79, no. 2 (2005): 215–36.

26. See also "Strict Shelter Rules Force Many Families Out," *New York Times,* November 29, 1999, www.nytimes.com/1999/11/29/nyregion/strict-shelter-rules-force-many-families-out.html.

27. Homelessness has long-lasting effects, especially for children; "Effects of Homelessness on Families and Children," *Institute for Children, Poverty, and Homelessness,* www.icphusa.org/wp-content/uploads/2015/09/Effects-of-Homelessness.pdf (January 14, 2018).

28. "Know Your Rights: In Prison—Disciplinary Sanctions and Punishment," *ACLU,* www.aclu.org/know-your-rights/prison-disciplinary-sanctions-and-punishment (January 14, 2018). For New York State guidelines, see "Prison Safety in New York," *New York State Department of Corrections and Community Supervision,* www.doccs.ny.gov/PressRel/06commissionerrpt/06prisonsafetyrpt .htm#VI (January 14, 2018).

29. Bruce Arrigo and Jennifer Leslie Bullock, "The Psychological Effects of Solitary Confinement on Prisoners in Supermax Units," *International Journal of Offender Therapy and Comparative Criminology* 52 (2008): 622–40; Michael

Massoglia and Cody Warner, "The Consequences of Incarceration: Challenges for Scientifically Informed and Policy-Relevant Research," *Criminology & Public Policy* 10, no. 3 (2011): 851–63; Sara Wakefield and Christopher Uggen, "Incarceration and Stratification," *Annual Review of Sociology* 36 (2010): 387–406; Sara Wakefield and Christopher Wildeman, *Children of the Prison Boom: Mass Incarceration and the Future of American Inequality* (New York: Oxford University Press, 2014).

30. About one quarter of New York State's prisoners have been in solitary confinement over the course of a year; New York State Bar Association, *Solitary Confinement in New York State* (Albany: New York State Bar Association, 2013).

31. George Dvorsky, "Why Solitary Confinement Is the Worst Kind of Psychological Torture," *Gizmodo,* http://io9.gizmodo.com/why-solitary-confinement-is-the-worst-kind-of-psycholog-1598543595 (January 14, 2018).

32. "New York State Parole Handbook," *New York State Department of Corrections and Community Supervision,* www.doccs.ny.gov/Parole_Handbook.html (January 14, 2018).

33. See also reports from the Correctional Association of New York, e.g., "Report on Attica Correctional Facility," www.correctionalassociation.org/wp-content/uploads/2014/12/Attica-2014-CA-Updated-Report-Final1.pdf (January 14, 2018); "Greene Correctional Facility: 2012–2014," www.correctionalassociation.org/wp-content/uploads/2014/10/Greene-C.F.-Report-Final.pdf (January 14, 2018); "Voices from Clinton," www.correctionalassociation.org/wp-content/uploads/2016/05/Voices-From-Clinton-FINAL-6-2016.pdf (January 14, 2018).

34. Frances Fox Piven and Richard Cloward, *Poor People's Movements: Why They Succeed, How They Fail* (New York: Vintage Books, 1979), 6.

35. "Afro-American" is James's own description of his ethnoracial identity.

36. This is the term used in New York State prisons, at least.

37. "Postdoctoral Researchers—Facts, Trends, and Gaps," *National Institutes of Health,* https://nexus.od.nih.gov/all/2012/06/29/postdoctoral-researchers-facts-trends-and-gaps/ (January 14, 2018).

38. Erin Hatton, *The Temp Economy: From Kelly Girls to Permatemps in Postwar America* (Philadelphia: Temple University Press, 2011).

39. Ken Jacobs, Ian Perry, and Jenifer MacGillvary, *The High Public Cost of Low Wages* (Berkeley: UC Berkeley Labor Center, 2015); Sylvia Allegretto et al., *Fast Food, Poverty Wages: The Public Cost of Low-Wage Jobs in the Fast-Food Industry* (Berkeley: UC Berkeley Labor Center, 2013).

40. *New York State Temporary Assistance and Food Stamp Employment Policy Manual* (New York: New York State Office of Temporary and Disability Assistance, 2009).

41. Noah Zatz et al., *Get to Work or Go to Jail: Workplace Rights under Threat* (Los Angeles: UCLA Institute for Research on Labor and Employment, 2016).

42. Zatz et al., *Get to Work or Go to Jail,* 1.

43. Noah Zatz, "Carceral Labor beyond Prison," in *Prison/Work: Labor in the Carceral State,* ed. Erin Hatton (Oakland: University of California Press, forthcoming).

44. Collegiate Employment Research Institute, *Recruiting Trends 2016–17,* 46th ed. (East Lansing: Career Services and the Collegiate Employment Research Institute, 2017).

45. E.g., Evan Grossman, "The Lowest Paid Athletes in All of Professional Sports," *Men's Journal,* www.mensjournal.com/adventure/races-sports/the-lowest-paid-athletes-in-all-of-professional-sports-20141125 (January 14, 2018); Kevin Draper, "It Is Time for All NBA D-Leaguers to Be Paid a Living Wage," *Deadspin,* https://deadspin.com/it-is-time-for-all-nba-d-leaguers-to-be-paid-a-living-w-1792344265 (January 14, 2018); Andy Martino, "AFL Players Cry Foul at Owners While Trying to Survive Shutdown," *New York Daily News,* www.nydailynews.com/sports/football/arena-football-league-players-cry-foul-owners-survive-shutdown-article-1.423904 (January 14, 2018).

46. This is particularly true for African American men; Devah Pager, "The Mark of a Criminal Record," *American Journal of Sociology* 108, no. 5 (2003): 937–75.

47. Guy Standing, *The Precariat: The New Dangerous Class* (New York: Bloomsbury, 2014).

48. Foucault, *Discipline & Punish.*

49. Karl Marx, *Capital: A Critique of Political Economy,* vol. 1 (New York: Penguin, 1992 [1906]).

CHAPTER 3. SUBJUGATION, VULNERABILITY, AND THE BODY

1. E.g., Kirstie Ball, "Workplace Surveillance: An Overview," *Labor History* 51, no. 1 (2010): 87–106; Alex Rosenblat, Tamara Kneese, and Danah Boyd, "Workplace Surveillance," Open Society Foundation's Future of Work Research Paper 2014, http://dx.doi.org/10.2139/ssrn.2536605 (March 25, 2018); Paul Thompson and Diane van den Broek, "Managerial Control and Workplace Regimes: An Introduction," *Work, Employment and Society* 24, no. 3 (2010): 1–12.

2. E.g., Blake Ashforth and Glen Kreiner, "'How Can You Do It?': Dirty Work and the Challenge of Constructing a Positive Identity," *Academy of Management Review* 24, no. 3 (1999): 413–34; Harry Braverman, *Labor and Monopoly Capital: The Degradation of Work in the Twentieth Century* (New York: Monthly Review Press, 1974); Randy Hodson, *Dignity at Work* (New York: Cambridge University Press, 2001); Everett Hughes, "Good People and Dirty Work," *Social Problems* 10, no. 1 (1962): 3–11; Tom Juravich, *Chaos on the Shop Floor: A Worker's View of Quality, Productivity and Management* (Philadelphia: Temple University Press, 1985);

Robin Leidner, *Fast Food, Fast Talk: Service Work and the Routinization of Everyday Life* (Berkeley: University of California Press, 1993); Steven Lopez, Randy Hodson, and Vincent Roscigno, "Power, Status, and Abuse at Work: General and Sexual Harassment Compared," *Sociological Quarterly* 50, no. 1 (2009): 3–27; Pamela Lutgen-Sandvik, "Intensive Remedial Identity Work: Responses to Workplace Bullying Trauma and Stigmatization," *Organization* 15, no. 1 (2008): 97–119.

3. Erik Olin Wright, *Understanding Class* (London: Verso Books, 2015).

4. Loïc Wacquant, *Punishing the Poor: The Neoliberal Government of Social Insecurity* (Durham: Duke University Press, 2009).

5. This is specific to my informants from New York State prisons and is likely not always the case, historically as well as across contemporary prison systems. Indeed, exploiting prisoners' labor was a primary focus of southern prisons after emancipation; Douglas Blackmon, *Slavery by Another Name: The Re-enslavement of Black Americans from the Civil War to World War II* (New York: Doubleday, 2008); Alex Lichtenstein, *Twice the Work of Free Labor: The Political Economy of Convict Labor in the New South* (New York: Verso, 1996); David Oshinsky, *Worse than Slavery: Parchman Farm and the Ordeal of Jim Crow Justice* (New York: Free Press, 1997).

6. Michel Foucault, *Discipline & Punish: The Birth of the Prison* (New York: Random House, 1977); Michel Foucault, *History of Sexuality*, vol. 1: *An Introduction* (New York: Random House, 1978); see also, e.g., David Garland, "'Governmentality' and the Problem of Crime: Foucault, Criminology, Sociology," *Theoretical Criminology* 1, no. 2 (1997): 173–214; David Lyon, *Surveillance Society: Monitoring Everyday Life* (Buckingham: Open University Press, 2001); Alan McKinlay and Ken Starkey, eds., *Foucault, Management and Organization Theory* (London: Sage, 1998); Nikolas Rose, Pat O'Malley, and Mariana Valverde, "Governmentality," *Annual Reviews of Law and Social Science* 2 (2006): 83–104.

7. I did not explicitly ask the ex-prisoners about this mode of subjugation. Like many of my findings in this book, this analysis emerged from my informants' spontaneous descriptions of their labor.

8. Kaaryn Gustafson, *Cheating Welfare: Public Assistance and the Criminalization of Poverty* (New York: New York University Press, 2012); see also Peter Edelman, *Not a Crime to Be Poor: The Criminalization of Poverty in America* (New York: New Press, 2017); Wacquant, *Punishing the Poor*.

9. Jane Collins and Victoria Mayer, *Both Hands Tied: Welfare Reform and the Race to the Bottom in the Low-Wage Labor Market* (Chicago: University of Chicago Press, 2011); Gustafson, *Cheating Welfare*; Sharon Hays, *Flat Broke with Children: Women in the Age of Welfare Reform* (New York: Oxford University Press, 2004).

10. See also Northwestern Football, *2013 Team Handbook*.

11. E.g., *NCAA Division I Manual–January, 2015–16* (Indianapolis: National Collegiate Athletic Association, 2015); *Northwestern University Athletics, 2013–2014* (Lafayette: School Datebooks, 2013); Northwestern Football, *2013 Team Handbook*.

12. Steven Lopez, "Power, Status, and Abuse at Work: General and Sexual Harassment Compared," *Sociological Quarterly* 50, no. 1 (2009): 3–27; see also Jeff Hearn and Wendy Parkin, *Gender, Sexuality and Violence in Organizations: The Unspoken Forms of Organizational Violations* (London: Sage, 2001); Denise Salin, "Ways of Explaining Bullying," *Human Relations* 56 (2003): 1213–32; Christopher Uggen and Amy Blackstone, "Sexual Harassment as a Gendered Expression of Power," *American Sociological Review* 69 (2004): 64–92; Marjan Vaez, Kerstin Ekberg, and Lucie LaFlamme, "Abusive Events at Work among Young Working Adults," *Relations Industrielles/Industrial Relations* 59 (2004): 569–84.

13. Shock prisons, also known as "boot-camp prisons," are intensive shorter-term programs usually intended for nonviolent offenders. They are modeled on military boot camps in order to "shock an offender into changing poor behavioral patterns"; "Lakeview Shock Incarceration Correctional Facility," *PrisonPro*, www.prisonpro.com/content/lakeview-shock-incarceration-correctional-facility (April 1, 2018).

14. Such a slur challenges male prisoners' embodiment of hegemonic masculinity as well as their presumed heterosexuality; C.J. Pascoe, *Dude, You're a Fag: Masculinity and Sexuality in High School* (Oakland: University of California Press, 2007).

15. Many reports corroborate Lindsay's claim; e.g., Alan Goldberg, "Coaching Abuse: The Dirty, Not-So-Little Secret in Sports," *Competitive Advantage*, www .competitivedge.com/%E2%80%9Ccoaching-abuse-dirty-not-so-little-secret-sports%E2%80%9D (April 22, 2019); John O'Sullivan, "Why Is Abusive Coaching Tolerated in Sports?" *Changing the Game Project*, August 15, 2018, https:// changingthegameproject.com/abusive-coaching-tolerated-sports/.

16. Mignon Duffy, "Doing the Dirty Work: Gender, Race, and Reproductive Labor in Historical Perspective, *Gender & Society* 21, no. 3 (2007): 313–36; Hughes, "Good People and Dirty Work"; Ruth Simpson, Natasha Slutskaya, Patricia Lewis, and Heather Höpfl, eds., *Dirty Work: Concepts and Identities* (London: Palgrave Macmillan, 2012).

17. Though to be clear, I did not initiate questions about physical violence in prison. I only followed up on informants' accounts, and therefore such incidents are almost certainly undercounted in this book.

18. This prisoner had to serve a longer sentence in another prison because he lost his position—and shorter sentence—in the "shock" facility.

19. This has likely been a cultivated response to the Attica prisoner uprising of 1971. For more, see Heather Ann Thompson, *Blood in the Water: The Attica Prison Uprising of 1971 and Its Legacy* (New York: Pantheon Books, 2016).

20. Edward Said, *Orientalism* (New York: Random House, 1978), 108.

21. Hannah Arendt, *The Origins of Totalitarianism* (New York: Harcourt, Brace, 1951).

22. Talking "in any kind of way" means overt verbal disrespect and mistreatment, including racist slurs.

23. "Student-Athlete Data," *NCAA*, http://web1.ncaa.org/rgdSearch/exec/saSearch (October 28, 2017).

24. E.g., Hodson, *Dignity at Work;* Tracy Vargas, "Employees or Suspects? Surveillance and Scrutinization of Low-Wage Service Workers in U.S. Dollar Stores," *Journal of Labor and Society* 20, no. 2 (2017): 207–30.

25. Foucault, *Discipline & Punish*, 25–26.

26. Foucault, *Discipline & Punish*, 26.

27. Foucault, *Discipline & Punish*, 25.

28. Robert Sapolsky, "The Influence of Social Hierarchy on Primate Health," *Science* 308 (2005): 648–52.

29. Jason Schnittker and Andrea John, "Enduring Stigma: The Long-Term Effects of Incarceration on Health," *Journal of Health and Social Behavior* 48 (2007): 115–30; Helena Hansen, Philippe Bourgois, and Ernest Drucker, "Pathologizing Poverty: New Forms of Diagnosis, Disability, and Structural Stigma under Welfare Reform," *Social Science & Medicine* 103 (2014): 76–83.

30. Bruce Arrigo and Jennifer Leslie Bullock, "The Psychological Effects of Solitary Confinement on Prisoners in Supermax Units," *International Journal of Offender Therapy and Comparative Criminology* 52 (2008): 622–40; Mary Murphy Corcoran, "Effects of Solitary Confinement on the Well Being of Prison Inmates," *Applied Psychology OPUS* (2015), https://steinhardt.nyu.edu/appsych/opus/issues/2015/spring/corcoran.

31. Schnittker and John, "Enduring Stigma."

32. E.g., Grant Iverson et al., "Cumulative Effects of Concussion in Amateur Athletes," *Brain Injury* 18, no. 5 (2004): 433–43.

33. Teresa Evans et al., "Evidence for a Mental Health Crisis in Graduate Education," *Nature Biotechnology* 36 (2018): 282–84.

CHAPTER 4. AGENCY AND RESISTANCE

1. Michel Foucault, *Discipline & Punish: The Birth of the Prison* (New York: Random House, 1977), 26.

2. For summaries of such debates, see Steven Vallas, "Working Class Heroes or Working Stiffs? Domination and Resistance in Business Organizations," *Research in the Sociology of Work* 28 (2016): 101–26; Dennis Mumby, "Theorizing Resistance in Organization Studies: A Dialectical Approach," *Management Communication Quarterly* 19, no. 1 (2005): 19–44; Pushkala Prasad and Anshuman Prasad, "Stretching the Iron Cage: The Constitution and Implications of Routine Workplace Resistance," *Organization Science* 11 (2000): 387–403; Rose Weitz, "Women and Their Hair: Seeking Power through Resistance and Accommodation," *Gender & Society* 15, no. 5 (2001): 667–86.

3. Antonio Gramsci, *Selections from the Prison Notebooks of Antonio Gramsci* (New York: International Publishers, 1971).

4. Michael Burawoy, *Manufacturing Consent: Changes in the Labor Process under Monopoly Capitalism* (Chicago: University of Chicago Press, 1979).

5. Other scholars have drawn similar conclusions; e.g., Alessia Contu, "Decaf Resistance: On Misbehavior, Cynicism, and Desire in Liberal Workplaces," *Management Communication Quarterly* 21, no. 3 (2008): 364–79; Foucault, *Discipline & Punish;* Paul Willis, *Learning to Labour: How Working Class Kids Get Working Class Jobs* (New York: Columbia University Press, 1977).

6. James Scott, W*eapons of the Weak: Everyday Forms of Peasant Resistance* (New Haven: Yale University Press, 1985); James Scott, *Domination and the Arts of Resistance: Hidden Transcripts* (New Haven: Yale University Press, 1990). For other early conceptualizations of "everyday resistance," see Herbert Aptheker, *American Negro Slave Revolts* (New York: Columbia University Press, 1943); Gramsci, *Selections from the Prison Notebooks;* Patricia Hill Collins, *Black Feminist Thought: Knowledge, Consciousness, and the Politics of Empowerment* (New York: Routledge, 2000).

7. Scott, W*eapons of the Weak*, 136.

8. James Scott, "Everyday Forms of Resistance," in *Everyday Forms of Peasant Resistance*, ed. Forrest D. Colburn (New York: M.E. Sharpe, 1989), 22.

9. Scott, *Domination and the Arts.*

10. E.g., Stephanie M. H. Camp, *Closer to Freedom: Enslaved Women and Everyday Resistance in the Plantation South* (Chapel Hill: University of North Carolina Press, 2004); Peter Fleming and Graham Sewell, "Looking for the Good Soldier, Švejk: Alternative Modalities of Resistance in the Contemporary Workplace," *Sociology* 36, no. 4 (2002): 857–73; Randy Hodson, "The Active Worker: Compliance and Autonomy at the Workplace," *Journal of Contemporary Ethnography* 20, no. 1 (1991): 47–78; Randy Hodson, "Worker Resistance: An Underdeveloped Concept in the Sociology of Work," *Economic and Industrial Democracy* 16 (1995): 79–110; Pushkala Prasad and Anshuman Prasad, "The Constitution and Implications of Routine Workplace Resistance," *Organization Science* 11 (2000): 387–403; Catherine Kohler Riessman, "Stigma and Everyday Resistance Practices: Childless Women in South India," *Gender & Society* 14, no. 1 (2000): 111–35.

11. Cindi Katz, *Growing Up Global: Economic Restructuring and Children's Everyday Lives* (Minneapolis: University of Minnesota Press, 2004), 242.

12. Mumby, "Theorizing Resistance," 21.

13. Katz, *Growing Up Global.*

14. Katz, *Growing Up Global*, 111.

15. Katz, *Growing Up Global*, 247.

16. As evidenced, for example, by the significant limitations of the labor and civil rights movements of the 20th century; e.g., Nelson Lichtenstein, *Walter Reuther: The Most Dangerous Man in Detroit* (New York: Basic Books, 1995); Nelson Lichtenstein, *State of the Union: A Century of American Labor* (Princeton: Princeton University Press, 2002); Ronald Formisano, *Boston against*

264   NOTES TO PAGES 141–165

Busing: Race, Class, and Ethnicity in the 1960s and 1970s (Chapel Hill: University of North Carolina Press, 1991); Kevin Kruse, *White Flight: Atlanta and the Making of Modern Conservatism* (Princeton: Princeton University Press, 2005).

17. Michael McCann, *Rights at Work: Pay Equity Reform and the Politics of Legal Mobilization* (Chicago: University of Chicago Press, 1994).

18. Robin D.G. Kelley, *Race Rebels: Culture, Politics, and the Black Working Class* (New York: Free Press, 1994); see also Nan Enstad, *Ladies of Labor, Girls of Adventure* (New York: Columbia University Press, 1999).

19. Malcolm X (with Alex Haley), *The Autobiography of Malcolm X: As Told to Alex Haley* (New York: Random House, 1964), 59; as quoted in Kelley, *Race Rebels*, 162.

20. Kelley, *Race Rebels*, 163.

21. Kelley, *Race Rebels*, 169.

22. In this way, Kelley's analysis echoes Erving Goffman's conceptualization of the "underlife" in total institutions. Because the goal of such institutions is the "stripping" of the self, Goffman argued, any effort to preserve, protect, and/or express the self in such institutions is an act of resistance; Erving Goffman, *Asylums: Essays on the Social Situation of Mental Patients and Other Inmates* (New York: Doubleday, 1961).

23. See also Frances Fox Piven and Richard Cloward, *Poor People's Movements: Why They Succeed, How They Fail* (New York: Vintage Books, 1978).

24. Lisa Bernstein has also used the phrase "get by" to refer to similar types of survival strategies; Lisa Bernsten, "Reworking Labour Practices: On the Agency of Unorganized Mobile Migrant Construction Workers," *Work, Employment and Society* 30, no. 3 (2016): 472–88.

25. Rosemary Ricciardelli, Katherina Maier, and Kelly Hanna-Moffat, "Strategic Masculinities: Vulnerabilities, Risk and the Production of Prison Masculinities," *Theoretical Criminology* 19, no. 4 (2015): 491–513.

26. Kelley, *Race Rebels*, 162, 169.

27. Again, as for most of these findings, these numbers represent informants' spontaneous descriptions. I did not survey them about their use of such strategies.

28. Corcraft is the brand name for New York State's prison industries; "About Corcraft," *Corcraft.org*, www.corcraft.org/webapp/wcs/stores/servlet/WhoWeAreView (November 18, 2018).

29. E.g., "Inmate Grievance Program," *New York State, Corrections and Community Supervision Directive*, Dir. #4040, Dtd. 01/20/2016, www.doccs.ny.gov/Directives/4040.pdf (April 1, 2018).

30. E.g., "Fair Hearings," *New York State Office of Temporary and Disability Assistance*, https://otda.ny.gov/hearings/ (April 1, 2018).

31. This is largely because for both prisoners and welfare recipients formal grievance procedures were developed in response to legal challenges; Goldberg v.

Kelly, 397 US 254 (1970); Valerie Jenness and Kitty Calavita, "'It Depends on the Outcome': Prisoners, Grievances, and Perceptions of Justice," *Law & Society Review* 52, no. 1 (2018): 41–72.

32. E.g., "Graduate Education: Summary of Graduate Student Appeal and Grievance Procedures," *Carnegie Mellon University*, www.cmu.edu/graduate /policies/appeal-grievance-procedures.html (April 1, 2018); "Student-Athlete Grievance Policy and Procedures," *University of Washington*, https://static .gohuskies.com/old_site/pdf/genrel/grievance-policy.pdf (April 1, 2018)).

33. Though, Gustavo added, his advisor did get "some nominal slap on the wrist."

34. E.g., Martin Greenburg, "Open Letter to President Mark Emmert of the NCAA—Abuse Must End," *The Law Office of Martin J. Greenburg, LLC*, www .greenberglawoffice.com/open-letter-president-ncca-abuse-must-end/ (April 1, 2018); Alexander Wolff, "Is the Era of Abusive College Coaches Finally Coming to an End?" *Sports Illustrated*, September 29, 2015, www.si.com/college-basket-ball/2015/09/29/end-abusive-coaches-college-football-basketball.

35. This long-established distinction in the sociolegal literature likely originates from Roscoe Pound, "Law in Books and Law in Action," *American Law Review* 44, no. 12 (1910): 12–15.

36. A Correctional Emergency Response Team (often called a "CERT" or "CRT" team) is a specialized unit of officers trained to subdue "incidents, riots, cell extractions, mass searches, or disturbances in prisons"; "CERT and Emergency Preparedness," *CorrectionsOne.com*, www.correctionsone.com/cert/ (March 30, 2018).

CHAPTER 5. HEGEMONY AND COUNTER-HEGEMONY

1. Nancy Fraser and Linda Gordon, "A Genealogy of Dependency: Tracing a Keyword of the U.S. Welfare State," *Signs* 19, no. 2 (1994): 309–36; Evelyn Nakano Glenn, *Unequal Freedom: How Race and Gender Shaped American Citizenship and Labor* (Cambridge: Harvard University Press, 2002); Linda Kerber, *No Constitutional Right to Be Ladies: Women and the Obligations of Citizenship* (New York: Hill and Wang, 1998); David Roediger, *The Wages of Whiteness: Race and the Making of the American Working Class* (New York: Verso, 1991); Judith Shklar, *American Citizenship: The Quest for Inclusion* (Cambridge: Harvard University Press, 1991); Kathi Weeks, *The Problem with Work: Feminism, Marxism, Anti-work Politics, and Postwork Imaginaries* (Durham: Duke University Press, 2011).

2. Michael Burawoy, *Manufacturing Consent: Changes in the Labor Process under Monopoly Capitalism* (Chicago: University of Chicago Press, 1979); Alessia Contu, "Decaf Resistance: On Misbehavior, Cynicism, and Desire in Liberal Workplaces," *Management Communication Quarterly* 21, no. 3 (2008): 364–79; Paul Willis, *Learning to Labour: How Working Class Kids Get Working Class Jobs* (New York: Columbia University Press, 1977).

3. Indeed, slave rhetoric has long been deployed as a discursive tool to both challenge and reify sociolegal constructions of work. Prior to industrialization, for example, waged labor was often disparaged as "wage slavery" in an effort to highlight and challenge workers' enforced economic dependence on employers, who were cast as unfairly reaping the surplus value of their labor; Fraser and Gordon, "Genealogy of Dependency"; Roediger, *Wages of Whiteness;* Weeks, *Problem with Work.* "Slavery" was thus discursively deployed to build class-consciousness and urge workers to resist capitalist exploitation. Through industrialization, however, waged labor was construed less and less as a type of "slavery" and increasingly as the foundation of white male "independence"; Fraser and Gordon, "Genealogy of Dependency"; Glenn, *Unequal Freedom.* Cultural notions of slavery were still central to this social construction of wage labor, but they were more often used to buttress—rather than critique—it by differentiating "real" (white, male) work and workers from racialized and gendered others; Glenn, *Unequal Freedom;* Roediger, *Wages of Whiteness.* Even still, activists and workers have continued to deploy discourses of slavery in an effort to highlight workers' mistreatment and exploitation and to promote class-consciousness and labor solidarity; e.g., John Krinsky, *Free Labor: Workfare and the Contested Language of Neoliberalism* (Chicago: University of Chicago Press, 2007). In recent years, though, there has also been pushback against what is seen as the overuse and misapplication of the term "slavery"; e.g., Julia O'Connell Davidson, "The Making of Modern Slavery: Whose Interests Are Served by the New Abolitionism?" *British Academy Review* 24 (2014): 28–31.

4. This is an especially strong tenet of law and society scholarship; Mindie Lazarus-Black and Susan Hirsch, eds., *Contested States: Law, Hegemony, and Resistance* (New York: Routledge, 1994); see also Kitty Calavita, *Invitation to Law & Society: An Introduction to the Study of Real Law* (Chicago: University of Chicago Press, 2010).

5. Robert Benford and David Snow, "Framing Processes and Social Movements: An Overview and Assessment," *Annual Review of Sociology* 26 (2000): 611–39.

6. Antonio Gramsci, *Selections from the Prison Notebooks of Antonio Gramsci* (New York: International Publishers, 1971); see also Paul Apostolidis, "Feminist Theory, Immigrant Workers' Stories, and Counterhegemony in the United States Today," *Signs* 33, no. 3 (2008): 545–68.

7. Apostolidis, "Feminist Theory," 547.

8. Kenneth Neubeck and Noel Cazenave, *Welfare Racism: Playing the Race Card against America's Poor* (New York: Routledge, 2001); Kaaryn Gustafson, *Cheating Welfare: Public Assistance and the Criminalization of Poverty* (New York: New York University Press, 2012); Joe Soss, Richard Fording, and Sanford Schram, *Disciplining the Poor: Neoliberal Paternalism and the Persistent Power of Race* (Chicago: University of Chicago Press, 2011).

9. Shklar, *American Citizenship;* Weeks, *Problem with Work;* see also Fraser and Gordon, "Genealogy of Dependency."

10. Though recent reporting on this topic does not support M.K.'s view, see, e.g., Ray Glier, "Pets, Car Repairs and Mom: How College Football Players Use Their Stipends," *New York Times,* January 5, 2017, www.nytimes.com/2017/01/05/sports /ncaafootball/pets-car-repairs-and-mom-how-football-players-use-their-stipends .html.

11. E.g., "Amateurism," *NCAA,* www.ncaa.org/amateurism (October 22, 2018); "Frequently Asked Questions about the NCAA," *NCAA,* www.ncaa.org /about/frequently-asked-questions-about-ncaa (October 22, 2018).

12. E.g., "The Personal Responsibility and Work Opportunity Reconciliation Act of 1996," *US Department of Health & Human Services,* https://aspe.hhs.gov /report/personal-responsibility-and-work-opportunity-reconciliation-act-1996 (December 20, 2017); Michael Goodwin, "De Blasio Has Somehow Made the Homeless Problem Worse," *New York Post,* August 20, 2016, http://nypost .com/2016/08/30/de-blasio-has-somehow-made-the-homeless-problem-worse/; see also Gustafson, *Cheating Welfare;* Krinsky, *Free Labor.*

13. Herbert Gans, *The War against the Poor: The Underclass and Antipoverty Policy* (New York: Basic Books, 1995); Michael Katz, *The Undeserving Poor: From the War on Poverty to the War on Welfare* (New York: Oxford University Press, 1989).

14. For more on inmate grievance representatives in the New York State prison system, see "Inmate Grievance Program," *New York State, Corrections and Community Supervision Directive,* Dir. #4040, Dtd. 1/20/2016, www.doccs .ny.gov/Directives/4040.pdf.

15. For these and other prison wage rates, see "State and Federal Prison Wage Policies and Sourcing Information," *Prison Policy Initiative,* www.prisonpolicy .org/reports/wage_policies.html (November 17, 2018). For a more detailed description of food service jobs and their wages in New York State prisons, see "Food Service Operations Manual," *New York State Department of Corrections and Community Supervision,* Directive #4310, April 2018, www.doccs.ny.gov /directives/FSOM.pdf.

16. The calculation is based on the assumption that they work six hours per day five days a week, which was the most common work schedule among my ex-prisoner informants.

17. Indeed, many prison officials have also argued that prisoners' labor is essential to the institution, though not to justify higher wages for prisoners; e.g., "Adult Corrections: Inmate Work Program," *South Dakota Department of Corrections,* https://doc.sd.gov/adult/work/ (December 20, 2017); Michael Crowe, "Funding Approved for Blount County Animal Center after Inmate Reduction Left It Short-Handed," *WBIR 10News,* August 8, 2016, www.wbir.com/news/local /blount-county-animal-center-left-shorthanded-by-lost-inmate-labor/290760742; Defendants' Opposition to Plaintiffs' Motion to Enforce, Case No. C01–1351-THE, United States District Court, Eastern District of California and the Northern District of California (2014); Jimmie Gates, "Counties Opt for Free State Inmate

Labor," *Clarion Ledger,* August 8, 2016, www.clarionledger.com/story/news /local/2016/08/08/counties-opt-free-state-inmate-labor/88397914/; "Inmate Labor Work Crew," *Nassau County Sheriff's Office,* http://nassauso.com/inmate-labor-work-crew/ (December 20, 2017); "Inmate Labor," *Jackson County, Georgia,* www.jacksoncountygov.com/184/Inmate-Labor (December 20, 2017).

18. For an overview of fines and fees levied on prisoners and others in the New York State criminal justice system, see "Mandatory Surcharge, Crime Victim Assistance Fee and Other Fees," *New York State Unified Court System,* www .nycourts.gov/courthelp/Criminal/surchargesFees.shtml (November 17, 2018).

19. For an example of a commissary sheet, see Department of Justice, Federal Bureau of Prisons, July 2015 Commissary Price List, www.bop.gov/locations /institutions/nym/NYM_CommList.pdf.

20. I.e., toiletries such as deodorant, shampoo, and toothpaste.

21. Corcraft is the brand name for New York State's prison industries; "About Corcraft," *Corcraft.org,* www.corcraft.org/webapp/wcs/stores/servlet /WhoWeAreView (November 18, 2018).

22. As this calculation suggests, Jackie did not consider the value of her SNAP benefits (food stamps) as part of her remuneration, contrary to New York State policy; Matter of Carter v. State, 26 N.Y.3d 272 (2015).

23. Pauline, like Jackie Robinson above, likely did not include the value of the food stamps she received in her calculation.

24. This is a central tenet of sociological studies of poverty and inequality; e.g., Leonard Beeghley, *The Structure of Social Stratification in the United States,* 5th ed. (New York: Routledge, 2008); Edward Royce, *Poverty & Power,* 3rd ed. (New York: Rowman & Littlefield, 2019).

25. E.g., Jeffrey Dorfman, "Pay College Athletes? They're Already Paid up to $125,000 per Year," *Forbes,* August 29, 2013, www.forbes.com/sites /jeffreydorfman/2013/08/29/pay-college-athletes-theyre-already-paid-up-to-125000year/#46540b622b82.

26. As quoted in chapter 2, though, at another point in the interview Zachary said that he felt that he had avoided getting "pimped." In my view, this is not a contradiction as much as an indication of Zachary's differing points of emphasis in those moments. When he recalled his hunger in the context of the many hours he worked as a college athlete, he felt that athletes "were getting pimped." But from his present-day perspective, when he talked about how he had succeeded in getting his college degree and being recruited to the NFL, he felt that he had avoided (at least the worst aspects of) that fate.

CONCLUSION

1. Suicide rates of prisoners in solitary confinement are disproportionately high; Thomas White, Dennis Schimmel, and Robert Frickey, "A Comprehensive

Analysis of Suicide in Federal Prisons: A Fifteen-Year Review," *Journal of Correctional Health Care* 9, no. 3 (2002): 321–43; see also Mary Murphy Corcoran, "Effects of Solitary Confinement on the Well Being of Prison Inmates," *Applied Psychology OPUS* (2015), https://steinhardt.nyu.edu/appsych/opus/issues/2015/spring/corcoran; Andrew Urevig, "The Confined Mind," *Lateral Magazine*, December 18, 2018, www.lateralmag.com/articles/issue-30/the-confined-mind.

2. E.g., Waverly Duck, "Becoming a Drug Dealer: Local Interaction Orders and Criminal Careers," *Critical Sociology* 42, nos. 7/8 (2016): 1069–85; Teresa Gowan, "American Untouchables: Homeless Scavengers in San Francisco's Underground Economy," *International Journal of Sociology and Social Policy*, 17, nos. 3/4 (1997): 159–90; Melissa Gira Grant, *Playing the Whore: The Work of Sex Work* (New York: Verso Books, 2014); Pierrette Hondagneu-Sotelo, *Doméstica: Immigrant Workers Cleaning and Caring in the Shadows of Affluence* (Oakland: University of California Press, 2001); Judith Rollins, *Between Women: Domestics and Their Employers* (Philadelphia: Temple University Press, 1985).

3. E.g., Jane Collins and Victoria Mayer, *Both Hands Tied: Welfare Reform and the Race to the Bottom in the Low-Wage Labor Market* (Chicago: University of Chicago Press, 2010); Alexandre Frenette, "From Apprenticeship to Internship: The Social and Legal Antecedents of the Intern Economy," *tripleC: Communication, Capitalism & Critique* 13, no. 2 (2015): 351–60; Chad Alan Goldberg, *Citizens and Paupers: Relief, Rights, and Race, from the Freedmen's Bureau to Workfare* (Chicago: University of Chicago, 2007); Philip Goodman, "Hero *and* Inmate: Work, Prisons, and Punishment in California's Fire Camps," *Working USA: The Journal of Labor & Society* 15 (2012): 353–76; Erin Hatton, ed., *Prison/Work: Labor in the Carceral State* (Oakland: University of California Press, forthcoming); John Krinsky, *Free Labor: Workfare and the Contested Language of Neoliberalism* (Chicago: University of Chicago Press, 2007); Noah Zatz, "Prison Labor and the Paradox of Paid Nonmarket Work," in *Research in the Sociology of Work*, vol. 18, ed. Nina Bandelj (Bingley: Emerald, 2009), 369–98.

4. E.g., Arlene Kaplan Daniels, "Invisible Work," *Social Problems* 34, no. 5 (1987): 403–15; Erin Hatton, "Mechanisms of Invisibility: Rethinking the Concept of Invisible Work," *Work, Employment and Society* 31, no. 2 (2017): 336–51; Nancy Folbre, *The Invisible Heart: Economics and Family Values* (New York: New Press, 2001); Amy Wharton, "The Sociology of Emotional Labor," *Annual Review of Sociology* 35 (2009): 147–65; Christine Williams and Catherine Connell, "'Looking Good and Sounding Right': Aesthetic Labor and Social Inequality in the Retail Industry," *Work and Occupations* 37, no. 3 (2010): 349–77.

5. E.g., Gretchen Purser, "'You Put Up with Anything': The Vulnerability and Exploitability of Formerly-Incarcerated Workers," in *Prison/Work: Labor in the Carceral State*, ed. Erin Hatton (Oakland: University of California Press, forthcoming); Gretchen Purser, "The Dignity of Job-Seeking Men: Boundary Work among Immigrant Day Laborers," *Journal of Contemporary Ethnography* 38,

no. 1 (2009): 117–39; Immanuel Ness, *Guest Workers and Resistance to U.S. Corporate Despotism* (Champaign: University of Illinois Press, 2011); Rhacel Salazar Parreñas, *Servants of Globalization: Women, Migration, and Domestic Work* (Palo Alto: Stanford University Press, 2001); Noah Zatz et al., *Get to Work or Go to Jail: Workplace Rights under Threat* (Los Angeles: UCLA Institute for Research on Labor and Employment, 2016); Noah Zatz, "Carceral Labor beyond Prison," in *Prison/Work: Labor in the Carceral State*, ed. Erin Hatton (Oakland: University of California Press, forthcoming).

6. National Employment Law Project, *Iced Out: How Immigration Enforcement Has Interfered with Workers' Rights* (New York: NELP, 2009); Southern Poverty Law Center, *Close to Slavery* (Montgomery: Southern Poverty Law Center, 2009).

7. Purser, "'You Put Up with Anything'"; Zatz et al., *Get to Work*; Zatz, "Carceral Labor."

8. George Steinmetz, "Odious Comparisons: Incommensurability, the Case Study, and 'Small N's' in Sociology," *Sociological Theory* 22, no. 3 (2004): 371–400.

9. E.g., Françoise Carré and Chris Tilly, *Where Bad Jobs Are Better: Retail Jobs across Countries and Companies* (New York: Russell Sage Foundation, 2017); Arne Kalleberg, *Good Jobs, Bad Jobs: The Rise of Polarized and Precarious Employment Systems in the United States, 1970s–2000s* (New York: Russell Sage Foundation, 2013); Arne Kalleberg, Barbara Reskin, and Ken Hudson, "Bad Jobs in America: Standard and Nonstandard Employment Relations and Job Quality in the United States," *American Sociological Review* 65, no. 2 (2000): 256–78; Chris Warhurst, Françoise Carré, Patricia Findlay, and Chris Tilly, eds., *Are Bad Jobs Inevitable? Trends, Determinants and Responses to Job Quality in the Twenty-First Century* (New York: Palgrave, 2012).

10. However, even though welfare benefits are not legally construed as "wages" (but see Matter of Walter Carver v. State, 26 N.Y. 3d 272, 2015), the sum of an individual's cash benefits plus food stamps divided by the number of hours worked is required to comply with the federal minimum wage; Stone v. McGowan, 308 F. Supp. 2d 79, 2004. Though graduate students and Division I athletes currently receive basic living stipends, such stipends are not legally construed as "wages."

11. However, they are often covered by some sort of legal protection from discrimination.

APPENDIX A. THE STORY OF THIS BOOK

1. In terms of recruitment, because New York State's Department of Corrections and Community Supervision did not grant me access to the state's prisons, I interviewed recently released prisoners, largely recruited from reentry programs in Buffalo and Rochester, New York. Though these 41 interviews mostly

took place in Western New York, these informants had been incarcerated in facilities across the state. Because prisoners are frequently assigned to such reentry programs upon release, moreover, this recruitment method did not introduce any significant selection bias; indeed, it likely yielded a more heterogeneous set of informants than had I interviewed them behind bars because, my informants told me, prison officials would have selected only those from the "honor block" to be interviewed. I also interviewed 42 current and former welfare recipients about their labor in exchange for public assistance in Buffalo, Rochester, and New York City. They were recruited from workfare sites and community advocacy organizations, which yielded a relatively heterogeneous set of workers with diverse workfare experiences. While those recruited from advocacy organizations were more likely to be critical of workfare (and more likely to deploy rights talk), such workers were a relatively small fraction of these informants ($n = 5$, 12%), and are proportionately represented in this book's findings. All of the informants in this study were offered (a meager) $10 for their time.

2. Because of the isolated, behind-closed-doors nature of domestic labor, I had a difficult time finding and recruiting such workers. I ultimately (and laboriously) used Craigslist, the classified advertisements website, to recruit and interview 20 domestic workers in Western New York: housecleaners, nannies, and caregivers of the elderly or disabled. They were 80 percent white, 85 percent female, and 95 percent native-born.

3. E.g., Grace Chang, *Disposable Domestics: Immigrant Women Workers in the Global Economy* (Cambridge: South End Press, 2000); Pierrette Hondagneu-Sotelo, *Doméstica: Immigrant Workers Cleaning and Caring in the Shadows of Affluence* (Oakland: University of California Press, 2001); Rhacel Parreñas, *Servants of Globalization: Migration and Domestic Work*, 2nd ed. (Stanford: Stanford University Press, 2015).

4. Both groups were recruited through snowball sampling via distant contacts, usually friends of friends of friends. None of the former athletes or graduate students I interviewed were affiliated—past or present—with my own university. Because these informants were located across the United States, moreover, I conducted these interviews via audio or video phone calls, in contrast to my other interviews, which I conducted in person.

5. Allison Pugh, "What Good Are Interviews for Thinking about Culture? Demystifying Interpretive Analysis," *American Journal of Cultural Sociology* 1, no. 1 (2013): 54.

6. Harel Shapira, "Who Cares What They Think? Going About the Right the Wrong Way," *Contemporary Sociology* 46, no. 5 (2017): 516–17.

7. Emphasis in original. Shapira, "Who Cares What They Think," 515.

8. E.g., Mario Small, "De-exoticizing Ghetto Poverty: On the Ethics of Representation in Urban Ethnography," *City & Community* 14, no. 4 (2015): 352–58.

9. Small, "De-exoticizing Ghetto Poverty," 354.

APPENDIX B. PEOPLE QUA DATA

1. Andrea Armstrong, "Race, Prison Discipline, and the Law," *UC Irvine Law Review* 5, no. 4 (2015): 759–82; Michael Schwirtz, Michael Winerip, and Robert Gebeloff, "The Scourge of Racial Bias in New York State Prisons," *New York Times*, December 3, 2016, www.nytimes.com/2016/12/03/nyregion/new-york-state-prisons-inmates-racial-bias.html; Jeremiah Wade-Olson, *Punishing the Vulnerable: Discrimination in American Prisons* (Santa Barbara: Praeger, 2018).

2. National Academies of Sciences, Engineering, Medicine, *Sexual Harassment of Women: Climate, Culture, and Consequences in Academic Sciences, Engineering, and Medicine* (Washington, DC: National Academies Press, 2018); Maria Ong, Carole Wright, Lorelle Espinosa, and Gary Orfield, "Inside the Double Bind: A Synthesis of Empirical Research on Undergraduate and Graduate Women of Color in Science, Technology, Engineering, and Mathematics," *Harvard Educational Review* 81, no. 2 (2011): 172–209.

Selected Bibliography

This bibliography represents only a selection of the scholarship and sources I used in researching and writing this book. It lists scholarly works on which I most often drew in formulating this book's central ideas and arguments. It does not include the primary documents I cite in this book, nor many important academic and journalistic studies. A complete list of my sources can be found in the endnotes.

Acker, Joan. "Hierarchies, Jobs, Bodies: A Theory of Gendered Organizations." *Gender & Society* 4, no. 2 (1990): 139–58.

Alexander, Michelle. *The New Jim Crow: Mass Incarceration in the Age of Colorblindness.* New York: New Press, 2012.

Arendt, Hannah. *The Origins of Totalitarianism.* New York: Harcourt, Brace, 1951.

Baptist, Edward. *The Half Has Never Been Told: Slavery and the Making of American Capitalism.* New York: Basic Books, 2014.

Beckett, Katherine, and Bruce Western. "Governing Social Marginality: Welfare, Incarceration, and the Transformation of State Policy." *Punishment & Society* 3, no. 1 (2001): 43–59.

Blackmon, Douglas. *Slavery by Another Name: The Re-enslavement of Black Americans from the Civil War to World War II.* New York: Doubleday, 2008.

Boydston, Jeanne. *Home and Work: Housework, Wages, and the Ideology of Labor in the Early Republic.* New York: Oxford University Press, 1994.

Brass, Tom. *Towards a Comparative Political Economy of Unfree Labour.* London: Frank Cass, 1999.

Braverman, Harry. *Labor and Monopoly Capital: The Degradation of Work in the Twentieth Century.* New York: Monthly Review Press, 1974.

Britton, Dana. *At Work in the Iron Cage: The Prison as Gendered Organization.* New York: New York University Press, 2003.

Burawoy, Michael. *Manufacturing Consent: Changes in the Labor Process under Monopoly Capitalism.* Chicago: University of Chicago Press, 1979.

———. *The Politics of Production.* London: Verso, 1985.

Byers, Walter. *Unsportsmanlike Conduct: Exploiting College Athletes.* Ann Arbor: University of Michigan Press, 1995.

Coates, Ta-Nehisi. *Between the World and Me.* New York: Spiegel & Grau, 2015.

Cockburn, Cynthia. *In the Way of Women: Men's Resistance to Sex Equality in Organizations.* New York: Macmillan, 1991.

Collins, Jane, and Victoria Mayer. *Both Hands Tied: Welfare Reform and the Race to the Bottom of the Low-Wage Labor Market.* Chicago: University of Chicago Press, 2010.

Collins, Patricia Hill. *Black Feminist Thought: Knowledge, Consciousness, and the Politics of Empowerment.* New York: Routledge, 2000.

Davidson, Julia O'Connell. "The Making of Modern Slavery: Whose Interests Are Served by the New Abolitionism?" *British Academy Review* 24 (2014): 28–31.

Evans, Louwanda, and Wendy Moore. "Impossible Burdens: White Institutions, Emotional Labor, and Micro-Resistance." *Social Problems* 62, no. 3 (2015): 439–54.

Evans, Robert. "Some Notes on Coerced Labor." *Journal of Economic History* 30 (1970): 861–66.

Ezorsky, Gertrude. *Freedom in the Workplace?* Ithaca: Cornell University Press, 2007.

Foner, Eric. *Reconstruction: America's Unfinished Revolution, 1863–1877.* New York: Perennial Classics, 2011.

Foner, Eric, and Olivia Mahoney. *America's Reconstruction: People and Politics after the Civil War.* New York: HarperCollins, 1995.

Foucault, Michel. *Discipline & Punish: The Birth of the Prison.* New York: Random House, 1977.

Fraser, Nancy, and Linda Gordon. "A Genealogy of Dependency: Tracing a Keyword of the U.S. Welfare State." *Signs* 19, no. 2 (1994): 309–36.

Gans, Herbert. *The War against the Poor: The Underclass and Antipoverty Policy.* New York: Basic Books, 1995.

Garland, David. *The Culture of Control: Crime and Social Order in Contemporary Society.* Chicago: University of Chicago Press, 2001.

———. *Punishment and Modern Society: A Study in Social Theory.* Chicago: University of Chicago Press, 1990.

Genovese, Eugene. *Roll, Jordan, Roll: The World the Slaves Made.* New York: Random House, 1976.

Gilens, Martin. *Why Americans Hate Welfare: Race, Media, and the Politics of Antipoverty Policy.* Chicago: University of Chicago Press, 1999.

Glenn, Evelyn Nakano. *Unequal Freedom: How Race and Gender Shaped American Citizenship and Labor.* Cambridge: Harvard University Press, 2002.

Goffman, Erving. *Asylums: Essays on the Social Situation of Mental Patients and Other Inmates.* New York: Doubleday, 1961.

Goldberg, Chad Alan. *Citizens and Paupers: Relief, Rights, and Race, from the Freedmen's Bureau to Workfare.* Chicago: University of Chicago Press, 2007.

Gramsci, Antonio. *Selections from the Prison Notebooks of Antonio Gramsci.* New York: International Publishers, 1971.

Gustafson, Kaaryn. *Cheating Welfare: Public Assistance and the Criminalization of Poverty.* New York: New York University Press, 2011.

———. "The Criminalization of Poverty." *Journal of Criminal Law and Criminology* 99, no. 3 (2009): 643–716.

Haley, Sarah. *No Mercy Here: Gender, Punishment, and the Making of Jim Crow Modernity.* Chapel Hill: University of North Carolina Press, 2016.

Hays, Sharon. *Flat Broke with Children: Women in the Age of Welfare Reform.* New York: Oxford University Press, 2004.

Hawkins, Billy. *The New Plantation: Black Athletes, College Sports, and Predominantly White NCAA Institutions.* New York: St. Martin's Press, 2010.

Hinton, Elizabeth. *From the War on Poverty to the War on Crime.* Cambridge: Harvard University Press, 2016.

Hodson, Randy. *Dignity at Work.* New York: Cambridge University Press, 2001.

Hughes, Everett. "Good People and Dirty Work." *Social Problems* 10, no. 1 (1962): 3–11.

Jessop, Bob. "Varieties of Academic Capitalism and Entrepreneurial Universities." *Higher Education* 73, no. 6 (2017): 853–70.

Katz, Cindi. *Growing Up Global: Economic Restructuring and Children's Everyday Lives.* Minneapolis: University of Minnesota Press, 2004.

Katz, Michael. *In the Shadow of the Poorhouse: A Social History of Welfare in America,* 2nd ed. New York: Basic Books, 1996.

———. *The Undeserving Poor: From the War on Poverty to the War on Welfare.* New York: Oxford University Press, 1989.

Kelley, Robin D. G. *Race Rebels: Culture, Politics, and the Black Working Class.* New York: Free Press, 1994.

Kerber, Linda. *No Constitutional Right to Be Ladies: Women and the Obligations of Citizenship.* New York: Hill and Wang, 1998.

Kessler-Harris, Alice. *Out to Work: A History of Wage-Earning Women in the United States*. New York: Oxford University Press, 1982.Kim, Kathleen. "Beyond Coercion." *UCLA Law Review* 62 (2015): 1558–84.

———. "The Coercion of Trafficked Workers." *Iowa Law Review* 96 (2011): 409–74.

Kohler-Hausmann, Julilly. "'The Crime of Survival': Fraud Prosecutions, Community Surveillance and the Original 'Welfare Queen.'" *Journal of Social History* 41, no. 2 (2007): 329–54.

———. *Getting Tough: Welfare and Imprisonment in 1970s America*. Princeton: Princeton University Press, 2017.

———. "Guns and Butter: The Welfare State, the Carceral State, and the Politics of Exclusion in the Postwar United States." *Journal of American History* 102, no. 1 (2015): 87–99.

Kornbluh, Felicia. *The Battle for Welfare Rights: Politics and Poverty in Modern America*. Philadelphia: University of Pennsylvania Press, 2007.

Krinsky, John. *Free Labor: Workfare and the Contested Language of Neoliberalism*. Chicago: University of Chicago Press, 2007.

Lichtenstein, Alex. *Twice the Work of Free Labor: The Political Economy of Convict Labor in the New South*. New York: Verso, 1996.

Linton, Ralph. *The Study of Man: An Introduction*. New York: D. Appleton-Century, 1936.

Lipsitz, George. *How Racism Takes Place*. Philadelphia: Temple University Press, 2011.

Lynch, Mona. "Theorizing Punishment: Reflections on Wacquant's *Punishing the Poor*." *Critical Sociology* 37, no. 2 (2011): 237–44.

Marshall, T. H. *Class, Citizenship and Social Development*. New York: Doubleday, 1964 [1949].

Marx, Karl. *Capital: A Critique of Political Economy*, vol. 1. New York: Penguin, 1992 [1906].

McCann, Michael. *Rights at Work: Pay Equity Reform and the Politics of Legal Mobilization*. Chicago: University of Chicago Press, 1994.

McLennan, Rebecca. *The Crisis of Imprisonment: Protest, Politics, and the Making of the American Penal State, 1776–1941*. Cambridge: Cambridge University Press, 2008.

Moore, Wendy. *Reproducing Racism: White Space, Elite Law Schools, and Racial Inequality*. Lanham: Rowman & Littlefield, 2008.

Muhammad, Khalil Gibran. *The Condemnation of Blackness*. Cambridge: Harvard University Press, 2010.

Nadasen, Premilla. *The Welfare Rights Movement in the United States*. New York: Routledge, 2005.

Neubeck, Kenneth, and Noel Cazenave. *Welfare Racism: Playing the Race Card against America's Poor*. New York: Routledge, 2001.

Ngai, Mae. *Impossible Subjects: Illegal Aliens and the Making of Modern America*. Princeton: Princeton University Press, 2004.

Oshinsky, David. *Worse than Slavery: Parchman Farm and the Ordeal of Jim Crow Justice*. New York: Free Press, 1997.

Parreñas, Rhacel. *Servants of Globalization: Migration and Domestic Work*, 2nd ed. Stanford: Stanford University Press, 2015.

Peck, Jamie. *Workfare States*. New York: Guildford Press, 2001.

——. "Zombie Neoliberalism and the Ambidextrous State." *Theoretical Criminology* 14, no. 1 (2010): 104–10.

Piven, Frances Fox, and Richard Cloward. *Poor People's Movements: Why They Succeed, How They Fail*. New York: Vintage Books, 1979.

——, and Richard Cloward. *Regulating the Poor: The Functions of Public Welfare*. New York: Pantheon, 1971.

Pugh, Allison. "What Good Are Interviews for Thinking about Culture? Demystifying Interpretive Analysis." *American Journal of Cultural Sociology* 1, no. 1 (2013): 42–68.

Purser, Gretchen. "'You Put Up with Anything': The Vulnerability and Exploitability of Formerly-Incarcerated Workers." In *Prison/Work: Labor in the Carceral State*, ed. Erin Hatton. Oakland: University of California Press, forthcoming.

Rhoden, William. *Forty Million Dollar Slaves: The Rise, Fall, and Redemption of the Black Athlete*. New York: Three Rivers Press, 2006.

Roediger, David. *The Wages of Whiteness: Race and the Making of the American Working Class*. New York: Verso, 1991.

——, and Elizabeth Esch. *The Production of Difference: Race and the Management of Labor in U.S. History*. New York: Oxford University Press, 2012.

Said, Edward. *Culture and Imperialism*. New York: Vintage, 1994.

——. *Orientalism*. New York: Random House, 1978.

Scott, James. *Domination and the Arts of Resistance: Hidden Transcripts*. New Haven: Yale University Press, 1990.

——. *Weapons of the Weak: Everyday Forms of Peasant Resistance*. New Haven: Yale University Press, 1985.

Shklar, Judith. *American Citizenship: The Quest for Inclusion*. Cambridge: Harvard University Press, 1991.

Slaughter, Sheila, and Gary Rhoades. *Academic Capitalism and the New Economy: Markets, State, and Higher Education*. Baltimore: Johns Hopkins University Press, 2004.

Small, Mario. "De-Exoticizing Ghetto Poverty: On the Ethics of Representation in Urban Ethnography." *City & Community* 14, no. 4 (2015): 352–58.

Somers, Margaret. *Genealogies of Citizenship: Markets, Statelessness, and the Right to Have Rights*. Cambridge: Cambridge University Press, 2008.

Soss, Joe, Richard Fording, and Sanford Schram. *Disciplining the Poor:*

Neoliberal Paternalism and the Persistent Power of Race. Chicago: University of Chicago Press, 2011.

Steinfeld, Robert. *Coercion, Contract, and Free Labor in the Nineteenth Century*. Cambridge: Cambridge University Press, 2001.

Strauss, Kendra. "Coerced, Forced and Unfree Labour: Geographies of Exploitation in Contemporary Labour Markets." *Geography Compass* 6 (2012): 137–48.

Vallas, Steven. "Working Class Heroes or Working Stiffs? Domination and Resistance in Business Organizations." *Research in the Sociology of Work* 28 (2016): 101–26.

Wacquant, Loïc. *Punishing the Poor: The Neoliberal Government of Social Insecurity*. Durham: Duke University Press, 2009.

Weber, Max. *The Protestant Work Ethic and the Spirit of Capitalism*. New York: Scribner's, 1958.

Weeks, Kathi. *The Problem with Work: Feminism, Marxism, Antiwork Politics, and Postwork Imaginaries*. Durham: Duke University Press, 2011.

Western, Bruce. *Punishment and Inequality in America*. New York: Russell Sage Foundation, 2006.

———, and Katherine Beckett. "How Unregulated Is the U.S. Labor Market? The Penal System as a Labor Market Institution." *American Journal of Sociology* 104, no. 4 (1999): 1030–60.

———, and Becky Pettit. "Incarceration & Social Inequality." *Dædalus* (Summer 2010): 8–19.

Willis, Paul. *Learning to Labour: How Working Class Kids Get Working Class Jobs*. New York: Columbia University Press, 1977.

Wright, Erik Olin. *Understanding Class*. London: Verso Books, 2015.

Zatz, Noah. "Carceral Labor beyond Prison." In *Prison/Work: Labor in the Carceral State*, ed. Erin Hatton. Oakland: University of California Press, forthcoming.

———. "Prison Labor and the Paradox of Paid Nonmarket Work." In *Research in the Sociology of Work*, vol. 18, ed. Nina Bandelj, 369–98. Bingley: Emerald, 2009.

———. "Working at the Boundaries of Markets." *Vanderbilt Law Review* 61, no. 3 (2008): 857–958.

———, et al. *Get to Work or Go to Jail: Workplace Rights under Threat*. Los Angeles: UCLA Institute for Research on Labor and Employment, 2016.

Index

Founded in 1893,
UNIVERSITY OF CALIFORNIA PRESS
publishes bold, progressive books and journals
on topics in the arts, humanities, social sciences,
and natural sciences—with a focus on social
justice issues—that inspire thought and action
among readers worldwide.

The UC PRESS FOUNDATION
raises funds to uphold the press's vital role
as an independent, nonprofit publisher, and
receives philanthropic support from a wide
range of individuals and institutions—and from
committed readers like you. To learn more, visit
ucpress.edu/supportus.